The Complete Guide to
Organic
Gardening
West of the Cascades

The Complete Guide to
Organic Gardening
West of the Cascades

by Steve Solomon

Pacific Search Press

Pacific Search Press, 222 Dexter Avenue North
Seattle, Washington 98109
©1981 by Steve Solomon. All rights reserved
Printed in the United States of America

Second printing 1982
Third printing 1983

Designed by Judy Petry

Library of Congress Cataloging in Publication Data

Solomon, Steve.
    The complete guide to organic gardening west of the Cascades.

    Includes bibliographical references and index.
    1. Organic gardening — Northwest coast of North
America. 2. Vegetable gardening — Northwest coast of
North America. I. Title.
SB324.3.S67   635′.0484′09795   80-28359
ISBN 0-914718-58-4

Wherever you go and whatever you do in the outdoors, move at Nature's pace, seeking not to impose yourself but to lose yourself. If you must leave footprints, make them not with blindness but with care and awareness of the delicate balance around you. And if you must take souvenirs, take them not in your pockets but in your mind and spirit. In preservation lies the promise of renewal.

—Pacific Search Press

Contents

Preface

This book is a *complete* guide to growing vegetables organically in the maritime Northwest. Because of our climate, gardeners in western Oregon and Washington have to be a little more educated than those in other parts of the country. Through the years I have seen many Northwest gardeners struggle along on advice in garden books written by East Coast and California garden writers. True, we all have to learn to make good soil and manage pests, and these techniques can be much the same in any area. But plants cannot be expected to respond in our damp, cool climate in the same way they respond in a warm, dry climate; maritime Northwest gardeners must learn which specific vegetable varieties are suited to our area and when and how to sow, culture, and harvest them. With this information in hand, Northwest gardeners can produce their own fresh food year-round.

I cannot claim responsibility for originating all the technology explained in this book, but everything I talk about here is a product of my own gardening experiences. I am offering you the easiest, most efficient methods I know of to produce food year-round in this climate. I assume that you want to be told with the least possible explanation how to accomplish your gardening goals in the simplest possible manner. While this book will tell you everything you need to know to have a thriving garden and thus is the only organic gardening book you need to own, it is not the only one you might want to have, because it is not a complete text in botany, geology, climatology, soil science, plant pathology, microbiology, and general horticulture. If you are serious about learning the whys and wherefores of what you are doing, then you should advance your studies above the level of "how-to-do-it" books—visit a used-book store near a university and purchase textbooks on these related subjects. All I can say in this book is "do this, and it will work." And it *will* work if you follow the steps indicated. You eventually should come to understand the processes in your garden well enough to create your own methods—superior to mine and more suited to your temperament and desires. Then you will be a truly self-sufficient gardener.

Helping gardeners in the maritime Northwest achieve that goal has become my full-time preoccupation in the last two years. When I was working on my first book, *Growing Organic Vegetables West of the Cascades* (the book you are now reading is a heavily revised, expanded, and—I think—improved version of this earlier book) I realized that specific varietal recommendations are needed for this area and somehow I had to find seeds that would grow well here. I began gathering them from four or five seed catalogs, including one from Europe. Knowing that most gardeners would not take the trouble to shop this way (buying seeds from Europe is a complex process that takes months to complete) and that many of those who tried would fall prey to the seductive descriptions and beautiful pictures, purchasing items they should not, I decided to create a single source that would provide a regionally correct selection. Thus I started the Territorial Seed Company. In addition to selling seeds of all the varieties known to be suitable to this area, it conducts ongoing research for other adaptable varieties, especially where there are gaps in the current selection. For example, we have a good tomato (several, in fact) for Willamette Valley gardeners but do not know of any that really *taste good* for people in the coastal fog belt.

My main purpose for the company and for this book is to combat the current tendency toward social, economic, and spiritual dislocations by helping people attain self-sufficiency and thus independence. We will have strong families only when individuals are surviving well. We will have a strong nation only when families are surviving well. We will have a strong planet only when nations are surviving well. The alternatives are frightening to contemplate.

The people of the maritime Northwest, with their independent spirit and desire for more self-sufficient living, provided a sounding board for me throughout the preparation of this book. After my first book came out, they enlightened me about what needed expansion, what was way off, and what was correctly explained. To them I offer my thanks. I also would like to express my appreciation to my wife, Susan, who read this manuscript many times and provided incalculable physical and spiritual support, and to the gardening experts at the Oregon State University Extension Service, who always helped answer my questions even though they did not agree with all aspects of my "organic" philosophy. Duane Hatch particularly provided support in many ways. Crossing swords with him over the doctrinaire issues of organic versus chemical methods enlightened us both. He came away much more tolerant of other approaches. I learned that those who advocate chemical farming and gardening techniques are only trying to help people grow food in the most inexpensive (in terms of dollars and cents) method possible. I still enjoy dropping in on Duane at his office in Eugene, Oregon, for a friendly argument. This book is dedicated to all of those whose support and assistance have made it possible.

Gardening Basics

I wrote this book to help you become more self-sufficient, but there is more to self-sufficiency than producing your own food. It also encompasses the ability to answer your own questions when things go wrong. And things do go wrong from time to time.

To help you become a truly independent gardener, I am going to review the basics of gardening. If the information in this chapter is new to you, or you find it very interesting, I suggest you eventually read a complete book about botany.

What Is a Vegetable?

A vegetable is a plant. All plants seem to be obsessed with a similar intention, which if expressed in human talk would amount to something like: "I want to have my children absolutely and completely take over the entire world and not leave room for any other kind of plant anywhere." I think it must make life interesting for plants—having goals that large.

To succeed in this goal, all plants operate in a similar manner. Their basic strategy is to produce as much seed as they can and distribute it as effectively as possible. In their seed lies hope for the future. Plants must manufacture and store up a great deal of food while producing their seed. Each seed is a capsule of life-sustaining food surrounding a tiny embryo. Each seed must be capable of keeping the embryo alive for several years and then must feed it heavily for a week or so during germination.

While making food, the plant must bring together several things from the environment. Carbon, the basic building block of all organic material, comes from carbon dioxide gas, freely available from the air. At least this one vital ingredient is never in short supply. Water is also needed, both to make up the general structure of the plant and to act as the basic solvent in all its manufacturing processes. Plants also need fairly significant quantities of certain mineral nutrients, which come from the soil. Finally, the sun acts as an energy source to power all the chemical reactions needed to make food and build tissue.

If all these needed ingredients are bountifully supplied, a plant is able to feed itself and have enough left over to produce a large crop of seeds. But it is never that simple. Plants do not grow in isolation: in nature there is competition for light, nutrients, and water that makes human wars look quite tame. While trying to suc-ceed at universal conquest, plants fight each other for these basics. The gardener must manage plants so they have an adequate supply of each one.

What Vegetables Need

Vegetables are special kinds of plants humans have tinkered with over the years. They have been bred to produce more-than-normal amounts of food and store that extra food for us to eat. We have encouraged them to be succulent at the expense of their ability to compete with other plants for water, nutrients, and light. To grow properly, vegetables require things that wild plants can do without. First, they need extra rich soil to provide the heavier than normal amount of nutrients that they require. Second, they need lots of water and light. Third, they need lots of help from people. Consequently, *vegetables need to be pampered*, and there is no escaping this fact. Provide vegetables with what they need to grow properly and they will feed you. Deprive them and they will not. It is that simple.

Your attitude toward your vegetables should be based on carefully studying them to understand what they need. Books and university educations are not necessary to complete this study, but, it will require a number of years of sincere interest in your plants combined with some basic knowledge. This book can pro-vide the basic knowledge. You must provide the sincere interest.

Weeds

Weeds are vigorous, competitive, unwanted plants. Unless you pull them out, they will always outgrow succulent, pampered vegetables and deprive them of needed water, nutrients, and light. In a very weedy garden, the vegetables will be utterly defeated. Fortunately, every weed does not have to be removed from the garden to let the vegetables win—only most of them.

The following are the priorities in weed removal. How far down this list you get in your weeding chores depends on the amount of time you have and your interest in the garden.

1. Completely remove any grass anywhere in the garden. As a family, grasses put out enormous root systems and rob all the soil under them of *all* nutrients they can get.
2. Pull any thistles, morning glories, or nightshade. All are persistent, vigorous, and extremely hard to get rid of once they are established. If they are already growing in your garden, keep after them and eventually they will succumb. Plants in this category store up a considerable amount of food in their roots and put up set after set of new growth for you to cut off. By immediately and repeatedly cutting off the new growth, you can even-tually exhaust their store of food so that they die.
3. Pull any weed that starts to get taller than the surrounding vegetables, since you want the vegetables to have all the light. A few spindly weeds that come along well after the vegetables are fairly large and that are shaded by the vegetables cannot do any harm.
4. As you start to get away from the vegetables' root systems, weeds get less important. If you are very energetic, pull all the weeds between the rows or beds. At least take a hoe to them once a month. These weeds will try to

reach into the softer soil around the vegetables and rob them of nutrients. Your foot traffic may be enough to keep them set back.

A few weeds left growing in the garden will actually help things. Weeds give insects something to eat besides your vegetables. Growing strong-smelling "weeds" such as chamomile, catnip, chives, dill, garlic, marigolds, and the like here and there in your garden also will help. Strong aromas confuse some insects, which use a smell location system to find the kind of plant they like to eat.

Thinning

The concept of thinning also follows quite logically. If unwanted plants can deprive vegetables of needed nutrients, water, and light, could not other vegetables do the same? Each vegetable needs a certain amount of space to develop properly. If other vegetables are too close to it, competition develops, and the vegetable does not do well. All the plant spacing tables and "how close can you plant information" in this book are provided because a gardener must be aware of this factor.

The extra work that thinning makes you do can actually be used to the gardener's advantage. Consider these facts. No plant makes seeds that are uniformly good. Many seeds contain deformed or damaged embryos, mutants, and what you might call "handicapped" embryos, and the like. In a batch of very good seed, these undesirable ones might make up 15 percent of the whole. Generally these seeds do not sprout at all, or if they do, they do not survive more than a few days after sprouting. Every batch of seeds also contains 10 or 15 percent exceptional seeds. These are the ones that are the most vigorous and the best adapted to your soil and will grow the finest plants. Now add to this another fact: most insects attack seedlings and are easily capable of destroying them. They usually can only set back a healthy, adult plant.

To use these facts to help you, simply plant five to ten seeds for every plant you want to end up with, and delay thinning until the insects have worked over the seedlings and it is clear that some are surviving quite well. This stage in the development of a planting is what I call "getting well established." Within a few weeks of planting there will be a few seedlings that stand head and shoulders above the others and that have not been damaged by insects. These are the ones to leave as you thin out the weaker seedlings. Sometimes, if you have planted far too many seeds, it is necessary to make a preliminary thinning within days of germination. This first thinning should get the seedlings only slightly out of each other's way and still leave many more than you will finally want to mature in that space.

Planting too few seeds and then thinning too soon causes you to have to fight the insects or have big gaps in your rows. Planting enough seeds and then thinning too late or not at all causes overcompetition and stunts all your plants.

Soil Improvement— The Essence of Pampering

Soil Types

Soil is a mixture of rock particles, decayed organic matter, air, water, and living things. The only scientific way to deal with soil is to understand these component parts. Otherwise, soil is just an amorphous mass to you, and what happens when you try to grow vegetables remains a mystery. Most failures of plants to grow vigorously can be traced to improper management of the soil.

The most important feature of soil is the size of its rock particles, which generally make up over two-thirds of the soil volume (air and water make up most of the rest). Breaking down soil into types is a handy way of describing the average size of particles in any particular soil and the quality of that soil (color, drainage, fertility). Going from small to large particles, soils are classified as clays, clayey loams, loams (silt), sandy loams, and finally sandy soils. It is not hard to tell roughly what type of soil you have. Take a small handful of soil and rub it between your fingers. If it is very gritty, it is a sandy soil. If it is composed of dustlike grit, it is a loam. If it is very fine stuff that gets gooey when wet, it is a clay.

It does not matter all that much which kind of soil a garden has. Each soil type except gravel (which will rarely grow anything) has definite advantages and disadvantages. Gardeners can afford (in money and time) to cope with whatever they have. Any soil type—even heavy "gumbo" clays—can, with the right techniques, be made into a fine garden.

Sandy soils drain well and make excellent winter gardens. They also are the first soils to dry up enough to be worked in the spring. Their lack of water retention, however, is a definite disadvantage in the summer. When planting, a gardener can add large amounts of water-retaining materials, which will improve this situation considerably. Sandy soils also have little ability to retain plant nutrients. This must be compensated for by more frequent use of fertilizers and other soil amendments.

Clay soils, on the other hand, retain considerable moisture and also retain nutrients well. Thus they do not require frequent watering, even in summer, and they provide the richest growing medium, all factors considered. Clay soils usually drain poorly in periods of heavy rain, however, and often require extensive ditching or the use of raised beds (see the section on raised-bed gardening in the "Tillage" chapter) if winter gardening is to be attempted. They are also very slow to dry out in spring and are hard to work up into a fine seed bed if there is too much or too little moisture. Gardeners can compensate for this by using no-till soil preparation techniques with raised beds and by initially adding considerable amounts of soil amendments to loosen up the land.

Loams are lighter than clays, drain fairly well, and require far less in the way of soil amendments than either clays or sands. Loams retain a fair amount of water and keep their nutrients quite well. I think clayey loams are the best garden soils, if they drain well. If your soil is not like that, do not worry. Sound organic gardening techniques adjust automatically for any soil type, changing the soil to a more loamy consistency.

Plant Nutrients

The basic nutrients plants require are minerals present naturally in rock particles. Those for which plants have the greatest need are phosphorus (P), potassium (K), and calcium (Ca). Some others that the plants need in much smaller quantities but no less urgently include magnesium (Mg), manganese (Mn), boron (B), iron (Fe), and copper (Cu). Plants also require several other nutrients in very tiny amounts, measured in parts per billion in the soil.

Any shortage of nutrients limits plant growth; severe shortages ruin plants entirely. Soil particles are the sole source of nutrients in unimproved land. Some soils contain highly mineralized rock particles, some do not. Whether a soil is rich or poor in nutrients has little to do with soil type. Soil type is mostly a statement of how finely broken down the soil particles have become, not their degree of mineralization.

Farmers have traditionally sought out lands with high levels of mineral nutrients in them. With careful management, rich lands can produce abundant crops for centuries (perhaps forever) without depletion. Fortunately, American gardeners usually can afford to make any land highly mineralized, no matter how poor it is initially. After all, gardeners are dealing with plots of only a few thousand square feet, not with the acres farmers must manage.

Generally, the gardener is concerned with supplying more phosphorus, potassium, and calcium to the plants. The other nutrients usually are available in large enough quantities or are present as trace elements in the organic substances used to increase soil phosphorus, potassium, and calcium.

Organic gardeners increase the mineralization of soils by imitating nature. We add rock particles that are very highly mineralized: for example, limestone is rich in calcium, dolomite lime contains both calcium and magnesium, rock phosphate is usually about 33 percent phosphorus, and granite and basalt flours are rich in potassium. Sometimes minerals can be added by amending the soil with organic substances. Kelp meal is 18 percent potassium and contains all the trace minerals in large quantities. Manures contain potassium and traces of phosphorus. Making soil rich this way appeals to gardeners not only because it imitates nature but also because these substances are very slow to break down and so provide abundant nutrients for many years. A few hundred pounds of rock flours can bring an average-size garden into a state of high mineralization.

Chemical Fertilizers

Farmers could not afford to spend five hundred dollars or more per acre adding rock flours to poorly mineralized land—at least not at present. The chemical fertilizing approach has seemed to them to be far more practical in this era when low-cost petroleum-based fertilizers are readily available. Chemical fertilizers are highly concentrated mineral compounds that dissolve rapidly into the soil and are immediately available as nutrients. Farmers see using tons of slow-releasing rock flours per acre as an unreasonable cost, even though that might be less work and expense in the long run.

Unfortunately, using *only* chemicals for soil improvements results in a rapid loss of humus, a substance that is vitally important to soil and plant health. Humus is decayed vegetation and is the food of most soil bacteria and other soil life-forms. These tiny creatures do more for soil than tons of chemicals ever could.

Soil Bacteria, Humus, and Tilth

Soil bacteria, called microlife, are the most important part of any soil, even though they rarely constitute more than 1 percent of it. They dissolve rock particles and release the nutrients to the plants. This is accomplished by the action of their breathing. The bacteria exhale carbon dioxide gas into the film of water surrounding soil particles, making the water slightly acid. This causes it to react with the rock particles and dissolve them. The slow power of this process has created giant caverns in limestone formations, because limestone is very easily dissolved by weak soil acids.

Soil bacteria maintain a balance of life in the soil, so plant disease rarely is a problem in soils rich in microlife. It is only in relatively dead soils that a pathogen can multiply greatly on a particular host plant.

Nitrogen is the only vital plant nutrient the source of which is not rock particles, but microorganisms in the soil have the ability to take nitrogen gas from the air and convert it to a mineralized form that all plants must have to manufacture their proteins. Any soil rich in microlife will be rich enough in nitrogen to produce good growth of most vegetables. There are a number of different kinds of nitrogen-fixing bacteria. Some live freely in the soil, and others associate themselves with the roots of certain types of plants.

A special group of fungi called microrhizae feed plants and make them healthy by penetrating the plants' root hairs and feeding nutrients the fungi have digested from the soil right into the plant.

I strongly suggest you read an excellent and classic book about soil bacteria, *The Soil and Health*. Its author, Sir Albert Howard, was the first scientist to understand the relationship between microlife and plants. He became the founder of the organic gardening movement. (*The Soil and Health*, published in 1947, is still in print—see "Further Reading.")

All microlife eat either decayed vegetation or other microlife. The decayed vegetation, called humus, is the basis for soil life and thus is the bottom of the food chain. Without humus, we get no naturally formed nitrogen, and the plants become diseased and more susceptible to insect attack. Humus has other beneficial effects besides feeding soil "germs." It mechanically loosens the soil itself and creates a texture we call good tilth. When soil has good tilth, it is soft and easy to work and crumbles easily into fine pieces. Water penetrates soil better when the soil has good tilth. Tilth prevents the formation of hard crusts on the soil's surface. It allows plants to put out larger root systems easily. There is lots of air in the soil, allowing bacteria to increase and speeding mineral release. The soil also holds more moisture. Good tilth allows delicate seedlings to poke through to the light and get a good start and also makes it easy to pull out a weed.

No matter what else you do to improve your garden's soil, you are going to want to improve its tilth. Good tilth is easily created in loamy soils with the addition of small amounts of humus. Perhaps a half-inch covering of humus incorporated into the soil each year would be enough, although I would recommend an inch or so to be safe. Sandy soils and clayey soils need more humus initially to create good tilth, but once it is established, a half inch to an inch of annual humus will maintain that condition. As an initial treatment, very sandy soils can generally use three inches of humus, and clayey soils need three to four inches. Manures and composts are the usual source of humus for gardeners.

Adding humus and mineralized rock to create rich soil is synergistic, meaning that the parts cooperate and produce something bigger than their simple sum. The humus feeds the microlife, which release minerals from the soil's rock particles. The humus also contains some minerals, which are released as it is consumed by the microlife. The microlife make mineralized nitrogen. The soil, rich in microlife, is surprisingly free of soil-borne diseases, for a balance of nature occurs and no single bacterial organism is prominent. Everything works together. The process is slow, and all the nutrients that are potentially available are not released in one month or one season, or even one year. The plants get a constant nutrient diet, grow in a soil relatively free of disease, and enjoy good tilth.

Adding both humus and fertilizer is working somewhat at cross-purposes. The humus feeds soil microlife, but the fertilizer (especially chemical forms of nitrogen) retards the activity of nitrogen-fixing bacteria and makes the soil dependent on outside nitrogen. Worse yet, nitrogen fertilizer overstimulates soil bacteria.

Suppose that in normal circumstances our soils consume an equivalent of a half-inch layer of humus each year. If you replace this, or if nature does (as it will if the plants grown on that soil rot back into it), a balance results—there is a fairly stable percentage of humus in that particular soil. Nitrogen stimulates humus-consuming bacteria. By adding concentrated forms of nitrogen to the soil, we cause it to consume two or three times the amount of humus it would ordinarily. Consuming soil humus does not help plants grow and simply "burns out" the soil. Once this has occurred, life level in the soil drops, new soil particles are not broken down as rapidly, and the plants become dependent on chemicals for phosphorus and potassium. If gardeners want to maintain good tilth and have over-abundant soil nitrogen, they will have to haul in a lot of humus and keep doing that every year.

Another liability of chemical fertilizers is that they act quickly. Since they are instantly water soluble, they make the nutrient level in soil shoot up and then drop off quickly after a few rains or irrigations wash the chemicals out of the soil. Using chemical fertilizer generally means paying attention to soil fertility every four to six weeks. With organic fertilizers, the release is slow enough that one application usually provides nutrients throughout the growing season. The organic approach is better, easier, and cheaper in the long run.

I am not saying that good vegetables cannot be grown with chemicals, especially if the plants are not sprayed. They can, particularly if careful attention is paid to keeping the humus levels in the soil and using chemicals only to *supplement* and *improve* already good soil. I prefer to use organic fertilizers to do this. Organic fertilizers consist of relatively fast-acting natural substances such as blood meal, fish meal, bone meal, and cottonseed meal.

Warning: When the chemical approach is used *without* adding considerable amounts of humus, very serious problems arise. The soil loses its tilth rapidly as humus is quickly used up, the airless soil compacts and will not absorb or release water well, drainage suffers, seeds do not germinate, root systems decrease, and plants suffer more from drought and disease. This description fits most of what was once America's finest farmland.

To sum it all up, if you add minerals to soil, it will grow vegetables. If you add humus to soil, the humus will develop microlife and good tilth. If both humus and minerals are present in large amounts, the soil will grow excellent vegetables—excellent, that is, if they also get lots of light and water, and grow without competition. All gardening failures may be traced to the factors outlined in this chapter, with the occasional exceptions of old seed that fails to germinate, summerless "summer" that inhibits growth and harvest of hot-weather crops, and varieties of vegetables that, because they are poorly adapted to our climate, do not grow or produce well.

Starting a New Garden— Or a New Gardener

Many novices are faced with the most difficult task of all—starting a new garden. A site has to be selected, and the initial tilling done. This job is often back-breaking, but it need not be heartbreaking. If you are establishing a new garden, please pay close attention to the following pages. The data they contain can save you an enormous amount of work and grief.

Location

You may have no choice about your garden's location—many gardens go in the sunniest part of the backyard, and that's that. But people on large suburban lots and country folk usually have a number of possible sites to choose from. If you do have a choice, selecting the correct garden site can make the difference between a horrible garden and an excellent one.

The ideal site would slope slightly to the south or southwest and have full sun all day, and it would be protected from the wind. The soil would be dark colored, fertile, and deep. The site would have good winter drainage, with no standing water no matter how hard it rained. It would also be close to the kitchen door, have abundant water piped to it, and be fenced to keep the critters out. If you have a spot where weeds grow tall and thick, that probably is the site to choose.

Sunlight

Most vegetables can use full sun all day. The light is their fuel, and the more of it they have the faster they grow. Full sun is vitally important for hot-weather crops. Often we have only a few weeks of really excellent growing weather in "summer." The more growth the plant can put on when growing conditions favor it, the more likely it is to mature.

The most valuable sun time is from ten o'clock until about four o'clock. Before ten and after four the sunlight has to pass through much more atmosphere and thus loses a great deal of intensity. The afternoon sun from four o'clock to sunset is much more useful than the morning sun. Most days, the sun has to burn off early morning clouds and cook out all the atmospheric moisture before strong light begins to hit the earth. On a really dry, hot, clear afternoon the sun stays strong and intense almost to sunset. If you have to choose between morning and afternoon sunshine, choose the afternoon exposure.

Most plants will make a fairly respectable amount of leaf growth in a shady location. They will tend to be spindly and grow slowly, but they will grow. They usually are not able to manufacture enough food to flower, fruit, and mature seeds well, but they will try. A shady garden or a shady part of a garden is not a bad place for growing greens, and if it has some sun it will grow good root crops.

Wind Protection

Strong winds can batter vegetables, slowing down growth. Winds also dry out soil in summer and make the site colder in spring and winter. The more protected the site is, the better.

This spring I found out for myself how much difference a windbreak can make. I built a small sunbathing enclosure so I could get an all-over tan. When the sun is shining, it is always five to six degrees warmer behind that seven-foot-high enclosure, which extends from a south-facing wall, than the temperature outside of it. I put a few test plants inside this sunroom, and they are weeks ahead of the same plants growing outside. They suffer a loss of sunlight, getting direct sun only from about ten o'clock to about four o'clock, but they grow better anyway. Now I want to erect an eight-foot wooden fence around the entire garden.

Numerous things can be used to protect a site from wind. High wooden fences are the most expensive. Allowing the weeds to grow up around the garden and letting some irrigation water get out to those weeds will be a help. Planting a hedge around the garden that eventually will get to be ten feet tall or so is another solution. Locating the site where an existing building blocks off some of the wind is an easy answer, and planning new buildings so they cluster around the garden without putting it into the shade is another. Keep in mind that the wind is an enemy.

Drainage

Soil drainage is crucially important west of the Cascades. In spring, bad drainage slows down tillage and planting. In late fall and winter, crops are killed by underwater soil. Minor drainage problems can be solved by adding humus and planting in raised beds, so that the paths become drainage ditches. These measures will not solve a really bad problem, however. If there is any lower area to which you can conduct water, dig shallow ditches through the garden to drain the rainwater off the site.

If you can, take time to live on the property for a while, or visit it monthly for a year to learn the nature of the land before you choose the garden site.

Soil Color

The color of soil is another consideration. If your land has more than one soil type, and all other factors are equal, choose the spot with the darkest soil. Black soil will be five degrees or so warmer in the spring than light-colored soil. This makes such a difference in growth that dark-soil gardens are often two to three weeks ahead of light ones.

My garden is located on an east-facing slope, in medium brown soil. It is a windy hillside, and the vegetables can take quite a battering at times. My garden is large—almost five thousand square feet—and I cannot afford to erect a three-hundred-foot-long board fence around it, so the vegetables have almost no wind protection. My house blocks a bit of the wind from one direction, but most days it does no good. The soil is so depleted that it barely grows two-foot-tall grass, so I cannot even get a natural windbreak to grow for me. I suppose I should make time to do something about the wind, but I am always busy with something more important.

I have a neighbor whose garden slopes not east but southwest. His soil is rich and black, and the weeds grow seven feet tall around the garden. He lives only a few miles from me, and we share the same chilly mountain climate. Yet his tomatoes are three feet tall when mine are a foot tall, his corn is always eighteen inches taller than mine, his peas are ready two weeks earlier, and so on. Both of us have fine gardens, but his is more productive and productive earlier. I have to do more work and pay more careful attention if I want abundant harvests.

Accessibility

Try to locate your garden where water can be gotten easily. A garden that is hard to water sometimes does not get watered. In the same vein, locate as close to the kitchen as possible. A garden too far away to go to for a sprig of parsley or a scallion is often neglected or not harvested. Sometimes the first settlers had two gardens. The main garden was located on the best site, no matter where it was in relationship to the house; the smaller kitchen garden, which grew salad greens, herbs, and other things that the cook needed a bit of from time to time, was right outside the back door.

Weeds

Any site that has not been used for cultivated crops is full of ungerminated weed seeds. The first year's gardening in such a spot can be a hell unless you first deal intelligently with the weeds. Otherwise they will swamp your vegetables, and you will have to choose between many hours of hand weeding and abandoning much of the garden. You will still be able to grow transplants, squashes, and corn, but all the small seeds will be engulfed with weed seedlings.

What you can do is cause most of the weed seedlings to sprout and then kill them off before planting your vegetables. If possible, start a new garden in late summer, with a good manuring and tilling. Begin to water it at this time; if you cannot, the end of summer rains will sprout a lot of the grass seeds and other weeds. Tilling again in October will kill off these plants. A good, thick green manure crop planted at this time will smother any weeds that sprout during the winter or early spring.

Tilling in the green manure in April or May will kill any weeds before they can make seed. But do not be in a hurry to plant that spring. If you wait three to four weeks after the first tilling, another large crop of weeds will appear. These too can be tilled up wholesale instead of trying to pull them out one at a time from between tiny vegetable seedlings. Then make raised beds and plant. Even if you do not get planted until June, there is still plenty of time to grow a fine garden. Mid-summer planting for fall and overwintered harvest can extend your growing season even further.

I have a neighbor who had an unusually bad weed problem. Someone had spread a thick covering of grass hay for mulch a few years before this neighbor purchased his property. That hay contained a great number of weed seeds, including thistles and nightshade. These are very tenacious weeds and difficult to eradicate. It seemed to him that the situation was hopeless. By midsummer his willingness to garden was expended, and he lost interest. The weeds simply took over—and went to seed! The next year his problem was worse. This year he came and asked my advice.

Knowing my questioner and his limited willingness to fight the weeds, I suggested that he put his garden into single, widely-spaced rows. That way he could run a rototiller between the rows every few weeks and cultivate the weeds out mechanically. I loaned him my tiller, which goes largely unused since I have put my garden into raised beds. This summer he runs the tiller up and down between the rows. He has a little hand weeding to do in the rows themselves, but he has so far managed to keep his soil completely bare of weeds. Next year he will have much less of a weed problem and the year after that he can go to raised beds if he wishes.

Size

If you have never gardened before, I strongly suggest that you limit your first garden to a thousand square feet or less. There are many things about gardening that can only be learned by experience; it takes a year or two to get over being a novice. Large gardens overwhelm new gardeners, resulting in losses. Their mistakes take so much time to correct on a large scale, and so many things are happening that they have never experienced before, that new gardeners do not learn nearly as much as they could or observe nearly as well as they might.

It also is a good idea for novices to grow only a few types of vegetables—only those they like the most. Then, after learning how to grow those by becoming acquainted with their entire life cycles, they can more easily expand to a few more types and perhaps a larger site. (This additional land should be prepared in late summer for use the following year.)

I learned this lesson the hard way, even though it appeared in the first gardening book I ever read. My first garden was an ambitious half acre. There was no way I could possibly haul and spread enough manure for the whole thing, and spending several hundred dollars on rock minerals seemed uncalled for, so I shortchanged the soil. I found myself working almost five hours a day to keep this half acre weeded and watered. Most of the food it produced was given away to anyone who would pick it.

The next year I reduced the garden's size to about 4,000 square feet (a half acre is about 21,000 square feet). However, I put as much manure and rock minerals into this "mini-garden" as I had carefully rationed over the entire half acre the year before. This little area produced almost as much as the space five times larger had, because it had enough nutrients in it.

The next year, the manuring and liming began to have their full effect (organics take over one year to fully take effect), and this 4,000-square-foot area produced too much food, so I cut the size again, to about 2,500 square feet. Only, believe me, I did not spend five hours a day on that small garden. My labor took only about fifteen minutes a day, except for harvesting time, and that 2,500-square-foot garden produced almost as much food as the half acre did initially. We still had lots of food to give away.

Many people have little idea of how much food, in terms of money value, can be grown in a well-managed garden. A "dollars per square foot" figure will vary greatly, depending on what you are growing, but as a general rule, I would say that fifty cents to a dollar per square foot is close—unless you are growing sweet corn, which has a value of about five cents per square foot.

Does your family use more than five hundred dollars worth of fresh vegetables in a season? Or even in an entire year, including canning and freezing? (They should, but they probably do not. Americans would be far healthier if fresh raw vegetables made up a major portion of their diets.) Do you need a garden larger than a thousand square feet to start with?

Root crops generally yield the highest food value per square foot. Next are leafy crops, and last, fruiting crops. One vegetable I would not suggest to anyone with a limited space is sweet corn. You are lucky to get one good ear of corn for each square foot planted, and that space is occupied during the entire prime planting season. You could get a crop of carrots *and* another late crop of spinach from the same space. And you would get twenty to thirty nice big carrots from each square foot. Or you could grow twelve to fifteen onions, a head of lettuce, or pounds and pounds of chard leaves.

From Lawn to Garden

A new home or the desire to turn your yard into a vegetable garden may have you trying to grow vegetables where grass once grew lushly. Such a site takes special handling when you turn it into a garden because it may have deep sod covering it. Tilling sod into soil leaves big clumps of grass that will not break down. These take root again and come up all over. If you till sod in the fall, again in spring, and again before you plant, everything will work out. But if it is spring and you are in a rush to plant but did not prepare the site last fall, you will have to remove the sod first.

You can rent a sod-stripping machine, or you can strip the sod with a shovel if you are athletic. A rear-end rototiller can also be used as a sod stripper. Run it over the sod at a shallow setting and go over it two or three times until the tines are cutting two inches deep or so. This will be just below the grass crowns.

When all the crowns are cut and stirred up with a small amount of soil, shovel them all up and make a compost pile with them. Sprinkle nitrogen fertilizer or about a half inch of manure between each six-inch-deep layer. The result will be a treasured "loam" compost, the best anyone could desire. Loam compost is regarded as a premium product for potting soil or starting bedding plants.

Some Advice for the City Gardener

I am a country person. I always have been one, even when I lived in a city back in Michigan. Every home I have owned has been on at least a half acre of land. I have never had to work around neighbors' trees or wonder where I could find space for the crops I wanted to grow.

One of the things I have noticed about city houses is that most of them have large, useless front yards, which are there and are maintained at great expense and trouble mostly to soothe the neighbors. Usually the front yard is sunnier than the backyard. This whole situation seems silly to me. I have always wondered why city people did not dig up those useless areas and put them to potatoes. In most countries, every bit of land around the house is used to grow food.

Even if you could not bring yourself to dig up a front yard, most houses in America have ornamental beds around them that are used to grow shrubs and flowers and other pretty things. Well, vegetables can be pretty things, too. Swiss chard, for example, can get to be thirty-six inches tall, and it has the most beautiful ruffled leaves imaginable. So do mustard greens. Little heads of lettuce are quite as nice as the succulents people grow for decorations. Why not have a border of purple cabbages? Even after the heads are cut, the large leaves around the stem can be left, and new smaller cabbages will form on the stem. Vegetables could be grown instead of flowers in beds along the walkways, or both can be grown together.

If you should want to sell that home later, the front yard garden could be tilled up and replanted to grass. In just a few months, it would come up better than any lawn you ever saw.

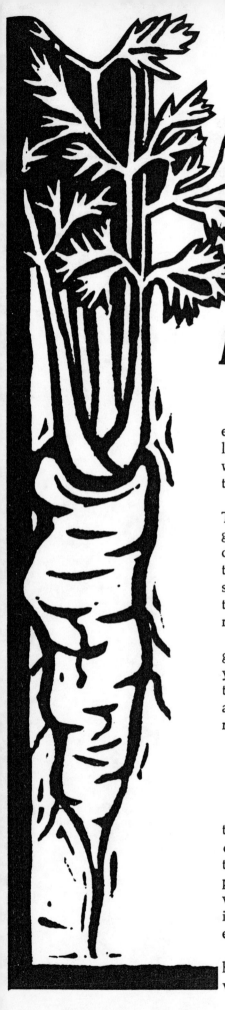

Improving the Soil

Almost no soil in our region is, in its virgin state, mineralized enough to grow excellent vegetables. And few soils, with the exception of some fine riverbottom loams, have sufficient humus or good enough tilth to grow excellent vegetables without improvement. Thus you probably will have to devote considerable attention to soil improvement.

Directing soil improvement by soil testing is not very useful to the gardener. The initial degree of soil mineralization is relatively unimportant when you are gardening. A good test from the Extension Service costs a minimum of twelve dollars in Oregon this year, and for your money you will receive a recommendation to use assorted chemicals you will not want to use anyway. Instead, why not simply add enough minerals to bring *any* soil to a high state of fertility, and continue to add enough thereafter to keep it there? With organic supplements there is no danger of overdosing soils.

Fertilizing is best considered a short-term expedient for making vegetables grow better. In the long haul, only soil improvement will make the kind of garden you will want to have. Remember, and remind yourself if you get lazy, that fertilization alone does not improve soil—it makes it worse. Only increasing the amount of soil humus and the amount of *potentially* available nutrients really results in long-term benefits.

Maritime Northwest Soils

Almost all soils west of the Cascades have several features in common. They tend to be rich in potassium and poor in phosphorus and nitrogen. This is a result of the geologic history of the Cascades and the surrounding region. The rocks that broke down to make up our soils tended almost uniformly to be low in phosphorus and high in potassium. Over the centuries, periodic dustings of volcanic ash have further increased the potassium levels in our soils without adding any phosphorus. The only places I know of west of the Cascades that experience potassium shortages are right along the coast where the rainfall is heaviest.

Nitrogen deficiencies are caused by several factors working together that inhibit legume growth. Legumes, including beans, peas, clovers, and vetches, are a valuable nitrogen-fixing family because they all share their root systems with a type of bacteria that takes atmospheric nitrogen and changes it to the mineralized form plants can use. A healthy crop of legumes can add enough nitrogen to soil in winter to grow a fine crop of corn or other vegetables the next spring. But our high winter rainfall levels tend rapidly to wash out calcium and magnesium from our soils, and without these alkalinizing agents soils get very acid. Legumes do poorly on acid soils with little phosphorus in them, and thus they do poorly west of the Cascades unless phosphorus and calcium are added to the soil.

Adding phosphorus and calcium, then growing a crop of legumes to supply nitrogen and increase the humus level—this is my plan for soil improvement, and I believe you can use it on any type of soil you are working with anywhere west of the Cascades, unless that land is pure gravel, or unless it goes underwater during the winter. Growing legumes also is a good test of your soil improvement efforts. If legumes, especially clovers, grow *lustily* on your soil, you know your soil is pretty good, and anything will grow well there.

Soil Amendments

Study the chart of soil amendments (Table 1) very carefully. You will see that manures are rich in potassium, which our soils do not particularly need, and low in phosphorus, which our soils desperately need. Adding manures will not make soil less acid, nor will it increase phosphorus levels significantly. Manures will add some nitrogen, greatly improve the tilth, and keep potassium levels high, so they should be used, but they are not the solution to the basic imbalance of our soils.

The best and cheapest source of phosphorus is rock phosphate. Bone meal also is good but more expensive, and it does not last as long in the soil. Bone meal is more of a phosphate fertilizer than a source of mineral phosphorus. The nice thing about rock phosphate is that it keeps on breaking down for many years. Adding some annually increases soil phosphate levels gradually without requiring any great expense in one year.

The calcium that soil needs to cure acidity is derived from limestone. This will be discussed at length later in the chapter.

The best and simplest source of potassium and all the trace elements is kelp meal. Generally, kelp for animal feed comes in fifty-pound sacks and is rather expensive, but one sack will last an average gardener many years.

Using Manure

Animal Manures

What goes in comes out. Manure derived from livestock fed on rich feed is much better than that derived from animals fed on poor rations. Try to find manure derived from alfalfa hay and grain feeding. Unfortunately, because of our climate, most of what passes for hay in our region is hardly worth feeding to animals. It fills their stomachs but contains very little in the way of nutrients.

Grasses grown for hay should be cut and dried at the peak of their vegetative growth stage. This occurs when the seed heads first start to form. After their formation, the plant begins to concentrate its energy into seed making, and the vegetative material of the leaves begins to lose nutrients and become less succulent. The longer hay making is delayed after this occurs, the worse the hay gets. Unfortunately, local grasses are usually ready to be cut around the first of June. But the

Table 1
Common Manures and Fertilizers

Type of Fertilizer*	Material	N%	P%	K%	Rate of Application (pounds per 1,000 square feet per year)†	Duration of Effect
1. Nitrogen plus humus	Steer manure	1–2.5	.4–.7	2–3	1,000–2,000	2 years
	Dairy manure	.6–2.5	.3–.5	2–3	1,500–3,000	2 years
	Horse manure	.7–1.5	.3–.6	2–3	1,500–3,000	2 years
	Compost	.4–4.0	.3–2.0	1–3	300–3,000	2 years
	Rabbit manure	2.5	1.5	0.5	300–500	2 years
	Goat manure	1.5	.25	1	700–1,500	2 years
2. Phosphorus	Rock phosphate	…	33	…	20–50	5–10 years
3. Potassium	Kelp meal	1	…	12	10[1]	4–6 months
	Wood ashes	…	…	10	10	1–4 months
	Granite/basalt	…	…	3–7	20–40	3 years
4. Humus	Sawdust	…	…	1–2	1,000[2]	2 years
	Urea	42	…	…	15–25	1–4 months
5. Fertilizers (primarily to add nitrogen)	Urea	42	…	…	5–10	1–4 months
	Blood meal	12	…	…	10–20	1–4 months
	Hoof/horn meal	14	2	…	15–25	8–12 months
	Fish meal	10	6	…	10–20	4–6 months
	Cottonseed meal	4	2	1	50–100	4–6 months
	Chicken manure	4	2.5	1–2	300[1]	2 years
	Bone meal	3	20	…	15–25	6–12 months

* Use one from group 1, one from group 2, and one from group 3. Or, use one from group 2, one from group 3, and both from group 4.

† When a range of amounts is given, such as 20–50 pounds, use the smaller amount if your soil is already producing well. If the last year's performance of your garden was poor, use the maximum amount. If it is a new garden site, use the maximum amount.

[1] Do not use more. Chicken manure is very strong. Kelp meal contains growth hormones that can adversely affect plant behavior if used in larger quantities.

[2] Sawdust is so low in nitrogen and phosphorus that it will badly unbalance soil if added without a nitrogen and phosphorus supplement. Add a healthy ration of nitrogen and a liberal amount of rock phosphate (or bone meal) along with the sawdust. Apply sawdust only in the fall and till it in with the extra nitrogen and phosphorus. This allows enough time for it to break down and for the soil to stabilize before planting in spring.

weather does not settle down and permit hay making until much later—some years not until mid-July. By this time, the hay has less than half the value it would have had if cut and dried at the right time. It also is full of mature seeds.

Manure from horses or cows fed on local grass hay has many ungerminated weed seeds in it. If the same hay gets in the bedding, even more seeds are present in the manure. If such manure is spread on a garden, lots of future weeds are being sown at the same time. To avoid this, pile up fresh manure and let it compost—which it will do naturally. After a few weeks of bacterial fermentation, the steaming manure pile will automatically begin to cool. When you could comfortably insert your hand into the center of the pile—probably eight to twelve weeks after it is piled up—spread it without fear. The high heat inside the pile will have killed most of the seeds.

Livestock is often kept on a bedding of sawdust or wood chips. Douglas fir is very acid, and you need to add at least fifty pounds of agricultural lime to each pickup truck load of manure and fir chips mixture. This can be done as it is being spread over the garden, or it can be incorporated into the manure as you pile it up, if it is going to wait in a heap near the garden.

If the livestock's bedding is red cedar do not use their manure for garden fertilizer. Red cedar contains a poisonous oil that prevents other plants from growing. It also prevents the cedar from rotting, which is why red cedar has been used for fence posts in this country for a long time. Other kinds of cedar are all right to use.

Hemlock is the best woody material to use in a garden, since it is neither acid nor alkaline. If you have neighbors who do not use their livestock's manure, persuade them to use hemlock sawdust or planer shavings for bedding. Offer to pay any extra cost, just so you get the manure-bedding afterward. That makes a good deal both of you will like keeping.

Chicken manure makes very rich fertilizer. Plants lucky enough to be grown with it do very well. However, it cannot be used to lighten up soil and add humus as horse or cow manure can. This is because the nutrients in chicken manure are so concentrated. If you added enough chicken manure to supply the humus needed (1,000 to 2,000 pounds per 1,000 square feet) the vegetables would be so overdosed with nutrients that they would be poisoned. Three hundred pounds of chicken manure per 1,000 square feet of garden supplies more than enough fertilizer. The humus has to be supplied with compost or some other less potent manure.

Old manure piles that have been out in the rain for years still have lots of humus in them, but very little else in the way of nutrients. Heavy winter rains have leached the nutrients out, so old manure piles are not worth the trouble to haul.

Some gardeners try to use sawdust in place of manure. *Be warned:* sawdust is very low in nitrogen and phosphorus—so low that you have to add extra fertilizer to it when it is incorporated into the soil. Twenty-five pounds of blood meal or urea is needed to balance the nitrogen deficiency created by a one-inch covering of sawdust over a thousand square feet of garden. Apply the fertilizer and the sawdust at the same time (in the fall) and till them both into the soil. I do not recommend using sawdust unless a horse or cow has been bedded on it first. Then the manure, which gets mixed into the sawdust, brings everything into a more natural balance.

A city gardener may have no choice but to make the best of using sawdust in place of manure. I suspect manure will be increasingly hard to buy inexpensively. If you do use sawdust, I strongly suggest you add it in the fall, till it in, and give it plenty of time to break down by spring. You could also grow a green manure crop on that land during the winter.

Green Manures

The word *manure* actually refers to any organic material applied to soil with the intention of increasing its fertility. Green manure does not come from animals but from plants grown in the soil and then tilled back into that soil at the peak of their vegetative growth.

Green manuring has three beneficial effects. First, it will very slowly increase the amount of humus in the soil. It might take three or four years, but regular green manuring can double the natural level of humus. Second, by preventing winter losses, green manuring increases the mineral supply in the soil. The most common Pacific Northwest green manure plant is annual ryegrass. Sown in autumn, it makes considerable growth before the chill of winter stops it. The most important part of that growth is below ground. Ryegrass makes enormous root systems that incorporate almost every bit of available nutrient. The winter rains cannot wash out soil minerals because the grass has captured them. In the spring, when things start growing again, the ryegrass is tilled into the soil and within a week or two, the plants rot. All those captured nutrients are released again for spring and summer crops to use. The third benefit of green manuring is that the roots break up the soil and rapidly improve the tilth. This is quite a bonus for a few dollars' worth of seed and a little work with a rototiller. Soil left hard and bare under the drenching rains of winter is often an indication of a careless or inexperienced gardener.

Other green manures accomplish the same beneficial effects. Legumes, when grown as green manure, add humus and nitrogen in large quantities. Austrian field peas or crimson clover make a beautiful stand of thick vegetation by spring when sown with annual rye. But legumes will grow lushly only in soils that are not acid and that contain fairly good amounts of phosphorus. Ryegrass will thrive on any soil.

To plant a green manure crop, scatter seed thickly over the garden toward the end of September. Do so right among the standing crops. Feel free to lift the big cabbage leaves and scatter some seed under them, too. Rake the seed in about a half inch deep wherever the soil can be easily scratched up. When the fall rains start, the green manure will sprout. Let it grow all winter. Surprisingly, the green manure will not interfere with fall and early winter vegetable production. The grass and clover have only shallow root systems until winter, and do not compete with remaining vegetables. Unfortunately, green manuring cannot be used in those areas that are growing overwintering vegetables for spring harvest, because sometime in February the green manure will begin to grow rapidly and will overtop any vegetables.

As soon as the soil dries out enough to till, work the green manure into the soil, wait two or three weeks, and you are ready to do the final tilling and make up a good, crumbly seed bed. During those two or three weeks, the green manure will have rotted and disappeared completely, leaving only humus and a lot of minerals that would have been lost to winter leaching. A good rear-end rototiller is necessary for all mechanical tilling of green manure crops.

Gardeners who do not have a rototiller capable of chopping up green manure, or those who use raised-bed systems, have traditionally not green manured but instead have imported manures and made composts from crop waste and kitchen garbage. But it is very easy to green manure on raised beds, and doing so lets you work the soil much earlier in spring. With tillerless green manuring, you do not even try to incorporate the vegetation but instead you compost it in piles.

Certain kinds of green manures, such as grain rye and, to a lesser extent, ryegrass, form clumps of large, strong roots that take time to break down. Grasses have to be tilled into the soil, and weeks must pass before the root clumps disintegrate. Then a seed bed can be worked up. Grasses cannot easily be pulled by hand because large clumps of soil come up with the roots, or the root clumps remain in the soil after the grasses break off them. Other kinds of green manures have fine, delicate root systems that remain almost unnoticed in the soil after the plant is easily ripped out by hand. Plants like this leave a fine, soft soil, which immediately can be raked into a seed bed.

A raised-bed or tillerless gardener can grow Austrian field peas, crimson clover, fava beans (which will overwinter in milder areas), or corn salad (which makes an edible green manure crop). Any of these can be planted in early fall and pulled up in spring just before you want to plant. The tops are composted, and half the weight of the plant (the root system) remains in the soil. If the soil is not too wet at this time, it can be loosened a little with a spading fork. If it is too wet to till even gently, it will tolerate a rake on the surface.

The bed will retain its shape, even after a winter of hard rains, for the green manure crop will have prevented erosion. After the soil has been bared, add about a half inch of compost or manure, and any lime, rock phosphate, or fertilizer needed. Then use a rake and mix the amendments into the top inch of soil. Rake out a fine seed bed and plant.

With a system like this, I can plant easily in spring after only two days without rain. I find this quite an improvement over the old timers' attitude that you "can't plant until the end of May, and if you're lucky, you'll be able to till by then."

The vegetation removed to make the bed goes into the compost pile. If you pulled it up in late spring, it may be used as a mulch. Careful attention to producing lots of green manures should eliminate most need for imported manure.

Soil pH

The only soil test a gardener needs to perform is for soil pH, which is a scale for measuring acidity. On the pH scale, 7.0 is neutral, less than 7.0 is acid, and above 7.0 is alkaline. Vegetables grow best when the soil is close to neutral. East of the Cascades gardeners have to correct alkaline soils. On our side of the mountains, we have acid ones to deal with.

It is not hard to find out the pH of your soil. Most nurseries sell an inexpensive test kit for a few dollars, and one kit will make years of tests. Try it! Test your soil. It will almost certainly be below 6.0 unless it has been well limed within the last five years.

Agricultural lime (calcium) is traditionally used to correct acid soils. It will *gradually*, over the course of a year or two, raise the pH in the direction of 7.0. If your soil test indicates a pH of between 5.5 and 6.0, spread fifty pounds of agricultural lime per thousand square feet of garden. If the pH is between 5.0 and 5.5, double the application. The best time to lime is in fall, but before you plant in spring will do. Work the lime into the top few inches of soil when you rototill, or spade and rake the soil. Lime not well incorporated into soil will do very little good. Experiments on my pasture seem to indicate that if the lime were simply dusted on the surface and not tilled in, it would take about ten times more to have the same effect on pH.

Be sure to use agricultural lime, not hydrated lime. Hydrated lime is for making cement, disinfecting animal pens, and curing smelly outhouses. Hydrated lime also dissolves quickly in the soil and leaches rapidly. You should use dolomite if you can find it. It is a type of agricultural lime but contains more magnesium than other types do. The magnesium is useful in some soils and will not hurt any of them. It also makes fruits sweeter.

Once each year, retest your soil and add lime as indicated by the pH test.

If testing seems like too much of a complication to you, here is a pat formula that will not overdo the lime and will improve things. If your garden soil is sandy, add twenty-five pounds of lime per thousand square feet *each year*. If it is loam, add about forty pounds. If it is clay, add about fifty pounds.

Mulching

Mulch is a layer of organic material (and sometimes sheets of plastic) laid on the soil's surface around growing plants. There is much controversy about mulching and much interest in the subject. It all started with a lady named Ruth Stout, whose book *Gardening Without Work* was quite revolutionary when it was published over twenty years ago. Ruth developed a system in which a mulch of hay and straw is spread about six inches deep over the garden and is kept there throughout the year. The thick mulch prevents weeds from sprouting, and it keeps the soil soft and workable with no tilling or spading. The only garden chores consist of planting and harvesting.

Unfortunately, year-round permanent mulching does not work well in

Table 2
Effects of Soil pH on the Availability of Plant Nutrients

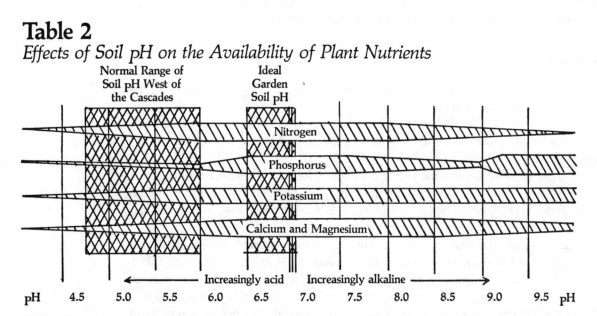

Width of the bar indicates the availability of some plant nutrients at various soil pHs. Increasing acidity below 6.5 makes nutrients more and more unavailable to plants. Simply by changing soil pH upward in the direction of 7.0, a far higher percentage of the soil's nutrients becomes available. If the soil is potentially rich, but acid, a healthy dose of agricultural lime will often turn it from an apparently poor soil to one that is quite good. In the same way, if you add nutrients to an acid soil, they only become immediately unavailable to the plants. The most basic, important step in soil improvement is adjusting the pH.

western Oregon, and I doubt that it would work anywhere this side of the mountains. One problem with mulching is that you need basically rich soil to start with. West of the Cascades, where we have to use lime and rock phosphate, and sometimes even rock potash, to maintain or increase soil fertility, mulch prevents the incorporation of these materials into the soil. Another difficulty with a year-round vegetative mulch is that it is an ideal breeding ground for many insects and slugs. In continental climates, such as in Connecticut, the soil freezes solid every winter, often as deep as three feet, which kills off most of the overwintering pests. We do not have sufficient cold to do that, so with permanent mulch the pests almost ruin your garden.

Mulch also slows the soil's warming up in spring. This is crucial, since vegetables will not grow well until the soil is warm enough. Some seeds will not even germinate until temperatures are over sixty degrees. Low temperatures also cripple root systems and send tomatoes, peppers, and eggplants into shock. Where I have tried a permanent mulch, it has taken as much as three weeks longer to get the soil warm enough to plant than in the areas in which I did not mulch.

I do use mulching under certain conditions, however. For example, where there is limited water, mulch can reduce evaporation by as much as 70 percent. An inch or so of grass clippings or straw (grass seed, barley, or wheat) will do the trick. Because mulches cool the soil, they must not be applied before mid-June. If it is a rainy summer, I would not mulch at all, so that the soil temperature can rise as much as possible. It is very important that any mulch left in the fall be raked up and composted.

Hay does not make good mulch, since it is usually full of ungerminated weed and grass seeds. To be used as mulch, it first needs to stand out for a winter in the rain and rot well. Then the bales can be broken up and the hay used. Even after one year of rotting there will still be some ungerminated seeds, but not so many that I would not use it. Some years, when it is rainy during haying season, it can be purchased for next to nothing.

Mulching with Manure or Compost

Another way to mulch is with manure or compost. I use this technique myself and have worked out a system in which I never have to till my soil. (Unfortunately, our climate prohibits a thick enough mulch to stop weeds, too, so I cannot escape that chore—yet.) Here is how it works.

When preparing my beds before planting, I rake them until they are smooth, then mulch them with an inch of compost or well-rotted manure, rake it into the top inch of soil, and plant or transplant. This mulch also greatly reduces evaporation, but not as much as grass or straw would. It also is completely gone—rotted into the soil—by fall.

Because I use raised beds (for an explanation of this method see the "Tillage" chapter) and do not compact my growing soil with foot traffic, I find that this inch of compost-mulch is all the humus my soil needs to maintain its high level of tilth. At first it was necessary to till considerable amounts of humus and nutrients into my soil, but after a few years of this, a mulching is all I need to do to *maintain* my garden.

This same kind of maintenance can also be done with sawdust, as sawdust mulch will not deprive soil of nitrogen if it is not deeply tilled into the land. However, it contains no nitrogen by itself so a bit of nitrogen fertilizer must be mixed into the sawdust when it is raked into the top inch of soil. Any of the nitrogen fertilizers in Table 1 can be used for this purpose at the recommended rate.

Plastic Mulches

Plastic mulches raise soil temperature several degrees and enhance growth of such hot-weather plants as tomatoes, eggplants, peppers, cantaloupes, and watermelons, which are not really adapted to our climate. It is nearly impossible to grow melons without plastic mulch this side of the Cascades, except in certain banana belts such as the Umpqua Valley and along the Rogue River. Eggplants and peppers are greatly benefited by plastic, although they can be raised without it. Tomatoes get a slight assist. Black plastic is the type to use, as it also prevents weeds. I have also used tarpaper, and the plants have not suffered from the tar.

Composting

Compost is the result of vegetation or manure rotting until it becomes something like soil. Most people think composting is done in piles, but this is not necessarily so. Another, easier method of making compost is done in the soil and is called sheet composting. To sheet compost, spread organic material on the surface of the garden and till it in. That is all there is to it. Sheet composting is best done in fall, after the summer's crops are harvested, and is good to do before planting a green manure crop.

When people spread manure and till it in, or do the same with sawdust, they actually are composting the material. It is important to compost organic matter before growing plants on soil containing it. This is because soil bacteria rapidly go to work devouring any fresh organic matter and change it into humus. While this initial rotting is going on, humus-forming bacteria take into their own bodies all the available nutrients in the rotting material, *plus* any nutrients that are in the surrounding soil. This results in very poor plant growth for a time. The duration of this effect is controlled by the amount of nitrogen in the material being rotted or in the soil itself if the material has little or no nitrogen of its own. More nitrogen means more bacteria, which means faster rotting.

Once the primary rotting has occurred and the bacteria have made humus of the vegetation or manure, they die off in large numbers. The nutrients they captured are released into the soil as the bacteria's bodies rot. Even fresh horse and cow manures rob the soil of nutrients, although they usually go through their initial rotting phase within a matter of weeks—often before the seeds you plant after tilling in the manure have germinated.

Only compost can be added to soil without unbalancing it for a while. Composting in piles is a way to accomplish primary rotting quickly and outside the soil. A compost pile must contain organic material, air, water, and enough nitrogen to feed the enormous colony of decay bacteria that will multiply in the pile and rapidly convert it to humus. If there is too little nitrogen, composting takes a long time—sometimes over a year.

Everything organic can be composted, either in the soil or in piles. Leaves, grass clippings, vegetable trimmings, cornstalks, peavines, weeds, kitchen garbage, hair, manures—all are excellent sources of humus. The only things to keep out of the compost pile are animal fats, which will not rot, and any part of a red cedar or walnut tree, which contains oils that may be poisonous to other plants.

A compost pile should contain at least one-third manure or have one pound of any strong nitrogen source such as blood meal or urea added to each cubic foot of material. The only exception is compost piles of *fresh* legume vegetation. Legumes are so rich in nitrogen that they will compost rapidly without any additional help.

For the city gardener, sloppy compost piles are usually out of the question. Neat compost bins can be fairly attractive, however, and not offend neighbors or guests. The simplest bins I ever used were made of two-by-four-inch welded wire, which is sometimes called "turkey wire." It comes in various heights, but the three-foot-high wire fencing makes the best compost rings. A piece fifteen feet long will form a self-supporting circle about four feet in diameter, which can be easily unhooked and removed after the pile is constructed. The pile will retain the cylindrical shape all by itself after it has settled for a few weeks. People have also made composting bins out of cinderblocks, snowfencing, boards, and even large garbage cans or oil drums.

Composting is best done with a two bin system. Make your bins at least three by three by three feet but no larger than four by four by four feet. Begin filling one bin with materials as they are available. The pile will naturally be built in layers, and none of these should be more than a few inches thick. Optimally, the layers will alternate: vegetation, manure, garbage, vegetation, manure, garbage, and so on. A sprinkling of garden soil from time to time will "seed" the pile with compost-forming bacteria and hasten rotting. The garbage can be set into the center of the pile and immediately covered with vegetation or manure to keep varmints out.

Serious composters will have a stock of manure on hand, even if it is in sacks, so it can be added to the pile as needed. They also will have a compost bucket or garbage-collecting container in the kitchen, where all kitchen waste can be stored for a few days. When there is finally sufficient accumulation, it is put in the compost pile.

Think of these materials as *vegetation:* seaweed, leaves, grass clippings, squash vines, cornstalks, hay, peavines, straw, sawdust, weeds, and any other crop residues. Think of these materials as *garbage:* fruit, meat scraps, fish waste, leftovers, burned food, and spoiled food. Think of these materials as *organic nitrogen fertilizers:* brewers' waste (usually sold as cattle feed), fish meal, coffee grounds, blood meal, cottonseed meal, hair, lobster shells, shrimp wastes, and urea.

When the first bin is full, start filling the second. By the time the second is half-full, the first should be ready to use. Composting takes eight to twenty weeks from start to finish. The outside few inches of the finished pile will not have rotted, so as the first pile is being used the outsides are shoveled into the middle of the second pile, which is now being built.

A dry compost heap does not rot. Water the materials well as you build the pile. If kept covered with a plastic sheet, the pile will not dry out so rapidly in summer. If it should dry out, water it again. A plastic cover in winter will prevent the pile from getting too wet and leaching out. A pile should be very damp to the touch, but not oozing water when a handful is squeezed hard.

Troubleshooting

Intense bacterial activity results in lots of heat. Within a few days of building the compost pile, the heat inside should approach 160 degrees. If your pile is built in stages, heating should begin once it gets about two feet deep. After a week or two of this very high temperature, the pile will slowly begin to cool off. Complete cooling means the composting is done.

If the pile gives off a smell of ammonia, it contains too much nitrogen or too much manure and will be too hot inside. Make your next pile with a greater percentage of vegetation. The presence of ammonia means nitrogen is escaping into the air. That nitrogen is better off in your soil.

If a compost pile does not get hot, or rotting does not take place inside, it means the pile is deficient in manure or nitrogen, it is not damp enough, or it is too small and the heat created by rotting is being lost to the air as fast as it is created. You do want the heat to be retained, as bacterial rotting goes much faster at high temperatures. Heat also kills fly larvae.

If the pile gives off bad smells, or the inside core is bad smelling and has a consistency of blackish goo, the pile is starved for air, and a different kind of bacterial action is going on—one that happens without oxygen present. Either you made the pile too large and air cannot penetrate, or it was constructed solely out of material such as grass and leaves that does not pass air. Using coarse materials such as cornstalks and brush, especially for the bottom layers, allows the pile to breathe.

If the pile is made correctly it will not smell, will not breed flies, and will turn into humus in less than four months.

Hole Composting

One simple method I use in my garden in the winter is hole composting. At this time there is no vegetation with which to make piles, but there is an abundance of kitchen garbage. I dig a hole about two feet deep and about two feet in diameter in the garden and toss the garbage into it. When it is two-thirds full, I heap the earth up over the garbage and dig a new hole. The next summer I plant winter squashes over these compost holes, and do they grow wildly! I can do this because my garden is fenced to keep the deer out, and this same fence keeps the dog out. And there are no rats around. I suppose a city gardener could cover the hole with a square of hardware cloth to keep the critters out. In an average winter I make and fill about ten holes, and there are only two of us to produce the kitchen garbage.

A Word of Encouragement

Compost making usually seems overwhelming and very complicated to a novice gardener. It isn't. Compost making is a little like baking bread. You can follow the recipe, but to get really good bread, you have to have experience. Remember, no matter how "bad" the compost turns out, it will still be good and usable. If the pile got too hot—so what? So you lost some nitrogen. Next time resolve to do better. If the pile is not heating, tear it down and see if it is dry inside, or add more manure or nitrogen fertilizer to it. If it smells, make it smaller or mix some coarse stuff into it, or wait a few weeks and the pile will stop smelling. Make a few piles, and you will get the feel of it.

Maintaining Soil

Once a soil is truly rich, a complete soil maintenance program can maintain a high level of humus in the soil without requiring manures from outside the garden. The soil requires only a little lime and rock phosphate from time to time. If it were one of the rare potash-deficient soils, it would also need a little rock potash or kelp meal.

What is rich enough soil? It is soil that is not acid and contains at least two to three times the natural level of humus. Natural soil humus rarely exceeds 2 percent. To get your garden soil up from there to a range of from 4 to 6 percent requires the initial addition of about twenty to forty pickup-truck loads of manure per acre or about one-half to one load per thousand square feet of garden.

Rich enough soil also supplies *abundant* phosphorus during the entire growing season. This concept of abundant phosphorus is the key idea that revolutionized my gardening, making me realize that more than manures were needed in an organic garden. When we moved to Oregon several years ago, I had never gardened in soil that was so phosphate poor. I was accustomed to good rich soils that have somewhere between 2,000 and 5,000 pounds of potentially available phosphorus in the top eight inches of soil in each acre. That really is not very much and is only a few parts per million by weight. I have never seen an Oregon soil that tested out at much better than 1,200 pounds of phosphorus per acre, and most are *much* poorer than that.

Curing phosphorus deficiencies is very simple if you make the assumption that the soil has no significant phosphorus at all and decide to add sufficient rock phosphate to raise it to at least 2,000—and 3,000 or 4,000 is better—pounds of potentially available phosphorus per acre. That translates to putting at least 6,000 pounds of rock phosphate (33 percent phosphorus) into each acre of soil. This works out to about 150 pounds per thousand square feet. You could go up to as much as 15,000 pounds per acre without causing any harm and getting additional benefit, but I do not know if the benefit is worth the high cost.

Some soils are so phosphate deficient that an application of fifty pounds of rock phosphate per thousand square feet seems to have no effect. The next year, corn and legumes grow very poorly despite the expense and effort. This is because rock phosphate takes several years to break down significantly. A good indicator of this situation is sweet corn. In phosphate-poor soils corn comes up dark green with purplish tints and is very stunted. (In nitrogen-poor soils it comes up light green.) If this has happened, sprinkle bone meal around the roots (this technique is called "side-dressing") at the rate recommended in Table 1, and add more rock phosphate the next year. The amendment will take full effect within a few years.

Once a high level of phosphorus is attained, it will maintain itself in the soil for many years. In these days of inflation, this looks like a terrific investment to me. The price of phosphate fertilizer has gone up 50 percent this year and will continue to increase rapidly because we are more likely to run out of phosphates than we are to run out of oil. What better security could you buy than the ability to produce your own abundant food supply without further inputs for many years?

All soil arrives at a balance—either the natural one or one the cultivator encourages. The balance is one of life processes. Each spot is capable of producing so much vegetation each year. If that vegetation rots back into the soil it will maintain a regular percentage of soil humus. The amount of vegetation is determined primarily by the soil's nutrient level and the climate. The higher the nutrient level, the higher the humus level.

If the gardener raises the basic nutrient level and then encourages the land to produce crop after crop and returns it to the soil, the humus percentage will increase. As humus increases, the soil produces even more abundant vegetation. You should see the stands of green manure I get!

I know that a gardener is better off to concentrate on nutrients rather than manure. A soil that has only 2 percent humus, abundant phosphorus and potassium, and no trace element deficiencies, and is not acid can produce more food than one that is highly nutrient deficient and yet has 6 or even 8 percent humus. But, of course, a soil with an abundance of nutrients and 6 percent humus does even better.

Fertilizing

There are considerable differences between fertilizing plants and improving soil. When fertilizing, the gardener thinks about the specific nutrient needs of individual plants and puts those nutrients where the plants can use them. It is a short-term effort made to get plants to respond rapidly. Improving soil, on the other hand, is a long-term project, designed to make a soil so rich eventually that the plants in the garden get all the nutrients they need in a natural and sustained manner.

Fertilizing is done either to make up for a lack of soil improvement or to feed those few types of plants that require larger quantities of nitrogen than most soils can possibly provide. Nitrogen is a very "dangerous" fertilizer. Using it is almost addictive (to the gardener) because it causes the most profound and rapid change in plant growth. Adding nitrogen makes plants' leaves change color to a darker green, evidence that nitrogen is the key to helping plants manufacture chlorophyll. Chlorophyll is vital to photosynthesis. With more of it, the plant can produce more food and so will grow more rapidly. If there is not a *severe* shortage of other needed nutrients, simply increasing the amount of available nitrogen will make most plants grow larger and more rapidly and will make them more productive.

One special time for using nitrogen fertilizer is in early spring. Then, low soil temperatures result in little bacterial activity and thus a very slow release of nutrients. Spring greens such as mustards and spinach demand high nitrogen levels to perform properly. A little blood meal worked into their planting bed just before sowing the seed makes a world of difference.

Fertilization is also useful when growing cauliflower. A generous dose of nitrogen applied when the plants are about ten inches tall will kick them into a vigorous growth cycle and produce a curd often twice as large as if no fertilization were given.

Nitrogen can also be used when transplanting tomatoes, peppers, and eggplants. A good one-time nitrogen feeding results in about six weeks of fast vegetative growth, after which the plants settle down to some serious fruit making. It is also crucial for growing really big leafy greens such as cabbages. Rarely can soil supply all the nitrogen these kinds of plants could use.

On all occasions where a short period of vigorous growth is desired, I use blood meal. Generally it is sufficient to sprinkle it on the ground around the roots. One-half cup is plenty for a large plant, and ⅛ cup will handle a transplant. If it is going into a planting bed before seeding, I use three to six pounds per hundred square feet of bed or hundred feet of row.

Another technique that produces rapid growth of leaf structure is the use of fish emulsion fertilizer, which is liquid, organic, and immediately available to the plant. A cup or two of this diluted fertilizer is enough to kick any plant into vigorous growth for a week or two. Fish emulsion is mostly nitrogen.

A gentler way to supply nitrogen is to make manure tea. To "brew" it, either spread a mulch of *fresh* manure around the plant and make the tea automatically as you water, or fill a five-gallon plastic pail with about one-quarter fresh manure and three-quarters water. Allow the tea to brew for twenty-four to forty-eight hours, and apply it sparingly to plants. A cup or two weekly should do it. Manure tea can replace fish emulsion and costs nothing. Blood meal tea is also very effective. Use about two cups of meal per bucket of water.

Another technique I have been experimenting with is foliar feeding. The idea behind this is that the plant's leaves are capable of absorbing nutrients. This will occur only while the sun is shining directly on the leaves. Under intense light, leaves will thirstily suck up a considerable amount of moisture. All you do is spray the leaves until all of them are moistened and the solution is dripping off.

Weekly foliar feeding will produce a considerable result. Spraying every two or three days will cause the plant to put on absolutely every bit of growth it can. Organic gardeners spray with fish emulsion, diluted to the concentration prescribed by its manufacturer. I have found that I can double that concentration without burning my plants.

I know that using nitrogen fertilizer sounds wonderfully positive and easy, but let me warn you that I am not sure that making overly large plants makes more nutritious or tastier ones. It certainly does cause the soil to get harder and lose tilth, if that nitrogen comes to the plants through the soil. It may also make plants less disease-resistant and more prone to insect attack. It certainly makes them less frost hardy. In the last chapter of this book you will find details of when and how to fertilize individual plants.

Although organic soil improvement does not necessarily supply plants with all the nitrogen they *could* use, it does supply them with bountiful phosphorus and potassium and the trace elements. No fertilizer has to be used to add these mineral nutrients—rock flours will provide plenty. But suppose it is already past planting time when you find yourself reading this. Your garden has been put in, without attention to soil improvement, and you have realized for the first time how important it is to provide plants with abundant nutrients. Or perhaps you are just about to plant, and there is not time to round up rock flours and manure, till them in, and still plant in time. If this is your situation, you will need a complete fertilizer that supplies all the nutrients.

You will also want something that breaks down quite rapidly and has an immediate effect. Commercial market growers—who are normally faced with this situation—side-dress their plants with water-soluble chemicals, either by adding them to the irrigation water or by spreading narrow bands of chemicals between the rows above the roots and then watering or waiting for rain. It is not as easy for someone committed to organic gardening to do this. Rock flours are not very quick-acting compared to chemicals and definitely are not very water soluble. Organics have to be *in* the soil to do all the good they can, unless you foliar feed with fish emulsion.

If I were faced with a garden already growing in poor soil or with poorly growing plants in a new garden, I would make a mixture of three parts blood meal, eight parts bone meal (either steamed or raw), and one part kelp meal (if I could find it). Then I would sprinkle about ten pounds of this material as a side-dressing along each hundred-foot row of plants and rake it into the top half inch of soil. This same fertilizer could be raked into the row or bed before planting. A mixture like this one contains both fast and slow releasing forms of nitrogen, considerable phosphorus, some potassium, and all the trace elements plants can use. It should last for about four months. Then, as soon as I could, I would begin a serious soil improvement program that would eliminate the need for most fertilizing.

Outflow Equals Inflow

There is a principle that operates in this universe like a physical law. The principle is that *outflow equals inflow*. If you want a garden to produce, it is absolutely necessary to put in nutrients, care, concern, attention, intention, and perhaps even some love. The two sides of the equation must balance.

Few people want to believe this about their gardens. They will try anything, except doing what they know is really required, and then wonder why things will never work as well as they should. I have almost had to force some of my neighbors to put a sack of lime into their soil—even after they have seen how much better my garden grows than most of theirs. And I am gardening on just about the most ruined, worn out pasture in the Lorane Valley.

Some lucky people realize that outflow equals inflow and operate their lives

Table 3
Comparative Production Techniques

Crop	U.S. Average Yield Per Acre (in pounds)	Intensive Yield Per Acre (in pounds)
Bush beans	2,200	19,000
Beets	13,000	65,000
Brussel sprouts	10,000	45,000
Celery	45,000	200,000

Table 4
Amounts of Organic Fertilizers Used by Ecology Action

Fish meal . . . . 50 pounds
Rock phosphate . . . . 100 pounds
Kelp meal . . . . 10 pounds
Manure or compost . . . . 10 cubic yards
(about 5,000 pounds)

Table 5
Amounts of Organic Fertilizers Used after Two Years of Treatment

Fish meal . . . . 30 pounds
Rock phosphate . . . . 50 pounds
Kelp meal . . . . 10 pounds
Manure or compost . . . . 3 cubic yards

as though the principle were as true as the law of gravity. These people are usually successful at whatever they do. Those of you who doubt the principle would do well to give it a fair try.

If you still need to be convinced, take note of the work of Ecology Action, a dedicated group of researchers located in Palo Alto, California. They have been studying French Intensive organic vegetable production techniques in an effort to develop useful methods of food production that have far higher than normal outputs but require less energy (gasoline) input. They hope to find the tools to prevent widespread starvation in the near future. Some of their results are described in Table 3.

As you can see, the experimenters are getting at least four times the average U.S. production. They believe their yields will increase considerably over what they are at present as more skill is acquired and their soil improves further. The U.S. farmers whose work makes up the average yield are using chemical fertilizers and are very skillfully managing their lands and crops. They are backed by university-trained agronomists and other researchers, both academic and commercial. The experimenters at Ecology Action are using only organic fertilizers. Their information is largely derived from experience.

Table 4 lists what each thousand square feet at Ecology Action receives each year. After two years of such treatment, the soil has reached such a high level of fertility that the amendments can be reduced to those described in Table 5.

It may well be that Ecology Action is using more amendments than most gardeners need, since they are working with an extremely heavy, infertile clay soil. Even the reduced amount they use after the first two years (three cubic yards per thousand square feet) is too high for gardeners west of the Cascades. Our cooler temperatures result in less bacterial activity and a corresponding reduction in humus loss. The manure amounts recommended in Table 1 are more in line with our area's requirements. But if you have a clay soil, you may well need to double or triple them for a year or two until your soil has loosened.

If you are interested in learning *How to Grow More Vegetables Than You Ever Thought Possible on Less Land Than You Can Imagine,* purchase the book with that title. It is listed in "Further Reading" at the end of the book.

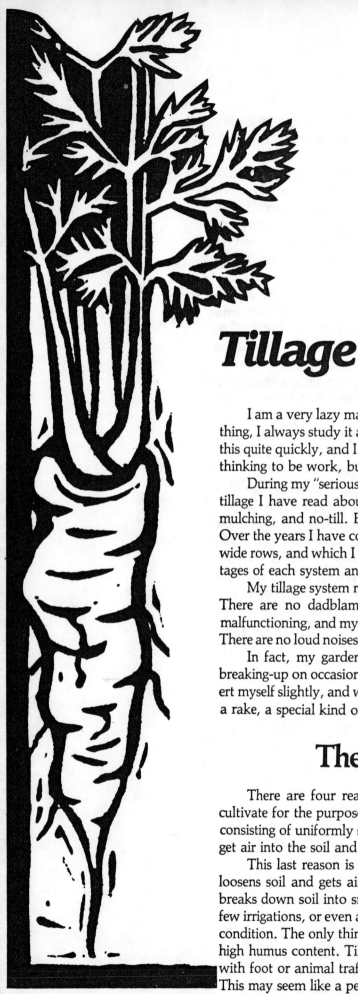

Tillage

I am a very lazy man who gets lots of work done. When I set out to do something, I always study it and find the easiest way to handle the job. I usually can do this quite quickly, and I believe my success is due to the fact that I do not consider thinking to be work, but fun.

During my "serious gardener" years I have experimented with every system of tillage I have read about or heard about—single rows, wide rows, raised beds, mulching, and no-till. Each of these systems has advantages and disadvantages. Over the years I have come to rely on raised beds, which I often plant in single or wide rows, and which I often mulch and rarely till. I think I have taken the advantages of each system and discarded the hard work of all of them.

My tillage system requires no rototiller. This means that my life is simplified. There are no dadblamed blankety-blank machines that are always breaking, malfunctioning, and mysteriously doing things that demand trips to the repairman. There are no loud noises or bad smells. I can hear the birds while I am in the garden.

In fact, my garden *requires* no tilling at all, although I do do a little soil breaking-up on occasion—when the soil is just right, when I am in the mood to exert myself slightly, and when it is not too hot. All I need is a spading fork, a shovel, a rake, a special kind of hoe, and very little effort.

The Benefits of Tilling

There are four reasons to till a garden: to incorporate soil improvers, to cultivate for the purpose of weed-killing, to make a seed bed (a well-worked soil consisting of uniformly small particles that allows seeds to germinate well), and to get air into the soil and loosen it up.

This last reason is not as straightforward as it sounds. The idea that tillage loosens soil and gets air into it is not totally accurate. Tilling very temporarily breaks down soil into smaller particles, makes it softer, and adds air. But after a few irrigations, or even after just a few weeks of time, the soil returns to its original condition. The only thing that keeps soil light, air-filled, and in small particles is a high humus content. Tilling will take compacted soil that has been beaten down with foot or animal traffic or tractor tires and make it return to its natural state. This may seem like a permanent improvement if no more animals or feet or tractors get on the soil. But actually it is only returning that land to its native condition. It has not really improved it.

Gardeners have traditionally followed the farmer's lead and imitated large-scale farming practices. Single long-row gardens look like little farms and may please the aesthetic sense of the gardeners who create them, but they make much more work than necessary. Each spring the soil is tilled to loosen it up and make a seed bed. After the seeds germinate, foot traffic in the garden rapidly compacts the soil. By the end of the season, the soil is very hard. It is so hard, in fact, that it must be loosened up again the following spring.

If that soil were placed in raised beds so there were no feet on the growing areas, once it had received enough humus to make it really loose it would stay that way until the humus was gone. The plants' roots could easily penetrate it without further loosening, and there would be enough air in it for the roots to breathe and for microlife to exist in large numbers. Unless excessive nitrogen fertilizer were used, the humus would remain for many years; very little would have to be replaced.

Raised-Bed Gardening

If you have been gardening in the traditional manner, I suggest you redesign your garden and put most of it into raised beds. If it is fall when you read this, add any needed lime or rock phosphate and put your garden into a green manure now. Then in spring, spread as much manure as you can stand to haul (up to three inches deep over the entire garden). If it is already spring when you read this, check the pH and add any needed lime and rock phosphate along with the manure. Then till your garden.

Lay out your beds and paths. Make the planting areas about four feet wide and as long as you like (up to about twenty-five feet), with two-foot-wide paths between the beds. Then shovel a few inches of soil from what are to be the paths onto what are becoming the beds. This raises them four inches or so above the paths. Using a rake, pull the clods from the top inch or so of the bed down into the paths. Then, spread about a half-inch mulch of fine compost or manure on top and rake it into the surface.

This mulch helps keep the bed from drying out, and when furrows are made for planting, the seeds are covered mostly by compost. The seeds stay damp, and there is no crust to prevent delicate seedlings from sprouting. The compost also acts as a mulch during much of the growing season, and when the bed is prepared again for later planting, it is rotted completely into the soil.

Maintaining the Raised Beds

If you make the soil rich enough the first time you raise the beds, surface applications of compost-mulch are the only humus your soil will ever need. In other words, no more tilling—ever. Once you have established raised beds they are very easy to maintain. Whenever you wish to replant, use the following procedure.

First, pull out any vegetation, including weeds, green manures, and the old crop, growing on the bed and put it in a compost pile. Then determine by the squeezing test if the soil can be loosened up. Grab a handful of soil and squeeze it hard. If moisture comes out in drops, forget it. If you till at this moisture you will ruin that soil for months until the clods you will form break down again. If the soil gums up and makes a tight ball when you squeeze it, you will have the same problem. But if the soil makes a ball that, when pinched firmly, breaks up into fine pieces, it is just right. If the soil will not form a ball at all, it is too dry to till and also too dry to be growing anything very well. You should be irrigating more.

This next step is optional. If the soil is at the right moisture to be worked deeply, loosen it up using a garden fork. Push the prongs into the soil to their full depth—twelve inches. Lever back the handle until the tines lift up the soil. It will come up in a big chunk as you first lift and will break up into several large pieces. Do not turn this soil over; let it settle back where it came from, and slide out the tines. This creates large air channels that will last quite a while. After removing the fork, work back four to six inches and insert the fork again. Continue this until the entire bed has been broken up twelve inches deep. A five-by-twenty-foot bed takes me twenty minutes.

Then go around the bed with a shovel and scrape up about one-half to one inch of soil from the path and shovel it up onto the top of the bed. This takes only a minute or two. Next, spread any needed soil amendments on the bed—lime, rock phosphate, fertilizers, and a half inch or so of well-rotted manure or compost (sawdust can be used if additional nitrogen fertilizer is used with it).

Then, using a garden rake, work the surface up into a seed bed. It is hard to describe in writing exactly how to use a rake—it takes experimentation. If you are expert at raking, however, you can make the surface inch of the bed into fine soil. The manure or compost will be completely mixed in, so this surface layer is incredibly rich and humusy. Any clods of soil or clumps of manure or compost will be pulled to the outside of the bed, so that some will be on the outside slopes of the bed and some in the path. The bed will be flat and well shaped. All this work takes about twenty minutes.

Making a good seed bed is extremely important. It is the key to making seeds germinate well. Consider: what are you doing when you plant a seed? A seed is an embryonic plant locked in the center of a small amount of stored-up food that keeps the embryo alive. Warmth and moisture start the seed sprouting. During germination it uses its store of food very rapidly, putting up leaves, starting roots, and pushing aside the earth as it seeks the light. If conditions are not just right, it dies. The delicate roots need to find soft soil they can penetrate to begin extracting water from. A big clod of earth on top of the weak stem could prevent the leaves from quickly finding the light, which must happen before the plant can start producing food.

If the soil has good tilth and is moist, the seed succeeds. If the soil is not soft and crumbly, most seeds will fail to germinate properly. If this does not make you realize again how important humus is, go back and reread the section about tilth.

Raised beds are permanent. I never step on a growing bed for any reason, since this prevents soil compaction and makes the beds much easier to work up later on. Raised beds eventually are soft and air-filled to a depth of two feet or more. Humus transported by worms and plants' roots that are left to rot in the subsoil after harvest do this naturally.

Raised beds eliminated my need for a rototiller. I would advise most gardeners working on a backyard scale not to buy a rototiller but to rent one for the first year's preparation, put the garden into raised beds, and spend the money you saved on rock phosphate, lime, and manure for the coming years. You will be able to work up beds easily by hand in coming years. I can do a five-by-twenty-foot bed in about one hour with hand tools and no sweat.

Of course, gardeners who still think that a garden has to be "put in" in one weekend late in May are going to need a power tiller. But this is not the best way to plant a garden. Having only one planting reduces the garden's production and limits the time during which it will provide you with fresh food to late summer and fall. Gardens can be put in from early February until the middle of September. Doing this results in nearly twelve months of food production—and fresh food is much better than canned or dried foods, no matter how well put up they are. Planting from February to September also means there is only one bed, or even one part of one bed, to be worked up at any one time. It is actually pleasant work, and not overwhelming.

I do not use boards or bricks around the beds to "hold them up." This seems like needless work to me. It can be quite attractive and might appeal to someone with a manicured yard, but retaining walls are more of a hindrance than a help. For one thing, you want to be able to rake the clods down into the paths where they are broken down by foot traffic. For another, what little soil erodes off the bed is mostly compost from the top. This mixes with the clods in the paths, and by the time you toss an inch of soil from the paths back on to the bed, which you do when re-forming the bed, the clods will be rich, humusy soil that will not form clods again.

Double Digging

There is a lot of interest among gardeners these days in the French Intensive or Biodynamic French Intensive double-digging method of bed preparation. There is nothing wrong with this technique, but I feel it creates more work than is usually justified. The idea is essentially to incorporate humus and other amendments to a depth of two feet by the strenuous work of double digging. Doing this allows the plants to make more vertical root systems, and thus they can be planted much closer together than they normally could be and still get enough nutrients and water. The yields are much higher than with standard methods, as I mentioned in the last chapter.

I have found that if a copious amount of humus is incorporated at one time to a depth of six inches or so, the soil will gradually soften deeper and deeper as long as additional humus is added to the surface each year and the gardener avoids soil compaction by using raised beds. Allowing nature to soften your beds gradually is a lot less work. My present garden is three years old, yet the beds are now soft to a depth of twelve to sixteen inches, and next year I expect them to be soft to nearly eighteen or twenty inches. Each year the yield goes up, and each year I plant a little closer together.

If you are gardening in a very small space and need maximum production *this* year, you will have to use double digging. (Read *How to Grow More Vegetables Than You Ever Thought Possible on Less Land Than You Can Imagine* to find out how to do it. See "Further Reading" at the end of this book.) But if you can wait a few years for production to steadily increase, save your effort.

A Strategy
for Heavy Clay Soils

I have had numerous people ask me about how to handle their "gumbo" clays. These people have a very, very difficult task ahead of them, but you *can* garden on heavy clay. Properly handled, clay makes the finest gardens for every kind of crop except carrots and parsnips.

The problem with clay is that it must be worked when it is *just right*. Other soil types allow some latitude about soil moisture, but not clay. If it is too wet, you get impossible clods, If it is too dry, you get dust, or you cannot even put the shovel into it. And it never seems to dry out in spring.

The first thing you should do with clay is to see about improving drainage. Dig a test hole to see if there is a hard, compacted layer eight to twelve inches down. This hardpan, if you have one, will often be a slightly different color from the other soil and will resist the shovel. Under the hardpan, the soil is much softer and easier to dig. Hardpans can be two to five inches thick, are impervious to water, and make rainwater sit on the surface. If there were no hardpan, rain would penetrate and flow through the soil, and the surface would dry out much sooner.

If there is a hardpan, break it up. Double dig, or have a tractor with a subsoil plow come in and open up the drainage, or rent a ditching machine and run ditches up and down the garden every three feet or so. Even when filled back in, these breaks will provide the water with a way out.

Putting the garden into raised beds will improve drainage. More importantly, it also will stop soil compaction in the growing areas and eliminate the need to till. Instead of tilling, grow a green manure crop that can be removed by hand pulling of the vegetation.

Incorporate three to four inches of well-rotted manure when you make up the beds the first time. Clays need this much humus to become lighter. They will not use up any more humus than any other soil, however, so after that an annual addition of about one inch will maintain the lightness. Using a manure-compost mulch in summer helps clays avoid crusting over and keeps them breathing.

Cultivation

With raised-bed gardening there is no need for cultivation, as there is with row crops. In summer, traditionally managed soils get crusty, which shuts out air, limits soil bacteria activity, and reduces nutrient release. Crusted soil requires hoeing to break up the field and let in the air. Hoeing also eliminates the weeds, but it is a lot of work.

Just as vegetables germinate well in raised beds, so do weeds grow better there than in any other soil. But they also are easier to remove. The need to weed is the limiting factor on the width of the bed, since you have to be able to reach the center of the bed from the path without stepping on it.

All closely planted vegetables have to be hand weeded. If the vegetables are set out farther apart, it is possible to use weeding tools. The normal hoe is just about useless on a raised bed. A special tool is needed—the "hula hoe," or action hoe. These hoes have a thin, sharp, metal blade that cuts weeds off just below the surface as it slides backward and forward through the soil. Using one is nearly effortless in the humusy surface of a raised bed, and an entire bed can be weeded in about two minutes. Action hoes will do a respectable job on compacted paths as well. One person who came to visit my garden asked about weeding raised beds, and I showed him the hoe. He said that just finding out about that tool made the trip out to see me worthwhile.

Like any other hoe, an action hoe must be kept sharpened, or it will not work properly. Most people do not realize that weeding hoes are cutting tools, not chopping tools. They are supposed to have a sharp chisel edge that can slice off the weeds. The steel in a traditional hoe is soft, so that rocks will not crack it or chip the edge. An action hoe has harder steel than a traditional hoe, but both get dull very fast. I carry a file in my back pocket when hoeing and touch up the edge every hundred feet of row or every few beds. The brief time it takes to sharpen it is paid back many times over in the next few minutes of effortless weeding.

Garden Planning

I must have read fifty gardening books in the last ten years, and almost every one of them was full of ready-made garden plans. Not one of those plans did me any good, even when I was a novice myself. No ready-made plan is ever going to match what you like to eat, the space you have to work with, and what this climate makes easy or hard to grow. If I have learned anything from studying gardening and gardeners it is that there are as many kinds of gardens as there are gardeners. A garden becomes so much an expression of the gardener that I can tell more about people by looking at their gardens than I can by looking at the titles on their bookshelves.

It is quite important to make a garden plan for yourself. Otherwise you can easily get carried away by an annual phenomenon I call the "short of space" syndrome. Our climate has a peculiar psychological effect on gardeners each spring, when fresh food seems quite scarce and dear. Even if you have successfully over-wintered a large garden, there are only a few things producing, and you are getting tired of spinach and corn salad salads, broccoli, and onions. The occasional cabbage or cauliflower that matures relieves the situation, but that is about all there is. The beets are gone, the carrots have sprouted, and the leeks have gotten woody. Pretty sad! The little seedlings you have just put in are growing so slowly it seems there will never be enough food, so you compensate by planting too much. Come mid-June, there is not enough room for the fall/winter garden, you are over-whelmed with food that needs to be preserved, and the whole cycle starts over again. If you make a good plan and stick to it, the proper amount of vegetables gets planted and things work out.

Each garden plan must fit the gardener. Some people want to preserve enough food in late summer to last until the next garden "comes in." Their gardens are "put in" around the last frost date in May and grow large quantities of green beans and tomatoes for canning, cucumbers for pickles, and sweet corn for freezing. There may be one big spinach patch for freezing and one broccoli crop. Sometimes a pea patch is put in early. Other people primarily want a salad garden—a particularly good idea for small spaces. The salad garden contains several successive plantings of lettuce, scallions, and spinach. There usually will be a cucumber vine, a cherry tomato plant, and a couple of vines of larger slicing tomatoes, and carrots. The salad gardener may also grow a few sweet pepper plants. Starting with mustard greens in the spring and ending with winter spinach, corn salad, and endive, salad gardeners can keep themselves supplied nearly year-round.

I cannot plan your garden. I cannot even tell you how many square feet of bed to plant in beans. I cannot do this because I do not know how good your soil is, how the weather will affect this year's crop, and how much you like beans. But you will find out for yourself after a few years of growing beans. One year you will have too many, the next too few, and eventually you will grow just a few too many, which is what you should want. To get you started, I have tried to give you a rough idea of what to expect in terms of yield from each vegetable in the chapter entitled "How to Grow Them: The Vegetable Families" at the end of this book.

Planning Factors to Consider

There are a few basic things to keep in mind when making a garden plan. Most of them are fairly obvious to anyone who has actually grown vegetables. Keeping these factors in mind could prevent a novice from making a lot of mistakes.

Sweet corn needs a large block of space to grow properly. One long row of corn will grow a lot of empty ears. This is because corn is wind pollinated, and with a single long row the wind could carry the pollen away without it landing on any silks. A minimum of four rows usually will be quite successful. Try to locate the corn patch at the north end of the garden, have a wide path at the north end of the patch, or grow shade-tolerant plants on the north side of the patch. Corn will also put anything growing to the east or west of it into partial shade. Cucumbers may be planted at the south end of the corn patch and actually will prefer to grow into the semi-shade of the corn.

Winter squashes and pumpkins take up a lot of space—at least five feet in all directions. Some varieties take an eight-foot circle. These are not for small gardens. The root system on squashes is less than three feet in diameter, however, so the vines can be planted at the edge of the garden and trained to run out on the lawn or through the fence. Many eastern garden books recommend growing squash in the corn patch. This works in Iowa, where the corn matures in *early* August. West of the Cascades, we are lucky if our corn matures by the middle of September. Squash will use the entire month of August to grow all over the corn, climbing the stalks as they compete for the light. When the squashes begin to mature, their weight pulls down the corn and makes an impenetrable tangle.

The salad garden should be as near to the kitchen as possible. The canning garden may be farther away. Once-picked-and-done crops like winter squashes and sweet corn should be in the most inaccessible locations.

Leave adequate paths. You will want to take a wheelbarrow into the garden to prepare a bed from time to time or to haul out the harvest. You may also want to run hoses down the paths or put sprinklers on them.

Grow things on the fence, especially in small backyard gardens. Pole beans, cucumbers, and peas are all climbing plants that grow well on fences. Why bother to erect a trellis when there is one already there? Most people do not realize that cucumbers climb, but when they are allowed to they take up much less space and the fruits are much easier to find. Melons and squashes can also be grown vertically, but their maturing fruits have to be supported in nets or they will break their own vines. Tomatoes can also be tied to a fence, or if the fence has an open mesh the vines can be woven in and out as they grow.

Locate all the perennials in one spot or one bed, in a corner if possible, so they will not interfere with tilling.

Making a Plan

I assume you are taking my advice and are putting your garden into permanent beds. On a large piece of paper, make a sketch of the garden and outline where the beds and paths will be. Make the beds between three and five feet wide. If there is a fence in the sun, make a half-width bed about eighteen inches wide beside it. Make the paths at least eighteen inches wide—twenty-four inches if possible. Having one much wider access path will be very useful if you have space for it.

Then make a list of the vegetables you want to grow in the order of their importance. Then look up each vegetable in the "How to Grow Them: The Vegetable Families" chapter. There you will find out how far apart to plant each one and their approximate yield. From this data you should be able to make a good guess about how much space you will want to give each vegetable. If your ranked list was corn, tomatoes, cucumbers, zucchini, beets, radishes, and asparagus, your resulting plan might look like Table 6. Notice that the asparagus was left out of the garden, since it often fails west of the Cascades and it takes several years to start producing.

Rotations

Practicing vegetable rotations is helpful, especially if it does not take up too much of your time or attention. The underlying principle of rotation is that the same vegetable families should not be planted in the same spot year after year. (See the chapter entitled "How to Grow Them: The Vegetable Families" for a list of the family groupings.)

Each family has similar nutrient requirements. If, for example, carrots are followed by beets, and the beets followed by parsnips in one spot over three years, a heavy potassium demand will be made on that one spot. After two years there will probably be so little available potassium left there that the third crop might well fail. But if crops are rotated, enough time passes between repetitions for rock particles to break down and resupply the needed nutrient.

Another good reason to rotate is that each family tends to fall prey to the same insects and diseases. A soil-borne disease organism must have a host plant to remain active. If the host family stays in the same spot for more than one season, the organisms build up, and serious disease problems can result.

Gardeners and farmers have worked out many formal crop rotations that are interesting but unnecessary. In rich garden soil that supplies abundant nutrients, a random shuffling of plants will give good results over the years. One rotation principle that should be followed, however, is to grow a legume at least every three years in every spot. This adds considerable amounts of nitrogen. If you green manure with clover or peas, you will meet this requirement annually.

With rotations in mind, the illustration in Table 7 might be what the garden plan from Table 6 would look like the following year. Notice that the radishes and beets are located north of the corn, where they will receive some shade. They do not "like" shade, but these roots will tolerate it better than the fruiting plants such as tomatoes and zucchini.

Successions

More than one crop can be grown in the same spot in one season. A crop planted in spring and harvested by early summer can be followed by something

Table 6
Garden Plan

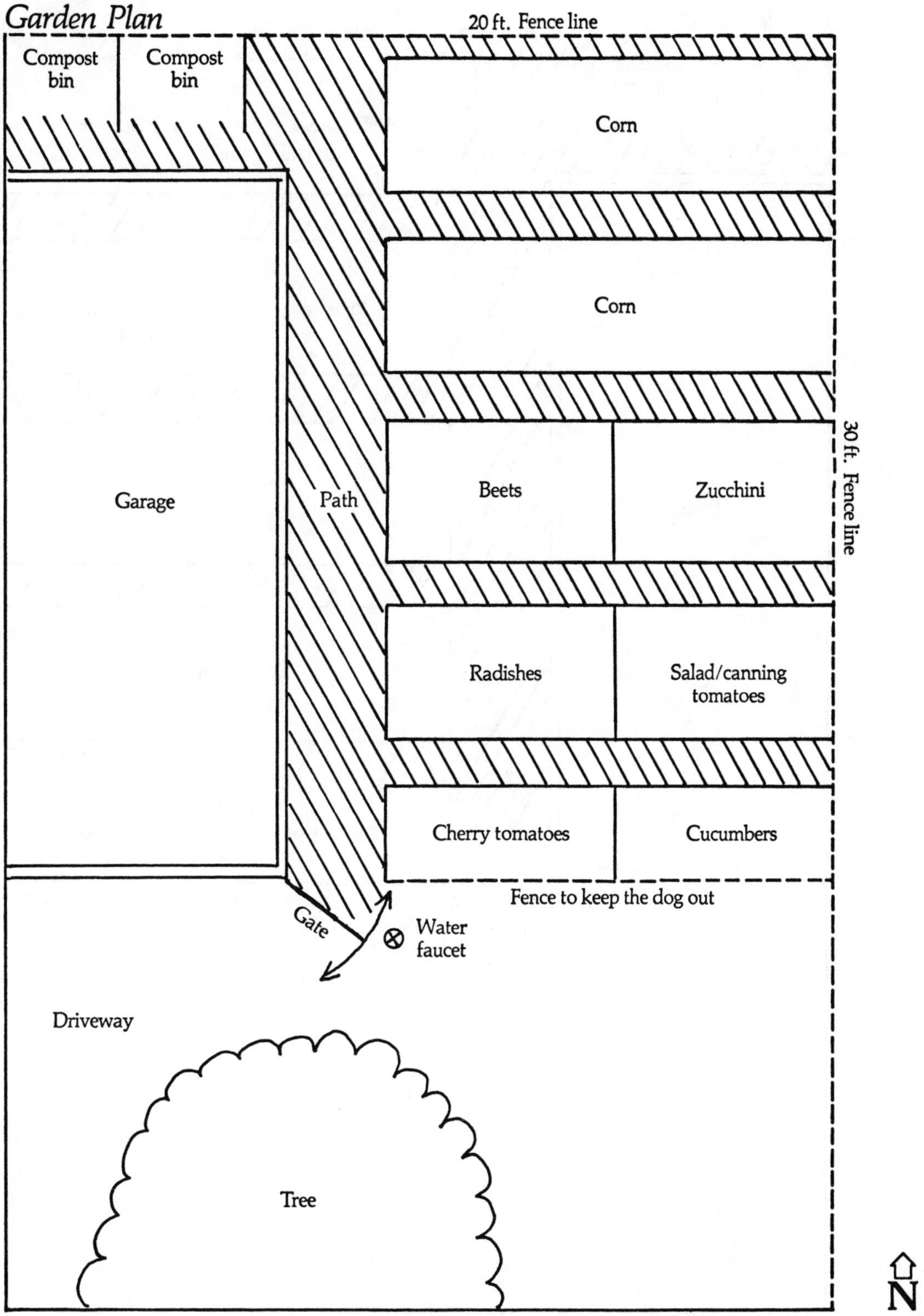

20 ft. Fence line

Compost bin | Compost bin

Corn

Corn

Garage

Path

Beets | Zucchini

Radishes | Salad/canning tomatoes

30 ft. Fence line

Cherry tomatoes | Cucumbers

Fence to keep the dog out

Gate

⊗ Water faucet

Driveway

Tree

N

Table 7
Garden Plan

20 ft. Fence line

Compost bin | Compost bin

Tomatoes | Zucchini

Radishes | Beets

Garage

Path

Corn

Corn

30 ft. Fence line

Cucumbers | Cherry tomatoes

Fence to keep the dog out

Gate

⊗ Water faucet

Driveway

Tree

N

else. Successions can make a small garden seem much bigger and can allow a big garden to become smaller and thus less work. Here are *some* possible successions:

1. *Peas,* followed by rutabagas, Chinese cabbage, late cabbage, fall cauliflower, lettuce, collards, storage beets, kale, fall broccoli, overwintered onions
2. *Spring greens (spinach or mustard),* followed by carrots, bush beans, parsnips, squashes, cucumbers, corn, peppers, eggplants, tomatoes
3. *Overwintered onions,* followed by carrots, parsnips, late brassicas
4. *Overwintered brassicas,* followed by carrots, parsnips, beets, onions, leeks, beans
5. *Spring roots (beets or radishes),* followed by late brassicas or late greens, or carrots, beets, or beans

When replanting with a succession crop, rake up a fine seed bed and plant. A light addition of compost or manure and any needed fertilizer before working up the bed improves tilth, encourages germination, and resupplies nutrients taken by the earlier crop.

To figure out more successions, note the maturity date of a vegetable and be prepared to plant something else in its spot as soon as it is harvested. One way to increase the number of possible successions is to start the succession crop as transplants and set them out later. This allows the first crop to have four to six more weeks of growing time before the transplants have to go into their bed.

Table 8 illustrates the same garden with successions included. Note that this garden is going to produce a lot more food than the first one planned.

Companion Planting

I think that far too much has been made of companion planting. I have found from my experience that alliums are bitter enemies of legumes. Onions certainly will set back the growth of green beans if they are interplanted. If their root systems are not intertwined, however, there seems to be no effect. Other than this relationship between these two families, I have noticed no other companionate effect in years of personal testing.

The entire theory of companion planting comes from a single book by Helen Philbrick and Richard Gregg called *Companion Plants and How to Use Them.* Ever since this book was published in 1966, the information in it has been used by gardeners and passed on by other garden writers as the absolute truth.

University-trained extension agents tear their hair sometimes when confronted with this or other pet ideas of certain gardeners and garden "authorities," whose theories certainly do not agree with the science that the professionals were taught in school. Why does salt prevent root maggot problems for one gardener but not another? Why do marigolds prevent aphids from attacking one garden and not another? Why does a dilute solution of insect bodies sprayed on plants act as an insecticide for some gardeners and not others? Why do soybeans help eggplants "grow"? Scientists dismiss all these phenomena as "anecdotal" and try to forget them. Gardeners keep passing them around, and they work sporadically.

I think the explanation for this situation is that gardeners are in contact with living things (other than just human beings). The plants, soil organisms, insects, and animals possess Life, as does the gardener. I have found that gardeners' intentions and thoughts and basic considerations will have a great effect on what happens in their gardens. Another way of saying this is that what happens in your garden is a reflection of your basic being, or soul. If there were a principle to ex-

Table 8
Garden Plan

20 ft. Fence line

Compost bin

Compost bin

Overwintered cabbages (transplanted in this bed in October) followed by corn, followed by corn salad and winter spinach

Overwintered onions (transplanted in this bed in late September) followed by corn, followed by overwintered cabbages (transplanted)

Garage

Path

Peas followed by winter beets and carrots

Spring radishes followed by zucchini followed by overwintered onions (transplanted)

30 ft. Fence line

Earliest spring beets followed by summer radishes followed by green manure

Corn salad (planted in October) followed by salad/canning tomatoes followed by green manure

Mustard greens followed by cherry tomatoes followed by green manure

Spinach followed by cucumbers followed by green manure

Gate

⊗ Water faucet

Driveway

Tree

N

plain this, it would be that *life affects and interacts with other life.*

If you truly believe, without doubt or reservation, that cabbage worms always will ruin broccoli, then this will probably happen in your garden. After all, you do "own" that space and are the primary cause for what happens there. If you believe that you should plant by the moon, then you had better do so or your seeds will not germinate properly. If you believe you can control the well-being of your garden by carefully associating certain plants with certain other plants, then you had better do that, too.

I never believed in companion planting, so it never worked for me.

The College of Gardening Knowledge

If there were one single thing gardeners could do to improve their gardens over the years, it would be to attend the college of gardening knowledge. This university is located right in your own backyard. Admission requirements are an intense interest in the garden and a willingness to spend some time thinking about it. The curriculum consists of a sturdy notebook in which you record your garden plans, thoughts, bits of interesting data, and the type of information illustrated in Table 9.

The class meets for ten or fifteen minutes every day or two in your garden. Go out and say hello to all your plants individually. Check them out and see how they are doing. Maybe this one has not grown at all for a few days and needs a little side-dressing or manure tea. Maybe that one has bugs. Maybe this one is maturing. Find out what is happening. The attention can double your garden's production.

Table 9
Information for a Notebook

Variety	Date Planted	Result	Remedy
Alaska peas	10 May	Turned brown and died before harvest	Must have gotten pea enation; plant earlier next year
Detroit beets	20 May	Smallish and a little woody	Had a hot, dry summer; next year, give beets more water
Leeks	20 May	Too small, size of scallions at maturity	Do as the book says, and start as transplants in Feb.
Jubilee corn	1 June	Wonderful!	
Illinichief corn	1 June	Didn't mature before frost	Grow earlier corn like Jubilee or try Earlivee next year
White top cauliflower	15 July	Beautiful heads, but all matured in late October	Plant several times, 1 June, 10 June, 20 June, 1 July, 15 July

Winter Gardening

Most people living west of the Cascades plant their gardens as though they were living east of the Cascades. This is quite understandable, since traditional gardening wisdom and most garden writers come from the other side of the mountains. So we try to garden like Ohioans and miss out on much this region has to offer.

In the northern United States the prime growing time is from mid-May until mid-September, when the sun is strong, the soil is warm, and the days are long. Plants grow fast! When the garden "comes in," the vegetables cannot be canned, dried, eaten, or given away fast enough. Then, after this great abundance, there is nothing to eat from October until the garden "comes in" again. This feast and famine is unnecessary on our side of the mountains.

Instead of having an Ohio garden in Oregon you could plant large quantities of vegetables in early spring that will mature from mid-April until July. Most people do not do this because they garden in single rows on flat ground. They cannot till their soil until May because of the rains. Using raised beds and wintertime green manures suitable to those beds solves this problem and allows you to plant whenever you want to. For summer harvest you could plant small quantities of vegetables in May or early June to mature in July, August, and September. This mini-garden will feed you handsomely during the summer, although there will not be much to preserve. Then you can plant large areas in June, July, and early August to mature from October until April and May. These late plantings grow slowly and are relatively unproductive compared to a tomato plant ripening in a hot September, but they will feed you well.

Old-timers around Eugene remember fields of winter cauliflower and other locally grown winter produce. But the competition from California put the local growers out of business long ago. For many years the concept of winter gardening was almost completely forgotten. Then a few years ago a group of Seattle gardeners rediscovered the idea and set out to study the subject cooperatively. They did test plantings and varietal research. One of their number, Binda Colebrook, seriously continued the research and eventually produced a pioneering book, *Winter Gardening in the Maritime Northwest* (now out of print).

Others were looking at the idea on a more "economic" level at the same time. Rising transportation costs raised the possibility that local vegetable growers might again be able to compete with California producers. The Oregon State University

Extension Service, ever alert to any good money-making opportunity for the small and threatened farmer, began to look into winter vegetable growing. Trials were conducted at the North Willamette Valley Experiment Station. The researchers looked primarily to Holland and England for the varieties needed by growers in Oregon and Washington, because our climates are similar, and because north-western Europe never had a southern California and so developed many fine vege-table varieties for growing in the winter.

I came across this research while working on my first book in 1978 and 1979. I also discovered that many of the vegetable seeds we need to grow good winter crops were not available to gardeners in America, so I decided to start a regional seed company. My interest in winter crops remains very high, and each year I have learned more about winter gardening than about any other aspect of vegetable growing west of the Cascades. I am convinced that it is more than possible to eat fresh food twelve months a year in most of the maritime Northwest—if you are willing to eat the kinds of food nature provides in winter and spring.

The Local Climate and Microclimates

The climate from the Cascades east to the Atlantic Ocean is what geographers call a continental climate. This means that the air masses that move across the area originate over land. The temperature of these air masses fluctuates widely. The summer weather is very hot and the winters very cold.

West of the Cascades we have a maritime climate, which means that our air masses originate over the ocean. Their temperatures are moderated by the relatively stable ocean temperatures, so our summers are cool like the ocean water. To grow hot-weather vegetables, we need quick-growing varieties. Eighty-day tomatoes do not even start to set fruit in ninety days west of the Cascades. Easterners must give up their preference for beefsteak tomatoes when they move here. Sixty-seven-day corn ripens in a hundred days if you are lucky.

As though in compensation for lack of heat in summer, our climate has a cor-responding lack of cold in winter. Spring comes early, and there is an extended season for growing quick-growing spring vegetables like beets, mustards, peas, and spinach. Our falls are long, so we can plant fall gardens that do not ripen quickly. Maritime fall vegetables stand in the garden well into the winter, growing slowly and waiting to be harvested. We can grow the quick-ripening fall crops used in continental regions, but doing so limits winter food production. We have the additional advantage of storing root crops in the ground where they grow, since winter temperatures are rarely very low. We can also overwinter certain vegetables planted in late summer and get a very early spring harvest.

Those areas most strongly influenced by the ocean make the best locations for winter cropping. Coastal winter temperatures are the most stable, with few really cold nights. The farther inland you go, the more likely the frosts are to be severe, because the more likely it is that unwanted air masses from east of the mountains will push over the hills and really drop the temperatures for a few days. Even in the harshest areas, however, such as high elevations in the coast ranges and north-western Washington, some winter crops can be grown.

While the ocean produces a positive effect for coastal gardens in winter, it has a negative effect for those gardens in summer because just as it kept winter temperatures from dropping low, it keeps summer temperatures from getting high. Most gardeners within a few miles of the ocean cannot raise tomatoes or peppers or even cucumbers without a small greenhouse. If coastal gardeners would only change their opinions of what a garden should be and would stop trying to grow corn and tomatoes, they would be happy to grow the best beets, cabbages, and carrots anyone ever imagined.

Choosing the Right Vegetables

Table 10 is a scale of winter severity. West of the Cascades, winter weather can encompass almost this whole range. You will need to consider the severity of the winter weather in your particular area when you plan your winter garden, because vegetables vary in their tolerance for cold weather.

No Frost
This category includes many of the "basic" vegetables—those most people think of when they think "garden"—such as beans, corn, tomatoes, peppers, melons, cucumbers, squash, and eggplants. All are completely intolerant to frost. They are not winter garden candidates.

Occasional Light Frost
Some kinds of tender head lettuces will take only a little frost once or twice.

Frequent Light Frost
Carrots and some leaf lettuces will handle frost without damage and continue growing.

Moderate Frost
Some lettuces will handle moderate frost and stand afterwards. So will beets.

Heavy Frost
Swiss chard will bounce back from below-twenty-degree nights. So will winter beets and many kinds of mustards. Kohlrabi will not take heavy frosts very well. Endive will generally stand a few. Chinese cabbage will not take them and has to be harvested before they come.

Occasional Light Freezing
Almost all members of the cabbage family will take occasional light freezing, and though they look a little sad after it, they bounce back and resume growth.

Moderate Freezing
At about fifteen degrees you begin to lose chard, beets, endive, and the more frost-sensitive members of the cabbage family. Varieties of cabbage and other brassicas that are bred to overwinter will all take this much cold in stride.

Strong Freezing
When plants are subjected to strong freezing, their breeding shows. Some survive and some do not. If you are in an area with frequent strong freezing in winter you probably should not try to overwinter members of the cabbage family. Almost all freeze out before zero degrees is reached. I have had collard greens take three degrees and come back, but no other brassica I have grown has handled this much cold. The only crops that dependably survive strong freezing are winter spinaches, corn salad, leeks, and overwintered onions.

Table 10
Scale of Winter Severity

No frost
Occasional light frost
Frequent light frost
Moderate frost—below 28 degrees Fahrenheit, warming the next day
Heavy frost—below 20 degrees at night, warming the next day
Occasional light freezing—between 20 and 32 degrees for many hours or the
   entire day; the ground does not freeze at all
Moderate freezing—temperatures above 10 degrees, staying below 32 degrees
   for a day or longer, but not so long that the ground begins to freeze
Strong freezing—temperatures above 0 degrees; the ground freezes temporarily
   (a couple of days) to a shallow depth, but after the cold snap is over, it
   quickly unfreezes
Severe freezing—temperatures stay below 32 degrees for long periods, and the
   ground freezes to a considerable depth and stays frozen for months

---

Severe Freezing

West of the Cascades, we have severe freezing only at high elevations. If you live high in the mountains, you should not try winter gardening.

Even if you are uncertain which of the freezing categories your garden is going to experience, go ahead and plant a bunch of winter vegetables. See for yourself which ones make it through the winter—all you will have invested is a little seed and some time. Actually, winter gardening is easier than summer gardening. For one thing, there is no need to irrigate anything. In fact, winter gardening offers some possibilities for dry-land vegetable production. Another advantage of winter gardening is that there is no weeding to do after September, and no insect pests either, except slugs, which are more unpleasant than dangerous. Winter gardening basically consists of harvesting from November to May.

For a successful winter garden, however, you must be careful to choose the right kinds of vegetable varieties. The chapter entitled "How to Grow Them: The Vegetable Families" explains the proper types to grow and exactly when to plant them for winter harvesting and overwintering for spring harvest. Please do not consider winter gardening a separate kind of gardening. It gets a separate chapter in this book because it is a novel idea to many people so they need special encouragement to try it. But it should be an integral part of your garden planning and work. Winter gardening means only that your planting is extended past early June into August or even later.

Locating the Winter Garden

If you have any choice about where you locate your winter garden, consider these factors. As soil temperatures drop, biological activity slows down, but it does not stop entirely. The more protection you can offer your vegetables and the warmer you can make your garden, the more growth the vegetables will make in the coldest months and the better chance they will have to survive a cold snap. Certain things can increase the garden's temperature by a few degrees, and those few degrees can make all the difference between surviving vegetables and frozen-out vegetables, between some growth and no growth at all. Everything I said in the "Starting a New Garden" chapter about choosing a garden site is even more important when winter gardening.

A south-facing slope will have a higher soil temperature than those facing other directions; even in winter it will often be several degrees higher. If you have a south slope, use it. Having a good windbreak around the garden can be a big help. Keeping the cold daytime winds out allows the soil and air to heat up. This warmer soil will reradiate the heat at night, keeping the nighttime lows a bit higher than they would be otherwise.

Do not despair, however, if you do not have a south-facing location. My east-facing garden with no windbreak at all does all right in winter.

Another thing to consider carefully is soil drainage. Waterlogged soils rot roots and kill plants. If you cannot locate in a well-drained site, perhaps there is a high part of your existing garden that does drain. If there is not, forget about winter cropping. Only grasses can survive being under water, which is why so much grass seed is grown on poorly drained soils in the Willamette Valley.

Another thing to consider when locating a winter garden is air drainage. When temperatures drop, cold air will flow down the hillsides like a liquid and settle in the lower parts of the valley. The upper parts of the hills are always a few degrees warmer than the valley bottoms—as long as the difference in elevation is only a few hundred feet or less. The only way to know for sure where frost pockets are located is to be living on that site and observe the frost patterns in the fall, very early in the morning when the frost is still on the grass. Staying out of frost pockets also can help protect frost-sensitive crops from the last freezes of spring and extend their ripening for a few weeks by avoiding the first frost of fall.

Again, do not despair if you cannot avoid the frost pockets. I garden in one, and my winter crops do fine. I know they could do better if I moved the garden, but I am too lazy and not willing to give up the investment I have made in the soil.

Special Skills and Techniques

Managing your soil correctly can extend the vegetables' ability to handle cold. It is widely believed that if a plant is well supplied with nutrients it is more cold tolerant. This is especially true of the trace minerals or micronutrients. The best single source of these micronutrients is kelp meal, so adding it to your winter beds before you sow seeds will improve your chances.

One thing you want to avoid is getting a lot of nitrogen in winter beds, since nitrogen encourages soft growth and increases the chances that the plant will freeze out. Winter crops have plenty of time to grow. You do not need to stimulate their development with strong manures or fertilizers, because there generally is enough left in the bed from the earlier crop. If you want to fully understand this phenomenon, get a botany text and read about the mechanisms with which plants handle below-freezing temperatures.

Extra Protection

It is not necessary to protect vegetables grown in winter with any kind of a greenhouse, cloche, or cold frame. Most winter varieties are hardy to around twenty degrees, and many will go below ten degrees. Gardeners trying to produce winter vegetables at higher elevations or in Washington's northwestern counties where winters tend to be colder, however, are probably going to have to use some sort of protection or limit what they plant for winter to the few most hardy vegetables.

The most effective and cheapest cold frame I know how to make is constructed with ten-foot lengths of plastic pipe or, better, with half-inch thinwall conduit. Conduit gives you a permanent structure that lasts as long as you are willing to prevent it from rusting. The tubing is bent into U shapes, and the ends are driven into the ground about a foot deep. This makes an inverted U that supports itself. The hoops are set down the beds every two to three feet, making a structure that resembles a giant croquet game. Greenhouse plastic is stretched over the tubing and anchored with soil. One end is left open, to be shut when it gets really cold. These structures can be twenty feet long or more. The temperatures inside are three to five degrees warmer at night and much warmer than that on sunny days.

Some areas west of the Cascades have so much winter rain that vegetables tend to rot. In these areas the same structures can be built and the vegetables grown under the plastic. In this case, I would leave both ends of the plastic tube open so moisture does not concentrate inside.

Growing Food Out of Season

Some gardeners are not happy eating what nature provides in its own season and want to produce out-of-season food. Using cold frames such as described above allows you to extend the season of such frost-sensitive vegetables as lettuce, radishes, mustards, chard, and celery. Even in the coldest areas, protective structures can nurse sensitive crops along until January with a fair degree of certainty.

Long cold frames constructed of tubing also can provide food much earlier in spring. Once the weather begins to warm up in mid-January, a frame creates a climate inside that is about six weeks ahead of actual conditions. Early mustard greens, radishes, spinach, fava beans, and peas can all be started under plastic in mid-January. Around the first of March the vegetables will think it is mid-April. Beets and carrots also could be planted—even lettuce could be attempted.

The protection will be useful for only about six weeks, until the weather catches up with the plants. Then it could be lifted off the bed and moved to another where the next batch of vegetables is to be started. Instead of starting hot-weather crops in mid-April for transplanting after the last frost, you could start them in early March and transplant them under plastic in mid-April. Even green beans and squashes could be seeded directly under plastic at that time. By the time all frost danger is past, the plastic could be removed—the large plants will be flowering and starting to produce food.

In late spring the tube must be tended daily. One end must be opened up each morning and closed again in the evening. On very sunny days, both ends must be opened or the vegetables will cook. Monitoring protected vegetables is more trouble than I am willing to take. I prefer to eat what the garden will provide in its proper season. Of course, I still can afford an occasional trip to the supermarket, where a bag of out-of-season tomatoes salves my hunger for a more varied diet. If I could not, perhaps all the work it takes to grow out-of-season food might be more appealing.

I suppose I am the world's laziest man.

Transplanting

The Advantages of Raising Your Own Transplants

Raising spring transplants is a skill many gardeners are reluctant to master. But semi-tropical vegetables must be transplanted if they are to mature west of the Cascades, and it really is not that hard to raise transplants—all it takes is some persistence and close attention for a few weeks.

Raising your own seedlings also offers many advantages over buying them from a nursery. First of all, when you go to the store to purchase plants, you have to accept the varieties offered. In many cases, there are much better types of vegetables. Unfortunately, nurseries have to sell what the public is used to, and the public often is used to what they knew back in Kansas or California or what some eastern garden writer has recommended in the latest fad book.

Raising your own can greatly increase production, especially if you have a small city garden. Instead of tying up large amounts of growing space for five or six weeks while almost invisible seeds become almost visible seedlings, transplants can be raised in flats or nursery beds and set out in their permanent location when they are larger. The main growing bed can be maturing another crop while the seedlings are developing in the nursery. Lettuce can be grown this way, as can midseason and late brassicas, onions, leeks, and celery. You will be saving money, too, because buying transplants often costs almost as much as the mature produce does in the market.

Although members of the curcubit family will generally produce if directly seeded, raising them as transplants gives them a big head start. Slow-growing winter squash varieties, especially butternuts, are greatly helped by an early start. Cucumbers, too, will mature several weeks earlier if they are set out in early June as five-week-old seedlings. You cannot grow good cantaloupes or watermelons without starting them under protection. Germination is very dependent on very warm soil, and early seedling growth simply will not happen unless temperatures are warm and stable. Rarely is the month of June conducive to early melon-seedling growth, and outdoor plantings often do not germinate at all. Starting melons in May and transplanting vigorously growing seedlings in June will at least quadruple yield, and most years it is the only way to get melons at all.

Using transplants also has a big advantage for people with heavy clay soils that are slow to dry out in spring. If you are in such a situation and are not using raised beds, starting much of your garden in a nursery and transplanting it out after the soil has finally been tilled will allow you to grow a good, early garden. But do not try to transplant anything with a long taproot, such as beets or carrots.

Another advantage is that if you are gardening with insufficient irrigation or without any, using transplants can make all the difference in fall. Since it usually begins to rain here by mid-September, many winter crops could be started around the beginning of August as transplants and be put out after there is sufficient field moisture. Starting this late with broccoli, cauliflower, cabbage, winter endive, lettuce, and so on, will only mean that the fall crops will be somewhat smaller at maturity, and the overwintered crops will hardly be affected at all.

Raising Your Own Transplants

Using Cold Frames

Home-grown seedlings can be so hardy they will grow vigorously from the moment they are in the garden and will never go into transplanting shock. In fact, well-raised home-grown transplants show strong, steady growth from the time they are seedlings a few weeks old. Seedlings this strong will produce much earlier than weaker ones.

Tough home-grown seedlings are produced by exposing them when they are quite small to the strongest shocks our climate dishes out. This allows seedlings to go into deep shock, recover, and resume growing long before they are in the garden. Then, no matter what comes along, they are already used to it. Once the seedlings are used to a certain unpleasant stimulus, like nighttime lows of forty degrees, for example, they will not be shocked by that again. They still will be shocked by a thirty-five degree night, however, and no amount of hardening could immunize them against frosts. Even a tropical plant like a pepper eventually can be brought to a tolerance for temperatures of forty degrees, and soil temperatures of only sixty or so. These "severe" conditions exactly match what our gardens are like around the first of June. If an unhardened pepper were suddenly to experience the first of June west of the Cascades, it would be severely shocked, would not grow for two to three weeks afterward, and might die. Such weakened plants are also far more susceptible to insect attacks.

Enough theory! This is how you do it.

You begin by germinating the seedlings indoors at room temperature under artificial light. Then you grow them indoors for a day or two or, in the case of some very sensitive plants like peppers, eggplants, and melons, for a few weeks. As soon as they can barely stand the cold frame, you put them out to be hardened off. (A frame is a miniature unheated greenhouse that you build yourself for very little money.) This process will take from four to eight weeks, during which time the plants will become accustomed to the conditions in the garden.

The cold frame protects the seedlings slightly. It warms up the chilliest days a bit and holds that heat during the night, reducing or preventing frost damage. A tightly built, well-insulated cold frame could provide more protection than this bare minimum, but *you* manage it so that it does not.

Many types of vegetable seedlings immediately go into shock when you first put them in the frame. With some types, a large percentage of the seedlings will die within a few days. This is all right! There are many more seedlings in a tray than you will eventually want. It also is all right because it is the weakest ones that die, and the tougher seedlings are the survivors. After a few weeks in the frame, the seedlings will be growing again—or at least *some* of them will be. These few that resume growth first are the toughest ones, and the ones you will allow to develop. Once they are hardened off, transplants grow vigorously in the frame—although that growth is still slower than it would be if the frame were heated.

The seedlings gradually are hardened off still further. On warm, sunny days, leave the cover off the frame so that the plants will be in direct light. On days like this, wind also bangs them around, and the stems thicken. You should also leave the cover off on warm nights, allowing the temperature in the frame to drop as low as forty degrees. It does not seem to be useful to allow the seedlings more shock than forty-degree lows. Leave the cover partially off any day that the air temperature is over fifty degrees. For their last week, the seedlings should be able to grow in the frame without the cover on at all. (Should there be a surprisingly severe night during this week, you can cover them again.)

Cold frames are not suitable for commercial purposes. For one thing, often over 50 percent of the seedlings die in the frame from disease brought on by cold. For another, they take much longer to be ready for transplanting than those grown in a heated greenhouse—six to eight weeks instead of four. But cold frame seedlings are so tough they will take almost anything, and the insects never seem to trouble them after transplanting. This is true even of tomatoes, which are plagued with hordes of flea beetles in typical summers.

Constructing Grow-Light Boxes and Cold Frames

You will need two pieces of equipment to raise your own seedlings—the cold frame and a fluorescent grow-light box. Both are easily constructed and will last many years.

Grow-Light Boxes

A grow-light box consists of one or two fluorescent fixtures suspended above the growing plants. I have found that four four-foot tubes will supply all the light bedding plants need and will accommodate enough plants for even the most serious gardener. Various arrangements can be used to keep the fixtures in place: they can be suspended from ropes or chains or attached to the inside top of a four-foot-long wooden box about sixteen inches tall and open on the long sides. The entire setup will cost you less than thirty-five dollars (in 1981, anyway) and will last for at least fifteen years without your having to change the tubes. The only requirement for success is that you use Gro-Lux fluorescent lights made by Sylvania. Gro-Lux lamps produce the right light spectrum for good plant growth.

If you have one double-bulb fixture, the plants should be about four inches below the lights. If you have two double-bulb fixtures, the plants should be kept about six inches from the lights. You can keep the growing plants the proper distance from the lights by raising the lights or by supporting the plants on platforms that can be lowered. I use old compressed-peat nursery trays for growing most of my seedlings and have found that one or two turned upside down make a fine platform for the growing seedlings. As they grow taller, I unstack the trays and lower the plants.

The lights must be on fourteen to sixteen hours a day. This is the only difficult part of the whole process, as I have found seedlings "dislike" irregular hours, while writers sometimes find it difficult to keep regular hours. I suppose I could buy an automatic timer to solve this problem.

Bedding plants could be started and grown in a light box without ever using a cold frame. There is room for up to fifty mature transplants under two tubes and up to one hundred under a four-tube setup. For several years I did just this and produced my own bedding plants every bit the equal of the ones I had bought from the nursery. Doing this also let me harden off the seedlings a little longer than I could have if I had purchased them, since I could begin the hardening process before the seedlings became rootbound. I began carrying them outside during the day about two weeks before transplanting them.

Cold Frames

When I discovered the cold frame, however, and how it helps *really* to harden off a seedling, I was able to improve what I grew.

A cold frame is simply a wooden box with a window sash on top. The window can be glass, fiberglass, or greenhouse plastic. It should open and close but need not be hinged, since it can be removed completely or propped open with a block of wood when the frame needs cooling. The box should be at least three feet wide and four or five feet long. It should not be much wider than three feet, because you cannot reach the plants in a wide box any more than you can weed a too wide raised bed. Overly wide boxes also need large sashes, and these can be unwieldy or weak. The box can be as long as you like and be covered with as many sashes as you like.

A cold frame should face south, with the sashes tilted to face the sun. The angle is not critical, but I have found that a low angle is best since less window will illuminate more area. I made mine with a front panel about twelve inches tall and a back panel about twenty-four inches tall. It is about three feet deep and has three identical window sashes covering it.

The whole secret of a good frame is to construct it tightly and insulate it well. Walls should be thick wood, or even two layers offset so the cracks between the boards are overlapped by the other layer. The sashes should be sealed with weather stripping. You often can buy used window sashes with the glass still in them for as little as a dollar each. If the frame will not maintain a nighttime temperature of at least ten degrees above that outside, on chilly nights you can cover it with a blanket. The frame should not be much more than ten degrees warmer than the outside temperature, or the transplants will not harden off well enough. When there is a good hard frost in mid-April with a temperature of about thirty degrees, the frame *should* drop to about forty degrees. A thermometer left in the frame overnight will tell you how it did. I always check the thermometer when I go out to remove the blanket just after dawn. A thermometer also reminds you to remove the sashes or open them when the inside temperature rises above fifty degrees. You do not want to overprotect the seedlings, and fifty degrees during the day is enough for a minimum growing temperature. Some days the air temperature is higher than that, of course, and the seedlings will grow very vigorously. But even at fifty, they will grow slowly.

The Proper Soil

The primary requirement for growing seedlings hardy enough to take a cold frame is good soil. It must be rich and full of nutrients, of course, but that is only the beginning. The soil in the tray must have sufficient reserve to hold lots of water. Outdoors, moisture actually rises up through the soil from below by capillary action, so the top few inches are never much drier than the soil a foot down, even when the sun shines strongly. In a growing tray, there is no soil down below. If your seedlings cannot get enough water, they will wilt, and once wilted they are badly shocked and may take many weeks to recover—if they recover at all.

Garden soil high in humus will generally hold enough moisture to grow pretty good seedlings without watering them three times daily. I have found, however, that a mixture of two-thirds soil and about one-third sphagnum moss (not peat moss) greatly improves the moisture-holding ability of soil and also prevents the soil from getting compacted in the trays. This is very important, since when it comes time to separate the seedlings from their trays and put them into individual pots or transplant them into the garden, compacted soil is hard to manage and makes it impossible to avoid damaging the roots.

There are a number of bacterial and fungal diseases, called damping-off diseases, that can attack seedlings. Some types of vegetables are more susceptible than others to damping-off diseases. Nurseries think that it is important to protect all their seedlings by sterilizing the growing mixture with heat or fungicides. I think this approach is a mistake (for noncommercial transplant raising), since the presence of soil disease selects out the weaker plants, leaving only the hardier ones.

Using poor soil is inviting epidemic damping-off. If your growing mix is reasonably rich, damping-off will reduce the number of seedlings by only 25 to 40 percent. Most losses occur within the first few days after germination; seedlings are increasingly resistant to damping-off as they get larger. Moving seedlings to the cold frame often triggers another flurry of damping-off, so plant enough seeds that a good percentage of them can die and still leave enough for your garden.

If your garden soil is not rich enough to support vigorous seedling growth, or if it is very heavy clay that is almost impossible to lighten enough to prevent compaction in the trays, you might want to make a special mix for growing seedlings. I think the best artificial mix is equal parts of vermiculite and finely ground sphagnum moss. Many garden stores do not carry this kind of mix because it is strictly a professional greenhouse item. Wholesalers do stock it, however, so you can order it. This soil mix does not compact at all and holds a great deal of water. In addition, vermiculite has the ability to bind to itself many water-soluble nutrients and release them gradually to the plants. Inexpensive potting soils are not good for raising seedlings. They contain perlite, which cannot hold nutrients, and peat moss, which tends to compact badly.

Prepared soil mixes usually come with small amounts of chemical fertilizers mixed in, but fertilized or not, they do not contain enough nutrients to create and maintain eight weeks of vigorous plant growth. The best way to enrich bedding plant mix or garden soil for the purposes of growing bedding plants is to use bone meal. I prefer to use raw bone meal because it releases its nutrients a little more slowly than steamed meal does and has a lower ratio of nitrogen to phosphorus. A half pound of bone meal per cubic foot of mix is plenty. A half pound of lime and a half ounce of kelp meal also are very helpful.

Bedding plants are overstimulated by high levels of nitrogen. This causes legginess and puny, spindly stems, particularly if the nitrogen is combined with warm growing temperatures. Only bone meal approximates the right proportions. Do not use liquid fertilizers on transplants unless they are not growing at all. If you think your planting soil is not rich enough, get a better one or enrich it with bone meal before you sow the seeds. The problem with liquid fertilizers is that they all contain large proportions of nitrogen and insufficient phosphorus. This is true even of fish emulsion, which is 7 percent nitrogen, 2 percent phosphorus, and 2 percent potassium, a composition that is represented by the code 7-2-2. If you could find something that was about 1-10-5, it would do excellently. I have never seen anything like that for sale. Bone meal is at least 3-10-0.

Growing Trays

Any used nursery container at least 2½ inches deep can make a fine growing tray. You also can build flats out of lathing strips. Aluminum cake pans work fine if they are deep enough and if you punch drainage holes in the bottom (all growing containers must allow water to drain out). Small paper or styrofoam cups also work well.

I use a growing tray to start most seedlings. In many cases, I like to transplant these seedlings to individual peat pots after the initial shocks of hardening off have selected out the most vigorous ones. In some cases, mostly with brassicas, I like to thin out the original seedlings and leave the best six or eight in the tray to mature without further transplanting. For hard-to-transplant vegetables like melons, squashes, and cucumbers, I start six or eight seeds directly in each three-inch individual peat pot. These thin, fragile containers are available from most garden stores. Peat pots are simply transplanted with the seedling and decompose within weeks.

Detailed information on growing transplants for tomatoes, peppers, eggplants, melons, squashes, cucumbers, cabbages, broccoli, cauliflowers, leeks, onions, and celery can be found in the "How to Grow Them: The Vegetable Families" chapter.

Buying Transplants

If you would rather buy transplants than raise your own, keep in mind that not all nurseries are entirely reliable. As in any other American business enterprise, the general rule is "buyer beware." Few nurseries make every possible effort to sell only the finest seedlings. Being able to recognize a vigorous and healthy flat of bedding plants is useful if you do not grow your own.

There are several indicators that will help you distinguish good transplants from bad transplants. Good plants are deep green and short and have thick, stocky stems. The flat or tray is fully rooted but not rootbound. To determine this, place your fingers among the seedlings and carefully tap the bottom of the tray while holding it upside down. Eventually, the entire mass of soil and roots should slip from the tray. When it does, there should be evidence of roots filling up the soil and holding it all together, but the roots should not be going in circles around the outside of the soil. If they are, the plants are said to be "potbound," which means that the transplants are too old and needed a larger container several weeks ago. Potbound transplants take several weeks to begin to put roots into the garden soil. They do not grow until they do and are very susceptible to wilting. Potbound cauliflowers fail to make a decent curd.

Suppose that, upon slipping the seedlings from their pots to inspect the roots, you see that the roots have not filled the tray, but the seedlings are fully developed. These seedlings have made top growth at the expense of root development and often will wilt when transplanted. If the stems are thin and tall, the greenhouse was too warm or too much nitrogen fertilizer was used in the growing mix. Spindly seedlings also often wilt upon transplanting. If the seedling has a thin, calloused section of stem at the soil line, it has had damping-off disease. Damping-off did not kill the seedling outright, but it ruined it. Transplants like this do not develop a healthy stem and grow poorly. Brassicas generally suffer most from this phenomenon.

Hardening Off

Taking a flat or tray of seedlings directly from a nursery or greenhouse (or your own house) and immediately transplanting them is a certain invitation to disappointment. Many gardeners never do figure out why so many transplants die or are attacked by insects. I suppose they think this is just the way it is with transplants.

The actual reason is that seedlings that have been grown indoors are not used to outdoor conditions. They need to be hardened off by being introduced to the outdoors gradually.

Use the following steps to reduce the strain that nursery-raised bedding plants will go through. On the first day, put them outside during the warmest part of the day in bright shade where it is not too windy, and bring them indoors before dark. The second day, put them out all day and give them the morning and afternoon sun, if there is any. Bring them indoors after dark. Do the same on the third day, except increase their strain by leaving them outdoors all night if it is not going to drop below forty degrees. Early in spring, brassica transplants can be left out if there is going to be a *light* frost but not in temperatures below thirty degrees. The fourth day, move them into full sun all day and keep them watered. Do the same on the fifth and sixth days. If there are several seedlings in a tray, cut them apart with a sharp knife on the fifth day, but leave them in the tray. The seventh day, carefully remove them from the tray, doing as little damage to their roots as possible, and transplant them.

Ethical nurseries will harden off their bedding plants for a week before selling them, but it is always a good idea to be gentle with seedlings. Another week of hardening off will not hurt unless the seedlings are getting very potbound.

If they are hardened off for one week, bedding plants generally will survive transplanting and will resume growing in a short time—if the weather is not too bad. Should there be a spell of cold, cloudy, or rainy weather right after transplanting, the seedlings are likely to go into shock, stop growing, and try to hang on. They will resume growth after the weather improves. If the seedlings were hardened off for at least four weeks by the nursery, they will be much more rugged and will continue growing rapidly after transplanting, regardless of weather conditions. But nurseries cannot afford to grow transplants this way and sell them for a competitive price. So they do not. You can grow much better transplants at home than any profit-minded nursery ever will. After all, no nursery could survive if their product cost twice as much as the competition's and there was no difference *in appearance* between the products.

Hotcaps

One thing you can do to improve your success with nursery-raised transplants is to use hotcaps. These are wonderful devices that protect plants and do the entire hardening-off process almost automatically. Hotcaps accustom the seedlings to their new surroundings very gradually and ease shock, thus inducing more rapid growth. Ready-made hotcaps can be purchased at many garden stores. They are waxed paper cones that are placed over seedlings after transplanting. The caps are anchored with a little soil and last for three to four weeks—just long enough for the seedlings to outgrow them. Since they are too fragile to be opened up on hot, sunny days to prevent the seedlings from cooking, waxed paper hotcaps are best used in early spring on brassicas.

You can make your own permanent hotcaps by recycling clear glass or plastic gallon jugs. After the bottoms are removed, they make a far better mini-greenhouse than the commercial paper caps. The plastic jugs are the easiest to transform—simply cutting the bottom off with a sharp knife turns them into a hotcap. But they are light and blow away easily if it gets windy. To anchor them, push the bottoms into the soil about an inch. Glass jugs are better because they have enough weight to stand where you put them. To remove the bottom of a glass jug, soak a string in kerosene or turpentine, tie it in a circle around the jug about a half inch above the bottom, and ignite the string. When it starts to go out, plunge the jug bottom first into a tray of cold water. The bottom usually will snap off cleanly.

Hotcaps can help you get earlier production if you want to. The protection they offer is similar to that of a cold frame but not quite as good. Seedlings generally can be transplanted under hotcaps two weeks earlier than they could be without the protection. The increased heat also induces more rapid growth than they would show if they were planted two weeks later without hotcaps.

It usually is not necessary to water the seedlings after hotcaps are over them, since the caps trap moisture. On cool, sunny days you must remove the tops from the gallon jugs so the heat can get out, or the seedlings could be cooked. On warm, sunny days, the jugs should be lifted off completely, then set back down in late afternoon.

Hotcaps also can protect small transplants against late, surprise frosts. Jugs, baskets, buckets, or anything else you have that can serve as a covering will keep the frost off. A few dozen clear glass gallon jugs are some of the best pieces of gardening equipment you could have.

Outdoor Transplants and Succession Planting

Succession planting is greatly enhanced by using transplants. After the first of May, brassicas easily can be raised outdoors as seedlings for transplanting. Sow late and overwintering cabbages, fall and overwintering broccoli, Brussels sprouts, and cauliflowers in nursery beds right in the garden. While the transplants are gaining size, some other crop is finishing up. When it is all through, the seedlings are ready for transplanting into the now vacant space. Generally I follow my early sweet corn with autumn cauliflowers that were sown in July. The late cabbages I started in early June seem to fit in right after the peas are harvested in mid-July, and they love the nitrogen left by the peas. Overwintering onions can be started in a nursery bed at the beginning of August and set out as late as early October. There is always lots of room in the garden by early October, even if your planning has gone completely awry.

A nursery bed is no more than a special place in the garden convenient to water, where the soil has been worked to a very fine consistency and is highly humusy. Ideally it should be about three feet wide and about five feet long. Liberal amounts of manure, lime, and rock phosphate are worked into this small area, and then it is raked well to a depth of at least three inches.

Sow the seeds in rows about six inches apart across the three-foot direction. Make a row of each kind of vegetable you want to transplant. Sow sparsely, and thin the seedlings to about three inches apart when they are well established. When the plants are four to five inches tall it is time to dig them out carefully with a *sharp* trowel. Taking care not to disturb their roots, plant them out in their final locations. During the summer it usually takes about four weeks to get a brassica to transplanting size; lettuce is ready in about three weeks, onions in about six.

Watering

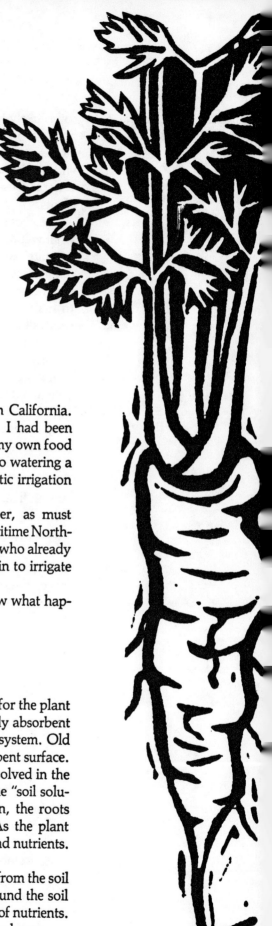

I came to understand the principles of irrigation while living in California. Without dependable rainfall, a California gardener has to irrigate. I had been gardening for about three years, quite seriously trying to produce all my own food myself, before I was lucky enough to discover that there was more to watering a garden than making sure the sprinklers ran long and often. Systematic irrigation increased my garden's productivity about 50 percent!

We in Oregon must water from mid-June through September, as must gardeners in Washington. Irrigation is an important subject for the maritime Northwest gardener to understand: I would not be surprised if those of you who already garden experience a 30 to 50 percent increase in yield when you begin to irrigate scientifically.

The simplest way I know to explain correct watering is to review what happens if you water incorrectly.

Underwatering

The root system of a plant is not static but must enlarge steadily for the plant to stay healthy. At the very ends of the root system, there are actively absorbent root hairs that are constantly being replaced as the plant extends its system. Old root hairs disappear, and the root toughens and ceases to be an absorbent surface. Plants may do this to increase their nutrient supply. Minerals are dissolved in the film of water surrounding soil particles. Soil scientists call this film the "soil solution." Once the nutrients have been extracted from the soil solution, the roots move on to a new place where there is fresh solution to drink. As the plant enlarges, its roots extend farther and deeper in search of new water and nutrients. If there is no water in the soil, there is no soil solution!

The crucial point here is that the plant "extracts" the soil solution from the soil particles and moves on. Even though a new film of water may surround the soil particle, it will take that film quite a while to build up a concentration of nutrients. There is much more in the way of nutrients farther away and deeper down.

Suppose you were to water so that only the top eight inches of soil were moist. This is easy enough to do. Simply use a hand sprinkler to water your garden for a short time every night or two and every time it seems dry. By mid-July, the soil is likely to be dry deep down and moist on the surface, and all the active root hairs will be within the top eight inches or so of soil. Many potential nutrients will be out of reach in the dry zone. Vegetables growing in this environment probably will not be able to gather sufficient nutrients for good growth. Even if enough water is present to prevent the plants from wilting, it will not produce big, healthy plants.

As long as the subject is underwatering, consider wilting and learn exactly what wilting does to a plant. A plant's rigidity, or turgor, is maintained by osmotic pressure. Any good botany text will explain this process in detail. What is important for the gardener to understand is that as long as the plant can draw up enough water from the soil to replace what the sun is evaporating from its leaves, it is able to maintain turgor and the integrity of its leaf cells. But the moment there is a shortfall of water, osmotic pressure starts to drop and the plant quickly collapses. Loss of turgor causes severe stress and the death of many of the plant's cells.

Most gardeners have seen a plant wilt. For example, many squashes wilt a bit in hot weather even if the soil is quite moist. By drooping its leaves, the plant is able to reduce the amount of sun hitting it and lower its demand for water, increasing its chances to hang on in drought by preserving more soil moisture. As the sun goes lower in the sky, the drooping plants perk up again and recover. This happens because the rate of evaporation declines as the sun sets, so the roots can once again supply as much water as is being lost. In very hot, sunny weather, plants can wilt early in the day and suffer such a severe loss of turgor that they are dead by sunset. This has happened at one time or another to all gardeners as they were transplanting in late May on bright, sunny days. The stressed root system of the seedling could not keep up with the rate of evaporation.

Even when the plants seem to recover their turgor after a midafternoon wilting, or spring back after the gardener has rushed out and watered them, they have suffered a severe shock. Most vegetables will never grow well after being allowed to wilt severely, even once.

Overwatering

Most gardeners intuitively understand the liabilities of providing too little water and make sure the plants have enough by irrigating frequently and heavily, soaking the soil deeply and keeping it that way through the summer. Surprisingly, this is almost as big a mistake as underwatering, although with different consequences.

Gardeners go to a lot of trouble increasing the level of available nutrients in their soil. They add rock minerals and manures, and adjust the pH to increase the solubility of these minerals. The key word here is *solubility*. With the exception of those nutrients supplied through the *association* of microrhiza and fungi (explained in detail in *The Soil and Health*—see "Further Reading"), plant nutrients must be water-soluble to enter the root.

In damp soil the film of water called soil solution clings to each rock particle and does not flow into the soil, despite the force of gravity. The soil's ability to hold a water film is limited. Once the surface layers of soil are saturated, any surplus water flows deeper into the soil, where it becomes a film on deeper soil particles. As more water is added, the water goes deeper and deeper. While the water is flowing down through the soil, it carries with it all the dissolved nutrients in the soil solution of the particles above. The process in which watering or rain moves nutrients deeper into the soil is called leaching.

Plants have different rooting abilities. Most vegetables do not put down roots below 2½ feet. If a gardener saturates the soil below this depth, the nutrient solution so carefully created for the plants is moved deeper than the plants can reach. This little bit of extra water cancels out all the work of soil improvement! One oversaturation is seldom fatal, since more nutrients are being released from the soil particles and going into the soil solution. If overwatering happens regularly, however—say, weekly—considerably less nourishment will be available to the plants, and their growth will suffer.

The best way to visualize all of this is to get a sponge from the kitchen and immerse it in water for a few minutes, then take it in your hand without squeezing it. Notice that water drips from the sponge. If the sponge were soil, a scientist would say it was "oversaturated" with water. If there were minerals in the sponge that had dissolved into the water, they would be dripping into the sink, as in leaching. After a while the sponge will stop dripping, as the soil does after it has stopped raining for a few days in spring. The sponge is now at "capacity"; it is holding all the water it can without having it pass deeper.

Now pretend you are the plant's root extracting water, and squeeze the sponge gently. More water runs out, and the sponge is below capacity, but there is still a reserve of water that could be squeezed out. Now wring out the sponge until it is as dry as possible. Notice that it is still moist, but no more water can be extracted. In the soil, this state is called the "permanent wilting point." The goal of systematic irrigation is to keep soil very close to its moisture capacity to a depth of 2½ feet without oversaturation.

Now you can better understand why a green manure is so helpful in winter. Heavy rains keep soil oversaturated much of the winter, but green manures put out enormous root systems and capture many nutrients that otherwise would be leached. In spring, when the green manure is made into compost, all these nutrients are released to support crop growth. This practice is the ultimate in thrift.

Correct Watering

Regardless of the equipment you are using to irrigate, you have to strike a balance between overwatering and underwatering. When the soil has lost 15 to 25 percent of its moisture and is holding 75 to 85 percent of capacity, a small amount of water should be added to bring it back up to over 90 percent of capacity, to a depth of 2½ to 3 feet. But it is not as apple-pie-simple as that. Sandy soils do not hold much water at all, so an inch of water can bring a completely dry sandy soil to capacity to a depth of over two feet. It might take five inches to do the same to clay.

Fortunately, there is a simpler way to compute how much water to add than taking soil type into consideration. In the Pacific Northwest, west of the Cascades, summer sun and warm temperatures cause the evaporation of about 1½ inches of water per week from the soil, regardless of soil type. Less is lost during cooler, cloudy weather. Very hot, dry spells can take as much as 2½ inches per week if temperatures are continuously over ninety degrees. All you have to do is replace the loss.

To be safe and to keep it simple, add 1½ to 2 inches of water per week to your garden from mid-June until mid-August, unless it rains. If it does rain, you should have something outside to act as a rain gauge, since it is helpful to know how much "free" water the garden has received. From mid-August to mid-September, add about ¾ of an inch of water per week.

There is no way to know how much water you have added without testing your sprinklers. Get three or four *straight-sided* glasses or tin cans. Put one near your sprinkler, one almost as far away as the water will reach, and one or two in between. Run the sprinkler for exactly one hour, then check the glasses or cans, which have become "irrigation rate gauges." You will find that they have water in them. Measure the amount of water with a ruler. That is the "rate of application per hour" for that sprinkler.

Most likely you will find much more water in the cans close to the sprinkler than in those far away. With many kinds of sprinklers there will be double the water in some parts of the pattern. This makes quite a problem. How do you add 1½ inches of water when some parts of the garden get twice as much as other parts? There is no simple answer to this question. You will just have to figure some way of evening it out. To get fairly even coverage, position the sprinklers in different places for varying amounts of time or install the type of irrigation system farmers use: a pattern of impact sprinklers. This results in close to uniform coverage but takes a lot of pipe and several sprinklers. The Rainbird Manufacturing Company is the oldest maker of impact sprinklers. Their catalog contains a complete set of tables and specifications for setting up sprinkler systems. It will tell you how far apart to set the sprinkler heads, how much water each sprinkler will require, and how many inches per hour the system will put down. Most farm suppliers and large plumbing suppliers have a catalog available for you to look at.

My own system consists of ten sprinklers that stand about two feet above the garden and are connected to permanent galvanized pipes. They are the smallest Rainbirds, and each uses only ¾ of a gallon of water per minute, so I can run all ten at one time and use only 7½ gallons per minute—an amount my limited well is capable of delivering. I turn them all on at one time with one valve outside the garden. The pattern of sprinklers delivers a uniform amount of water to an area about fifty by seventy feet, and less to the area immediately outside the pipe grid. The rate inside the pattern is about ⅕ of an inch of water per hour.

You should look for a small sprinkler that emits very little water. Large, "efficient" sprinklers spray large droplets that can compact soil and drive out air. Also, if you have a sprinkler with an hourly application rate of more than an inch, a great deal of leaching can occur if you forget it for an hour or two.

I know of one farmer who nearly doubled his potato yield simply by using a number of very tiny sprinklers in his field. He was able to afford enough pipe and sprinklers to cover the entire field without moving the system around. He never, never stepped on his soil once the potatoes were planted and let some weeds grow rather than compact the soil with tractor cultivation. Between his lack of ground traffic and the use of tiny sprinklers that emitted mistlike droplets, he avoided soil compaction and the potato plants developed more and larger tubers.

Irrigate your garden twice a week, giving it half its needed weekly ration of water each time. This will keep soil nearer to 100 percent capacity. It also prevents leaching of sandy soils. If you have a very coarse, sandy soil, you might consider irrigating three times weekly in even smaller amounts.

Watering should be done before eleven in the morning or after four in the afternoon. It also is a good idea to let the plants dry off before dark to prevent the growth of diseases and molds.

Mulched gardens require much less water than unmulched gardens. There is no exact rule of thumb to use. The depth of the mulch and the closeness of planting determine how much water is lost. When the soil under the mulch starts to dry out, add an inch or two of water.

Gardening without Irrigation

Before the advent of electric pumps, easily available pipe, and sprinklers, irrigation was a laborious task. Water was carried in buckets from a shallow well or stream, and kitchen and wash water often was saved and used. It was probably considered the height of luxury to order some water pipe and have gravity water. Yet, despite this, people gardened.

These days many people are turning back to rural living. Some settle on properties with very deficient wells (by modern standards) and have severe water shortages to contend with. Although I am not in this situation, I have been interested in trying to raise food independently of the electric utilities. I do not have all the answers yet, but it is clear to me that really self-sufficient homesteaders would have to rely heavily on fruit trees for most of their fresh food during August and September. Without irrigation the garden would dry out and be pretty skimpy until, refreshed by late summer rains, new fall crops filled out and began supplying food. A few feet of snap beans might be helped out by the bucket brigade, and a few deeply rooted tomato plants might be coaxed along by mulching them well. A large nursery bed full of late brassicas and onions could be hand-watered and held in readiness until the field moisture was sufficiently high to transplant them out. Root crops would be planted late and would be smaller than irrigated ones—but they would carry you through the winter. Spring gardens would be large and would get you through early summer, until the soil dried out. Peas would be a more important staple than beans, and we from the maritime Northwest might well be known as "pea-soupers."

If you are trying to plan a garden around a limited water supply, consult the chapter entitled "How to Grow Them: The Vegetable Families" for watering recommendations for each vegetable you want to plant. If you are planning to irrigate, however, you should ignore those recommendations and give all the plants 1½ inches of water per week; there is no need to make allowances for variations in plant requirements.

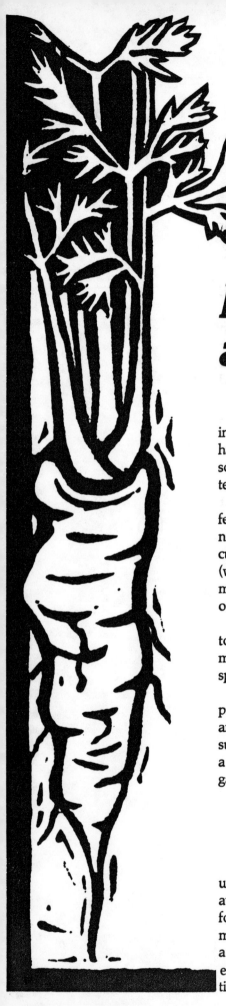

Insects and Other Pests

I am the wrong person to write an authoritative statement about insects and insect control. I actually have not learned much about the subject in all the years I have been gardening. Recently, because so many people had been asking me to solve their problems (because I have become an "expert"), I purchased a couple of texts on insects and plant diseases, but this data is only a curiosity to me.

In my garden only the most common and prolific pests make their presence felt at all. I am sure there must be others lurking around somewhere, but I have not noticed them. So I do not know all the whys and wherefores of the brown-spotted cucumber flower nibbler, the hybrid sweet-corn borer, the purple-poppy plucker (which has never raided my garden), or the sneaky, slimy weed-nabber. I am intimately acquainted with only a few varieties of bugs, and of course slugs, and some other critters that burrow under my garden beds.

I am not constantly at war with even these prolific pests. I rarely feel compelled to take any action against them. Oh, I could fight them at every turn, as many of my neighbors do, and contest every head of early cauliflower and every radish in spring, but I do not. It is mostly "live and let live" in my garden.

I like making my life relaxed. Being worry-free allows me to attend to the present rather than mulling over the past and future. I appreciate the things that are actually around me. Not battling insects that might be threatening my food supply allows me to see the pests as useful friends. I now use them to help me grow a better garden. By following the lead of the pests, I discover paths to more natural gardening.

Peaceful Coexistence

The first step along the road to worry-free gardening is to stop fighting insects unnecessarily. The solution is to grow enough vegetables so that the pests can take away a third of them and still not threaten your food supply. Do not fight for your food supply unless it becomes clear that the pests are going to get greedy and take more than their third. (Nature's tithe is rarely even 10 percent.) And when I suggest a one-third limit, I mean one-third of the entire garden. If insects practically ruin an entire crop, so what? There will be many other vegetables maturing at the same time that will not be bothered a bit.

And I ask you, is it all that important that you never find an insect in your food? What is actually wrong with soaking broccoli in water for a few minutes to dislodge a lurking worm or with peeling off the few outer leaves of a cabbage to get rid of any slugs resting harmlessly inside? The proponents of spraying vegetable crops are absolutely right: you cannot raise many types of commercial vegetable crops without spraying, because farmers would go broke if they did—the public would not eat the vegetables. But in your own garden, you can do as you please. If you still are repulsed by the idea of finding an insect or slug in your food, you are either going to have to change your mind or become a gardener who sprays a lot.

Why not coexist with the insects? There is a big difference between a plant showing the effects of a few insects and a plant that has been severely damaged or ruined by them. You do not have to spray a plant because there are a few pinholes in some of its leaves, or even because all the leaves are riddled with pinholes, as long as the plant is still growing vigorously. Only when plants are being set back, when their growth is being slowed or prevented, should you want to intervene. If the growth is being hindered only a little bit, do not bother to interfere; the vegetables will continue to grow vigorously.

Protecting Seedlings

Insects can do the most damage when vegetables are in the seedling stage. Newly germinated plants are very tiny in relation to insects, and seedlings are slow-growing. A leaf-eating insect can really wreck a seedling in short order, so it is very tempting to spray seedlings to "get them over the hump." But doing so is unnecessary and actually degrades the quality of your crop, because the vigor and genetics within any batch of seedlings is highly variable. Spraying allows many nonvigorous seedlings to survive and mature. If these had succumbed in the beginning, the survivors would have made much better vegetables—healthier, more vigorous, probably more productive, and certainly less susceptible to other disease or insect trouble later on.

I think insects that attack seedlings automatically head for the less vigorous plants and leave the healthy ones alone. Vegetable selection in the seedling stage is almost effortless when you let insects do it for you. This does entail some extra thinning, however. If the stand germinates well and the initial seedlings survive three or four days without insect attack, you will have to make a preliminary thinning to allow the seedlings room for proper development. At this stage I thin the plants to about a half inch apart. Then, a few weeks later, only the stoutest of the survivors are left to mature.

Planting at the correct time helps seedlings resist insect attack. If seedlings emerge into a hostile environment with cold air temperatures and chilly soil, they will go into shock. While acclimatizing themselves to the weather or trying to stay alive while they wait for it to improve, they do not grow, and the insects have a field day. If seedlings emerge into a warm, welcoming environment, many of them immediately begin to grow rapidly. The bugs do not stand a chance. Fertile seed beds and late plantings make gardening much easier. Trying for the earliest possible harvest makes for a lot of pain and strain.

Spraying

Despite all this fine rhetoric, there still will be times when spraying is called for. But apply spray to only the specific plants that need help. In any garden there are many beneficial insects—those that eat the insects that bother your plants. General spraying does more harm than good. Always use the smallest possible quantity of the weakest possible solution over the smallest possible area. And when you decide that you must intervene with a spray to help your plants, decide at the same time to improve the soil those plants are growing in at the first opportunity.

Slow-growing, unhealthy plants are the major cause of insect problems. Healthy, vigorous plants outgrow insect damage so fast that you do not even realize the insects have been there. This is why I am no expert on insects: I concentrate on soil improvement and have never had much reason to learn much about bugs.

Fish Emulsion Fertilizer

Fish emulsion fertilizer makes the best first line of defense against insect troubles. It has a profound effect on plant growth and health when sprayed on their leaves. Fish emulsion also makes the plants smell like fish for a few days. This smell confuses many insects and prevents them from finding the plants at all. The first thing I do any time I feel like helping my plants is spray foliar fertilizer.

Gardeners have been spraying bad-smelling liquids on their plants for years with good success. Garlic or onion extracts, hot-pepper water, and combinations of all three work from time to time. Fish emulsion combines the bad smell with active fertilization, repelling insects and eliminating the weakness that attracts them in the first place.

Rotenone

Rotenone is a true insecticide that is available all over the maritime Northwest. It is a natural, organic product, hardly toxic to people or animals (though it does kill fish quite efficiently). It works on most insects that eat leaves and also on some kinds of aphids. Rotenone also kills a lot of beneficial insects and should not be used indiscriminately. It can be dusted on or sprayed on in water. Rotenone only stays effective for a day or two after spraying, and you can eat anything treated with it twenty-four hours after spraying.

The "liability" of using rotenone is that you have to spray frequently if one dose does not handle the situation. But this fast biological breakdown of rotenone also means that you are not poisoning yourself with chemical residues or poisoning beneficial insects that happen along days after the pests are all gone.

There are other organic insecticides, such as pyrethrum, ryania, and sabadilla. Unfortunately, the only currently available natural insecticide is rotenone.

Bacillus Thuringiensis

Bacillus thuringiensis is another useful organic spray and is generally available under the trade name Dipel. Do not let the long name scare you. Dipel contains live bacteria that kill leaf-eating caterpillars, such as the ones that chew up cabbages and tomatoes. They also kill tomato fruitworms and sometimes are effective against cutworms and corn earworms. I would not hesitate to use Dipel any time a pest it might handle is present. It seems to be persistent, although its manufacturer cannot legally claim that it is. One spraying reduces the population of worms for the entire summer, but it would have to be sprayed weekly to eliminate all worms. Dipel is so effective that even some nonorganic farmers use it.

Water

Water is one of the most effective sprays to use against aphids: a fairly hard stream of water from the hose knocks them off the plant. They may not find their way back for over a week.

Chemicals

If you feel that more powerful sprays are needed, or if some insect that rotenone will not handle is ruining your crop, your friendly neighborhood garden store has shelves and shelves of potent substances to sell you. If you are not certain which of those substances to use, your local extension agent has lots of literature to give you and will even identify the pest for you if you show him a dead insect or sometimes even if you just describe what it does to the plant.

Keep in mind that once you start depending on chemicals to do the work of soil improvement for you, you will find it hard to stop.

Pests

I have made the acquaintance of some very common pests in the maritime Northwest and have had some success at handling them. I am sure many others have briefly come and gone in my garden, but I did not notice them. If your favorite plague is not covered in this section, you have real trouble, and you probably should reread the chapter on "Improving the Soil."

Slugs

Slugs do their worst damage in early spring. They are hungry then, and there is little natural vegetation with which they can fill their stomachs. They are migratory critters, so the ones attacking your spring seedlings are not necessarily from your garden, and the ones from your garden probably are busily traveling out of it as fast as they can. If you feel that they must be handled, go out at night with a flashlight, pick them off by hand, and drop the unfortunate victims of your desire to satiate your stomach with some fresh spring greens into a nice warm jar of gasoline. This will suffice most years.

Sometimes, if the spring is particularly damp or the winter has been particularly mild, the slug population will be high and you may want stronger measures. I have tried beer traps, oyster shells, and sprays made of dead slugs, all to no avail. One thing that does work, and is an improvement over handpicking, is to lay one-by-six-inch boards down in the paths between the beds. The slugs will hide under the boards at sunrise, and you can give greater quantities of them a gasoline bath every day or two.

Sometimes the stronger measure will be slug bait. Using poisons, even one as harmless as metaldehyde (a form of alcohol slugs love to intoxicate themselves with) is strictly a no-no with more religiously Organic gardeners. These same people would be unlikely to use rotenone for the same reason—it too is an effective poison. It seems to me, however, that the object of not using poisons is to avoid damaging your own body with residues and to avoid harming the environment. Metaldehyde is harmful to your body, but it does degrade into harmless substances rather quickly. And it does not have to be used in the garden to be effective.

Remember that slugs are migratory and that the ones in your garden are escaping as fast as they can. The ones from outside are blundering in. A band of slug bait about twelve inches wide around the outside of your garden will keep the slug population inside very low without getting any metaldehyde on your food. The minor damage done by a few slugs can be ignored.

Besides, are you absolutely certain that it is slugs that are causing the damage? Are they eating the plants or just *on* them or *near* them? I am not sure that slugs do any harm other than to offend the sensibilities of some gardeners. If you come to understand what they are about, you will realize that slugs are really beautifully efficient critters. Remember that slugs can only damage some seedlings, and do not fight them unnecessarily. Instead, plant enough extra seedlings for them.

Cabbage Root Maggots

Cabbage root maggots are the larvae of a small nondescript fly. The fly lays its eggs on the soil near the stem of the host plant and the newly hatched larvae dine on the roots and sometimes on the stems. They eat the roots of all brassicas to one degree or another. The larvae are unnoticeable until it is too late.

The fly is quite clever about picking the host. For example, the maggots do not hatch out near radishes or turnips until the roots are swelling up rapidly and can make a home for many maggots. Then when you cut the roots open, there are lots of brown tracks and little white worms inside. Tiny seedlings never seem to be selected, because there is not enough root on them to feed a family of hungry larvae. But once they are seven to ten inches tall and the stem is thick as a pencil, the fly alights and sows her brood. You will not be aware of this until a hot day comes along and the plant wilts and collapses. When you inspect the plant you will see that many of the roots have been eaten away, and there are little white worms in and around the roots. Cauliflowers, followed by broccoli, are the most susceptible to maggots. Rarely will maggots ruin a cabbage seedling, but they might stunt it. Brussels sprouts seem to be able to tolerate them, perhaps because the plants make the major part of their growth during a time when the maggots are not active.

The peak season for root maggots is from mid-April through May and in the early fall, although this varies somewhat from year to year. They are not present at all before the first of April, and they are not much of a problem from the first of June until September, when they come back with a vengeance to wreck my fall Chinese cabbage crop and slightly disfigure my rutabagas. (On Chinese cabbage they invade the stems and cause the entire plant to collapse and rot.) Once the fall frosts come, the maggots disappear until the following spring.

The degree of damage varies from year to year. Sometimes maggots are hardly noticeable. Sometimes they stunt the crop without the gardener realizing what happened. Only when damage is severe do most gardeners discover the cause.

It has long been thought that maggots dislike nonacid soils and that applications of wood ashes would deter them. This recently has been proved to be untrue. Applications of ashes around the stem seem to slightly increase the amount of damage. Apparently the highly alkaline soil produced by the ashes encourages maggot growth. Liming the soil in which brassicas are grown will help. Ten to twenty pounds of agricultural lime per one hundred feet of row will not make alkaline soil but will supply needed calcium. This induces more vigorous growth in the brassicas so they can resist the root loss.

One strategy for dealing with maggots is to make use of their life cycle. Planting before mid-March or after mid-May will help a lot. Before the larvae invade, the earlier seedlings have a chance to gain enough size to survive some damage. Using hotcaps at this time also is very helpful, since the caps prevent the flies from getting to the soil until the seedlings outgrow them, and they also induce more rapid growth, making an even more vigorous root system that can survive even more damage. Brassicas planted after mid-May rarely will be damaged much, except by the fall resurgence that hinders root crops and Chinese cabbage planted in late summer. I do not know how to grow the beautiful Chinese and Japanese radishes that mature in September and October without building wide cages of screen around them to keep the flies off. Maggots also make it very hard to grow very early cauliflowers. But all and all they are an adversary that can be lived with and worked around.

No organic insecticide is very effective against the maggots. The only techniques that can be used to fight them are those that prevent the fly from gaining access to the soil around the plant. There are several such methods. A thick mulch of sawdust (not chips) tightly packed against the stem and extending out about four inches will protect transplanted brassicas if it is applied *before* the flies lay their eggs—which means immediately after transplanting or immediately after the hotcaps are removed. Cones made of window screen also will prevent flies from getting to the plant. These cones could be as large as sixteen inches in diameter at the base and could be left over the plant for quite a while.

Radishes and turnips also can be protected in spring by sowing their seed directly on the ground without a furrow and covering the row with a one-inch-thick and four-inch-wide band of sawdust. The sawdust will protect the plants until the roots begin to enlarge and knock the sawdust aside, exposing the soil to the flies. The roots expand rapidly at this point in the plant's growth cycle and are usually harvested before the eggs even hatch out. This strategy does not work so well on fall radishes or turnips. Radishes grown in fall are so large and so slow to mature that the maggots have plenty of time to get into the root before harvest.

Since maggot damage is most severe in spring, one effective strategy is to avoid planting brassicas then by overwintering them. This is more a function of planning to avoid fighting than of fighting itself. A beautiful spring garden can be had most years. The harvest can include broccoli, cauliflower, and cabbage—all planted the previous year. These overwintered brassicas are so much larger than transplants that maggots do not do serious damage to them. Planting new crops in spring is less urgent and any losses sustained in new seedlings more bearable, when overwintered brassicas are being harvested.

Should maggots wreck a spring brassica, the thing to do is to sow a few seeds in that spot. Directly seeded brassicas will only be a little later than the transplanted ones. This will extend your harvest, which is not a bad thing at all.

Carrot Maggots

Carrot maggots come from a similar fly that lays its eggs near carrot plants. The larvae enter the carrot root and feed until they are large enough to become flies. Their season is much the same as that of cabbage maggots. Carrot maggots seem to be more troublesome in Washington than they are farther south. I have seen so few in my carrots that I have wondered why I do not have more. I suspect that I do not see many carrot maggots because I am living in an area where entire pastures are covered with wild carrots. These wild hosts must support a large population of both carrot flies and their predators, so I have a balance of nature. If I were gardening in the city or in the Willamette Valley, I suspect my difficulties with this pest would be more severe. It seems to be much easier to avoid insect problems if you are gardening in a rural setting not surrounded by sprayed farmlands. Additionally, large monocultural areas do not allow for fields of alternative hosts and stable predator populations. I think the situation in large cities is similar.

The same principles of control used for the cabbage maggot are used for the carrot maggot. What you must do is to plant carrots after mid-May when the infestation is past its peak. This usually is enough control even for Washington gardeners. Carrots, being very small plants, lend themselves well to the other method of protection, however—keeping the flies away. A great harvest of carrots can be gotten from a very small patch of soil. If you grow them in rows six inches apart and thin to one inch apart in the row, you can harvest about twenty-five carrots from each square foot of bed. A frame covered with window screen over part of a raised bed can protect a lot of carrots. This same method could be used on radishes.

I know of one Washington gardener who protects his carrots very nicely by growing them in single rows and hilling up earth around the stems as they grow. Eventually the root itself is covered by five or six inches of soil. The maggots cannot penetrate this deeply after hatching and are defeated.

Cucumber Beetles

Cucumber beetles look like ladybugs, except that their coloring is yellow with black spots on their backs. Unlike ladybugs, these beetles are vegetarian and can chew up a lot of leaves. Cucumber beetles seldom are seen on cucumber plants. They seem to make the most trouble for bean seedlings, but they do not pass up tasty, tender beet seedlings. In fact, there is just about no plant in the garden I have not seen them take a taste of.

Vigorously growing bean plants will tolerate a considerable amount of beetle damage without having their yield noticeably affected. If the beetles are ruining your seedlings, either you did not plant enough seed and they are just taking their share (which you begrudge them) or the seedlings are not growing very well. If beans germinate in cool weather, they are liable not to grow for several weeks. While they have little leaf area a few beetles can do a great deal of damage and can even kill them. Good, *warm* soil at planting time is the best protection. Sometimes, however, despite your preparations, clever weather predicting, and good soil, the weather will suddenly turn rainy for quite awhile after you sow beans, and the seedlings will germinate in the cool soil. At times like these, rotenone can save the day.

Another excellent control is to sprinkle some blood meal in the furrow before planting the seed. Blood meal contains so much nitrogen, and apparently some growth stimulants (judging by its effect), that it makes the seedlings grow very rapidly for about a month, helping them to outstrip predators. I have found this technique to be especially effective with beet seedlings, which tend to be puny and to grow slowly in poor soil.

Flea Beetles

Flea beetles are tiny black insects that also relish leaves. Flea beetles generally go for slow-growing, unhealthy plants. I have noticed that they will selectively damage certain seedlings and ignore others one or two inches away. The ones attacked are always the least vigorous. Flea beetles prefer members of the brassica family and particularly enjoy the seedlings. As with cucumber beetles and most other beetles, rotenone is an effective control, but planting thickly, and using a little blood meal in the furrow, and then not worrying about them is the best remedy.

If flea beetles are attacking tomato or pepper transplants after you set them out, spray rotenone to let the seedlings get established, and side-dress the seedlings with blood meal or give them a good feeding of fish emulsion. Then resolve to find a way to grow transplants that will not go into transplanting shock, since unshocked transplants are not bothered by flea beetles.

Moles and Gophers

Moles and gophers are very difficult to handle. There are traps that seldom work and poisons that seldom work. To compound the situation, the moles or gophers actually are often shrews or field mice that run in the mole or gopher tunnels. Different traps and poisons are needed to trap and poison shrews or field mice. Moles eat worms, insects, and occasionally carrots or other roots. Gophers will pull a plant down into the run and eat it. Mice prefer roots.

Moles and gophers make different kinds of mounds as they excavate new tunnels. Mole mounds are rough and conical; gopher mounds are fan-shaped, and the soil is fine, not rough. I usually have done more damage to my garden trying to trap moles than they have done as they inadvertently push seedlings out of the ground. The field mice that run in their tunnels, however, are very destructive. I would not say that I do more damage than gophers if I try to trap them. I had a lot of experience with gophers in California and got quite expert at trapping them. I would say we did an equal amount of damage, but once I got the critter trapped, it did not do any more damage.

Some people set up little windmills, believing these make vibrations in the soil that are unpleasant to moles. Some believe that mothballs inserted into the runs keep them away. Nothing I have tried works regularly enough for me to recommend it. The only successful technique I can think of is to get a couple of good hunting cats and give them a good meal when they present you with evidence of a successful hunt.

Deer

Many people in rural areas have deer problems. The only *reliable* way to keep the deer from your garden is with a 6½-foot fence. Blood meal hung around the garden in sacks does not work reliably, and barking dogs go to sleep at the wrong time.

However, there are a few plants that deer will not bother and that thus can be grown outside the fenced area. They are tomatoes and winter squash. One successful scheme used by a very reclusive young resident around Lorane involved digging holes in clearings in the woods around his house. He fertilized each three-foot-diameter hole with manure, lime, and bone meal, and planted a couple of squash vines and tomato plants in each one. Each hole was given a bucket of water each week—the water lasted that long because of the high humus content of the enriched soil. The vines spread out from the hole and grew abundant crops. He says the deer do not like to sleep in squash vines or get their noses into them because they are prickly. I am not sure that is true, because the local deer certainly like to browse on blackberries, but still, the method works.

Avoiding Trouble

When something has been attacking your garden, be sure you know what is actually causing the trouble before you spray or take other action. Go out and observe the plants carefully until you see the culprit. If necessary, go out at night with a flashlight. Are the "cutworms" really rabbits? One grower I know had wilting tomato plants. He was told that nematodes (little worms that infest roots) were at fault and that a soil poison was called for. He investigated himself and found to his chagrin that the soil under the tomatoes was bone dry starting at about eight inches. He had been underwatering.

The biggest single cause of insect trouble is poor soil preparation. I know I have said this before, but sometimes it is necessary to hammer something home before people will believe you. If you already believe me, please use the following stories when you want to convince someone else.

It is early September as I write this paragraph. Back in July, I planted some cabbage plants for my winter harvest. A few weeks after I sowed the nursery bed, I worked up a rich growing area for the cabbages. When the transplants were about four inches tall, I set them out into their growing bed, but I had eight transplants left over. Not wanting to destroy them, I searched the garden and finally found a spot in the corner where I had not done any soil improvement. The area had never been manured and had no rock phosphate. I had not needed that space before, but it was inside the deer fence. "What the hell," I said to myself. "I'll set those plants in that spot."

Now it is September. The cabbages set out in prepared soil are all about two feet in diameter, healthy, vigorous, and heading up. The ones in the unimproved soil are about eight inches in diameter, and they have been severely attacked by both cabbage worms (for which I sprayed Dipel) and slugs (which I handpicked every few days), and now aphids are settling on them in droves. The healthy plants were never bothered by anything. Needless to say, I have finally abandoned the little ones and am letting the bugs have them.

Some organicists believe that insects actually are like the wolves that trail a caribou herd. They fulfill the beneficial function of letting the strong ones reproduce. If you grow a strong plant in weak soil, it becomes a weak plant subject to insect attack.

Once I had a row of Brussels sprouts. Only one of the twelve plants was attacked by aphids, and it was repeatedly reinfested after I washed them off. Out of curiosity, instead of spraying, I eventually dug the plant out and found that the root system had been damaged when I had transplanted it months ago. There was a sort of a **J** in the root that crimped it and reduced the flow of nutrients to the leaves.

How to Grow Them: General Recommendations

This section of the book tells you how to go about raising individual vegetables. It recommends seed varieties and plant densities, gives planting dates and tells you how to grow your own seeds. It will not, however, tell you how to raise these vegetables commercially, with heavy equipment, or on a large scale. The data in this section are not untested, secondhand information but are based on my experiences in my own garden.

Vegetable Varieties

A maritime Northwest gardener is well advised to get smart about vegetable varieties. Planting the wrong types of vegetables greatly limits what a garden produces. My recommendations about which varieties to grow are very specific. This does not mean that some other variety not mentioned will not grow well—I am not familiar with every vegetable variety from every seed company. But you can count on those I do recommend. They are the best-adapted types I know of, and all will grow well.

I wish I could wholeheartedly recommend seed from racks, but I cannot. First of all, many seeds offered are not adapted to our region. Companies that sell seeds off the rack must try to make one selection do for as broad an area as possible. At the same time, their growing directions must be vague. This leaves you getting the short end of the stick many times. In addition, the pictures on those packets usually are not a good guide to what the variety looks like. The companies that make those packets have stock pictures of "representative" vegetables.

Seed-rack seed is good seed. It germinates well and grows vigorously. In order for the rack companies to be able to pay the store a large percentage of the sales price, however, and to support the person who installs and services the rack and pay for all those pretty picture packets, the packets themselves usually are filled with inexpensive seed in small quantities. First-class seed cannot be sold on a rack for less than fifty cents a packet.

If this book recommends a variety and you find it on a seed rack, go ahead and purchase it. It will grow well and will probably please you. But be wary of those other seductive pictures: unless you know, do not grow!

Buying from a mail-order seed catalog is often as risky as buying from a rack.

Mail-order seed companies usually are trying to service as large an area as possible. They do not tell the reader which varieties are adapted to which conditions. The number of days to maturity they list are not for our region but describe how that vegetable grows at the company's home office or where the seed is meant to grow. So eighty-two-day corn—which does take eighty-two days in the Midwest—may never ripen in our region because we do not have sufficient heat west of the Cascades.

Some mail-order companies are also guilty of selling inexpensive seed. They buy from low-priced seed wholesalers and present mediocre items in glowing terms and beautiful color photos. Often they change the name of an old, well-known variety to something foreign and exotic. There is a phrase circulating in the seed trade about this. It says that a seed company can get away with this or that because, after all, "the gardener isn't a critical trade." In other words, gardeners do not know or appreciate the difference, so why give them the best kinds of seeds? If the eventual results do not match the pretty picture, the gardener will always think the weather or the soil was to blame.

Not all seed sellers are participants in the American business "ethic." Some believe that they have a responsibility to their customers. These companies have an awesome task: providing you with the start of your year's food supply and financial stability. They take every precaution to bring you the best, even if it costs five cents more per packet. I am willing to stake my reputation on some companies. These are the ones I recommend to you. I do not know all about every American seed company, however, so an omission from my recommended list is not an indictment. My recommendation of a seed company also does not mean that I broadly recommend everything in its catalog. For one thing, not everything they sell is well adapted to growing west of the Cascades. You have to sort out their catalogs intelligently. *Caveat emptor!* Let the buyer beware.

I can broadly recommend two companies, since just about everything in their catalogs will grow well just about everywhere in the maritime Northwest. One is Johnny's Selected Seeds, the other is my own. Johnny's is a regional company servicing gardeners and growers across the northernmost tier of the United States and southern Canada. It is located in a very cool area of Maine and sells only varieties that do well in their location. Because northern Maine is similar to our region *in the summertime*, Johnny's summer vegetables do very well here. Their fall crops, however, are better adapted to a continental region. All their fall items will grow well here but limit winter gardening by the speed of their maturity. Johnny's sells only top-quality seeds and makes every effort to improve their offering. They grow a good percentage of their seeds organically, contract with local farmers for some, buy some from large U.S. growers, and import all their brassicas from a good Danish seedsman who is very much quality oriented.

My own company, Territorial Seed Company, serves only western Oregon and Washington. Everything in the catalog will grow well in the inland areas of western Oregon and southwestern Washington. All the cool-weather crops will do very well along the coast. (In the coastal fog belt, almost no hot-weather crops do well.) The dates to maturity in the catalog are for Lorane, Oregon, and will be similar to those in your garden. Territorial Seed Company does not grow its own seeds at this time but is concentrating on crop research and testing vegetable varieties from fine seed companies around the world for good adaptation to the maritime Northwest. We hope eventually to grow locally some of the varieties under test.

There are three other seed companies I can recommend for their quality and attitudes but not necessarily for the fine adaptation of all their seeds to our region: Stokes, Burpee, and Harris. These companies are very large and have a good piece of the national market. Stokes originated as a regional seed company serving the same territory Johnny's does now, but they have gone out for a larger territory, so their catalog contains many things not at all suited to our climate. I have been impressed by the quality of the products from Burpee and Harris and the general good adaptation of many of them. When I recommend specific varieties, these five companies will be abbreviated as follows:

Johnny's Selected Seeds	JSS
Territorial Seed Company	TS
Stokes Seeds, Inc.	STK
W. Atlee Burpee Company	BUR
Joseph Harris	HAR

Saving on Seed Purchases

Storing

It is not necessary to buy fresh seed yearly. You can save and reuse seed for a number of years, which will save you a lot of money. For example, a half-gram packet of cabbage seed sells for $.50. Four grams sell for $.70, and twenty-eight grams (one ounce) sell for $1.40. One ounce of cabbage seed is enough to plant a very large garden full of cabbages for three to five years without beginning to feel the bag is running low. Seed is sold like this because of packeting and handling costs. The seed itself is not all that expensive in many cases. The first $.50 of almost any packet pays for the envelope, packeting, sales, shipping, and other expenses. Anything above that is what you pay for the seed itself.

Taking a few simple precautions can greatly increase the shelf life of most kinds of seed. The cooler and dryer seed is kept, the longer it stays viable. Minimum precautions would be a tight glass jar in a cool closet. A large sachet filled with powdered milk placed in the jar can act as a dessicant and maintain much drier conditions. You can increase the protection simply by putting the jar in the refrigerator. Optimum storage conditions require a stable environment just a few degrees above freezing with a humidity of about 8 percent. Only research institutions and very large seed companies use this kind of storage to maintain their genetic stock.

The only exception to storage in sealed glass jars is for big seeds like beans, peas, and corn. These seeds have large embryos and need a fresh supply of oxygen around them so that the embryos do not die from air starvation. The best place for these large seeds is a paper bag in a dry, cool closet.

If minimal precautions are taken, you can expect several years of usable shelf life from most vegetable seeds. Leeks, onions, parsnips, spinach, corn, hybrid tomatoes, and lettuce are all short-lived seeds; they will last just one or two years. Even in their second year, the germination percentage is very likely to drop significantly. I would test any of these types of seed for germination before reusing them. Beans, carrots, and peas have a shelf life of three years, while beets, chard, mustard, pumpkins, peppers, rutabagas, and tomatoes can be kept for four years. Brussels sprouts, broccoli, cabbage, cauliflower, cantaloupe, celery, Chinese cabbage, collards, cucumber, endive, kale, kohlrabi, melons, radishes, squash, and turnips are the longest-viable vegetables; they can be stored for five years.

Testing for Germination

To test for germination if you are doubtful, fill a transplant tray with a small amount of your best, tilthiest, richest garden soil. Count out one hundred seeds and plant them in furrows in the tray. If you are lazy, reduce the number of seeds to ten. Try to separate the seeds neatly. Keep the tray moist by putting it inside a clear plastic bag. Put the tray in bright light but not direct sunshine. When the seedlings germinate, count them. The number of seedlings is your actual germination percentage. (If you used only ten seeds, multiply the number of germinated seeds by ten.)

If the germination is somewhat low, you can still use the seed by planting more thickly. If it is very low and the seedlings are not very vigorous, it is likely that the stresses and insects outdoors would ruin the stand before it got established.

Raising Your Own Seed

Even though I am in the business of selling seed to gardeners, I encourage you to save your own seed. Doing so breaks another dependency you have and contributes to your self-sufficiency. Additionally, your own seed can be superior to any purchased from a seed company.

Certain kinds of vegetable seeds are very easy to save. These types are all from annual plants that are self-fertile and require little or no isolation to prevent cross-pollination. Beans, peas, and tomatoes fall into this category. Peppers and eggplants almost fall into it but do require a small degree of isolation for safety and high purity. Other types of plants are more difficult because they require isolation and careful selection. Still, they are fairly easy to handle in a garden. These include corn, spinach, and radishes.

Many types of vegetables are biennials—they overwinter and make seed the following year. All root crops are biennials, as are the brassicas. Providing protection to overwinter them, isolating them while they are flowering, and carefully selecting them to maintain the quality of the strain is more than most gardeners are willing to do, especially when a packet of seed is available and affordable.

Whether or not you do save your own seed, you should have the data on how to do it, since there may be a time when the trouble it takes will be worth it. I have outlined seed-raising procedures for all types of vegetables.

Hybrid Varieties

If you are considering raising seed for yourself, the first thing to realize is that hybrid varieties cannot be grown by the gardener. A hybrid is produced by the controlled crossing of two different strains of vegetables, neither of which is likely to be a valuable plant. The results of their crossing, however, will be uniform, vigorous, and productive. When the hybrid makes seed, it reverts to every possible combination of the parent lines, almost all of which are deficient.

For example, large hybrid slicing tomatoes usually produce worthless, viney, low-yield cherry tomatoes, and every vine is different. Only seed companies, in possession of their "top secret" parent lines, can produce the hybrid year after year by making the same controlled cross.

Commercial growers like hybrids because they are uniform and often higher yielding. All plants in the field ripen at the same time, and all of the vegetables are the same size—often large. This makes growing more profitable. Seedsmen like hybrids because gardeners must buy new seed each year, and because other companies cannot duplicate their secret parent strains.

Hybrids are not necessarily a boon for the home gardener. Having twelve cabbages mature on the same day is not what you want. Vegetables that vary in size and date of maturity allow you to select a small one for dinner and a jumbo for company night, another next week, and another the week after that. The increased vigor and yield that come from certain hybrids is appealing, however, and may well be worth the extra money the seed costs. In some cases, only the hybrid vigor will allow really secure production at all west of the Cascades. This is true for Chinese cabbages, for example, and for watermelons.

Isolation and Selection

Two factors determine the success of attempts to grow seeds at home. One is sufficient isolation between different varieties; the second is selection. Many vegetables make seed through a process of pollen exchange. When this occurs, two varieties such as hot and sweet peppers can cross, resulting in a large assortment of combinations of the two parents. This is undesirable, though it is certainly interesting. Sometimes the isolation required is minimal—ten to twenty feet. This small distance can be handled easily by careful garden planning. Sometimes the isolation requirement is quite stringent. Beets, for example, need an isolation of nearly one mile to be effectively protected against chance wind-carried pollen. To grow pure strains of beet seed, the gardener needs to be fairly confident that there are no other *flowering* beet plants within a mile upwind.

The second factor is selection, which means that the seed grower chooses which plants are allowed to go to seed and by that selection determines the kind of strain that will result. This act of careful choice is vital. Consider what Luther Burbank, one of the world's greatest plant breeders, said about plants. Burbank thought that plants are very accommodating beings that adapt themselves rapidly to their environment. He believed that his plants changed in response to his will, because he had become their environment by cultivating them.

Certainly you will agree that plants adapt to the environment. If you and your desires do not shape that adaptation, natural factors will, and the plant will adjust on a random basis, becoming something you may not like. To maintain a variety over the years, you have to have an idea firmly in mind of what that vegetable is supposed to look like and how it is to develop and behave. You allow only those plants that conform to your image to make seed; the deviants are eaten or destroyed. This destruction of deviants is called *roguing*. The clearer your picture of the desired plant, the more effectively you can rogue and the finer your saved seed will become.

Selection by roguing allows you to adjust a strain gradually to fit your own requirements. Suppose you want to make a vegetable mature earlier than it now does. By selecting the earliest maturing plants to save seed from, you can gradually change the plants. After several years the strain probably will produce somewhat earlier. If you want a corn with a cob, selecting long-cobbed plants will gradually change the variety.

This is fun! Raising seed and backyard plant development has captured the hearts of many experienced gardeners. If you like a variable strain, with considerable differences in size, appearance, and maturity, do not rogue these factors and the strain will loosen up. If you want a highly uniform strain (which is probably what you initially bought from the seedsman), continue roguing it carefully.

If you want to adjust a strain to suit your growing style, site, soil, and climate, selecting those individuals that are most vigorous and successful in your garden will give you that.

Inbreeding

Only one other factor can interfere with home seed-growing. That is loss of genetic diversity through inbreeding—selection from too small a population. Self-fertile plants such as peas, beans, and tomatoes are not affected by inbreeding. Plants that exchange pollen can be made weak and useless through this phenomenon, which is sometimes called "running out."

Seedsmen grow plants by the acre for seed production, and the plant populations are in the many thousands. Gardeners grow plants by the dozens, and inbreeding is very easily introduced. If an entire patch of corn were planted from the seed of only one plant, all plants in the plot would have a very similar genetic structure. If only one plant from that plot were selected and its seed used the next season, and if this were done for several years running, the corn would be very likely to become genetically more homogeneous. Recessive genes would more and more often combine with recessive genes, and the line would become weaker, poorer, and smaller. Having large plant populations exchanging pollen and saving seed for replanting from as many plants as possible prevents inbreeding.

The more plants used to maintain the strain, the better. If you are saving seed from pollen-exchanging plants, I suggest you limit the number of varieties you use, plant as large a patch as possible, and let as many plants as possible in that patch contribute to your seed stock for coming years. You might have to devote 10 to 20 percent of your garden to seed production if you are trying to maintain a large number of varieties.

Planting Dates

In the next chapter, planting dates are given for each particular vegetable. The dates given are specifically for the Lorane Valley. Lorane is about a thousand feet above sea level. Its seasonal changes are several weeks behind those in the Willamette Valley in spring and several weeks earlier in fall. The temperatures average three degrees cooler than Eugene, the nearest large city. I suppose that Lorane is more like southwestern Washington than the Willamette Valley. Table 11 will help you convert the dates I plant by to your own situation.

Frankly, I think you will be better guided by natural phenomena than by a calendar date. The wild plants are carefully measuring the weather and regulating their actions to take advantage of the best possible moment. So for me, planting tomatoes when the apple trees begin to leaf out is a much more reliable date than "22 March." Apple trees will leaf out later where the climate is more severe and the spring later, so you can use apple trees just as I do to determine the planting dates. Consult Table 12 for guidelines. Should you find my natural phenomena a little off for your location, I suggest you use other plant activity nearby.

Plant Spacing

There is no hard and fast rule about how to space plants. The figures I have

Table 11
Local Planting Dates

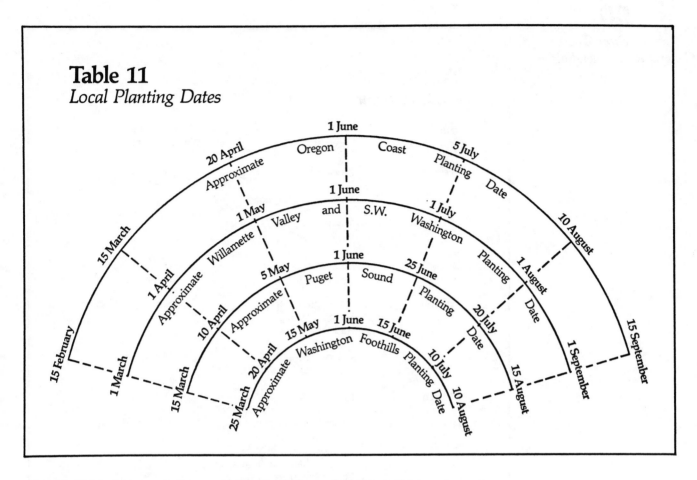

given in Table 13 are safe for someone who follows the basic soil improvement approach in this book. Your soil may be much more fertile than I am assuming or much poorer than it should be. To allow for either of those situations, you are going to want to adjust the plant spacing data.

The key concept used in making decisions concerning plant density is one of *limits*. If a plant is given unlimited amounts of what it needs, it will grow to the maximum size, flavor, and vigor that it can. But if one of the growth factors is reduced to the point that it fails to supply all the plant can use, it limits the plant's possible growth. For example, if you place vegetables so close to each other that they compete for light, the vegetables will limit each other. If they are farther apart and do not shade each other, all the plants will grow better. The availability of light seems to be the crucial factor in spacing. No matter how much water or nutrients you supply, you cannot increase plant density past the point that competition for light allows.

Soil fertility is another limit. The richer the soil, the smaller the root system plants need. Also, the deeper the soil is soft, the more plants can make roots that are going down instead of sideways, allowing them to be spaced closer. This is the idea behind French Intensive gardening—make soil so rich that the ultimate limit on plant density is light competition.

Another key limit is water competition. When water is in short supply and soil moisture drops, plants respond by enlarging their root systems. If too many plants compete for too little water, many of them will wilt. Spacing vegetables allows them to stand drier soil—although it does reduce yield.

Here is how to use Table 13. If you are working in a new soil that has not had

Table 12
When to plant

Date (approximate)	Vegetable	Corresponding Natural Event
1 February	Broccoli* Early cabbage* Sweet Spanish onions*	Pussy willows start to open
15 February	Peas† for the overeager Fava Beans†	
25 February	Midseason cabbage (next 10 weeks)*	Crocuses begin to come up
March— entire month	Asparagus roots‡ Mustard greens† Radishes† Parsley† Celery/celeriac* Early cauliflower*	Crocuses begin to bloom
1 March	Leeks*	
15 March	Sweet Spanish onions† Early potatoes† Broccoli (under hotcaps)‡ Early cabbage (under hotcaps)‡ Peas (next 10 weeks)†	First daffodils bloom
April— entire month	Early cauliflower (under hotcaps)‡ Onion sets† Spinach† Parsley† Scallions† Beets† Turnips† Kohlrabi† Chard† Carrots† Lettuce*† Broccoli*‡ Peas† Midseason cabbage*	First leaves open on apple trees
1 April	Tomatoes* Peppers* Eggplants*	
10 April	Early Brussels sprouts*	
15 April	Midseason cauliflower (next 10 weeks)*	
May— entire month	Beets† Kohlrabi† Parsley†	After apple trees flower

Table 12 (continued)

Date (approximate)	Vegetable	Corresponding Natural Event
	Chard†	
	Carrots†	
	Peas (enation-resistant varieties only)†	
	Lettuce†	
	Leeks‡	
	Brussels sprouts*†‡	
	Broccoli†‡	
	Sweet Spanish onions‡	
	Storage onions†	
	Midseason cauliflower*†‡	
	Midseason cabbage*†‡	
	Scallions†	
1 May	Bush beans (under plastic)†	
	Corn under plastic†	
	Melons*	
	Squashes*	
	Cucumbers*	
10 May	Tomatoes (under hotcaps)‡	LAST FROST! Cow parsnips bloom
15 May	Squashes (under hotcaps)†	
	Cucumbers (under hotcaps)†	
	Sweet corn (for next four weeks)†	
20 May	Late cabbage (for next three weeks)*†	
	Chinese cabbage (spring types)†	
	Tomatoes‡	
	Bush/pole beans†	
	Storage potatoes†	
	Parsnips (next eight weeks)†	
June—entire month	Lettuce*†	
	Early Brussels sprouts*†	
	Radishes†	
	Carrots†	
	Chinese cabbage (spring types)†	
	Chard†	
	Midseason cauliflower*†‡	
	Parsnips†	
1 June	Peppers‡	
	Eggplants‡	
	Melons‡	
	Squashes†‡	
	Cucumbers†‡	
	Soybeans†	
	Celery/celeriac†‡	

Table 12 (continued)

Date (approximate)	Vegetable	Corresponding Natural Event
10 June	Late cabbage*†	
15 June	Fall broccoli (next six weeks)*† Late cauliflower (next six weeks)*†	
July— entire month	Radishes† Late cauliflower*† Fall broccoli*† Lettuce (leaf)*† Carrots† Chard† Rutabagas†	
1 July	Late cabbages (last ones)*† Head lettuce (last ones)*†	
15 July	Collards (next two weeks)*† Overwintered broccoli*† Winter beets (next three weeks)† Endive (next three weeks)†	Wild carrots in full bloom
20 July	Kohlrabi (next three weeks)† Kale (next three weeks)† Chinese cabbage (fall types next three weeks)†	
August— entire month	Turnips† Radishes† Mustard† Winter spinach†	
1 August	Overwintered onions† Overwintered cauliflowers*†	
15 August	Overwintered cabbages*†	
1 September	Corn salad (next two weeks)†	
15 September to 15 October	Crimson clover† Austrian field peas† Annual ryegrass†	
1 October	Overwintered fava beans†	

Key *raise as transplants
†direct seeded
‡transplant

Table 13
Plant Spacing

Vegetable	Minimum Space in the Row (in inches)	Minimum Between-Row Space (in inches)	Vegetable	Minimum Space in the Row (in inches)	Minimum Between-Row Space (in inches)
Bush beans	6	12	Lettuce:		
Lima (bush)	8	12	head	12	16
Beets	3	10	leaf	8	12
Broccoli	18	18	Mustard	12	18
Cabbage	24	24	Onions	3	12
Chinese cabbage	18	18	Parsley	4	12
Melons	24	48	Parsnips	3	12
Carrots	2	8	Peas	1–2	12
Cauliflower	24	24	Peppers	18	18
Celery	10	18	Potatoes	12	18
Celeriac	8	12	Radishes	1	6
Chard	10	18	Rutabagas	8	24
Collards	12	24	Spinach	3	12
Corn	8	24	Squash:		
Cucumbers	36	36	summer	48	48
Eggplants	24	24	winter	60	60
Kale	24	24	Tomatoes:		
Kohlrabi	3	12	unstaked	48	48
Leeks	3	12	staked	36	36
			Turnips	2	12

much improvement, you could increase the spacings about 50 percent. You might double the spacings if you are short on irrigation water or are trying to raise vegetables on field moisture without any irrigation at all. You might be able to tighten them up a little if you double dig your beds and are a religiously obedient French Intensive gardener. Use them as they are if your soil is moderately fertile. If you find that the vegetables are getting too large (which is hard to imagine), tighten up the spacing next time you plant. And if many of them seem small and stunted, increase the spacing *and* improve the soil.

How to Grow Them: The Vegetable Families

Vegetables are grouped in families here, not in alphabetical order. Those who are scientifically trained might throw up their hands, because I have intentionally paid little attention to the niceties of botanical classification. Instead I have grouped the vegetables as I think of them.

Understanding vegetables as members of families has helped me to handle new and unfamiliar species. Thinking this way will encourage you to experiment with growing plants and may make you much more successful.

These are the groups:

1. Solanacae: eggplants, peppers, potatoes, tomatoes
2. Legumes: beans, clovers, peas
3. Greens: celery, celeriac, corn salad, endive, lettuce, mustard, parsley, spinach, Swiss chard
4. Brassicas: broccoli, Brussels sprouts, cabbage, Chinese cabbage, cauliflower, collards, kale, kohlrabi, rutabagas
5. Roots: beets, carrots, parsnips, radishes, turnips
6. Curcubits: cucumbers, melons, pumpkins, squashes
7. Alliums: garlic, leeks, onions
8. Miscellaneous: asparagus, sweet corn, dill

Solanacae

Solanacae are all semitropical or tropical plants that we in the Northwest must grow as frost sensitive annuals. Potatoes are the most hardy member of the group and are able to tolerate light frosts.

In the tropics, the fruiting solanacae are perennials, making a continuous yield for several years, until they have exhausted their soil and lose vigor. Growing them in the Northwest is very different. Here, solanacae must be coddled and rushed into maturity before frost ends their life.

Solanacae are to varying degrees intolerant of cool conditions, particularly in their seedling stage. Soils must be very warm for germination. Outdoor soils might not warm up enough to let seeds sprout until mid-June. Were solanacae sown directly in the ground like beets or beans, most types would not mature and start setting fruit until nearly the time that the first frost ended their lives. So solanacae should be started indoors and grown under protection until outdoor conditions suit them. This gives them a six-week head start, providing several months of fruit production at the end of summer (if it is a warm summer).

Transplanting into chilly earth puts solanacae seedlings into deep shock for several weeks or longer. A nighttime low temperature of forty degrees also will put unhardened plants into shock. This causes a problem. Our gardens usually have chilly soils when we want to transplant, and forty-degree nighttime lows are not at all uncommon in late May and early June. Raising quality transplants means walking a tightrope between hardening off seedlings as fast as possible and trying not to overshock them.

I begin hardening off solanacae as soon as the seedlings will survive the process in reasonable numbers. I expect many to die while being toughened up and use hardening off as a way of selecting vigorous seedlings that will be more likely to thrive in the Northwest.

Hardening off is accomplished by transferring the seedlings to a cold frame as soon as most of them will survive the conditions there. I hold my seedlings in the cold frame until they *must* go into the garden because they are getting rootbound. This reduces the risk of a really chilly night, and the soil will have had longer to warm up.

If you selected only the toughest seedlings that could take the severest conditions and then saved the seed produced by the earliest resulting plants, your solanacae strains would be selected for the ability to tolerate seedling chill and cold soils and to ripen a little earlier. This would be a useful piece of plant breeding, producing tomato, pepper, and eggplant strains better adapted to this specific climate.

All solanacae prefer acid soils—not highly acid, but somewhere around 6.0 on the pH scale. They will grow fine anywhere from 5.5 to 7.0. All are fairly heavy feeders, but overabundant nitrogen is not helpful to a fruiting plant. I suggest using a half cup of blood meal side-dressed around the stem when transplanting solanacae. For five to six weeks this will provide a very high nitrogen level that will then taper off rapidly. The plants respond by making abundant vegetative growth and then settling down to some serious fruit making. Plants need little nitrogen when fruiting, but they do require abundant phosphorus and potassium. If you have phosphorus-deficient soil, working a large handful or two of bone meal into the transplanting hole will help all season. Cottonseed meal is the finest all-purpose fertilizer to use on solanacae should your soil not yet be up to snuff. One cup under each transplant may produce results that will amaze you.

Solanacae generally are self-fertile. Some occasional crossing will occur in peppers and eggplants. Seeds are easy to save on a garden scale, and only a small degree of isolation is needed to ensure purity of pepper or eggplant strains. Hybridization of solanacae results in increased vigor but generally is not required to get an acceptable crop of tomatoes or peppers. It is a prerequisite for getting any crop at all when growing European eggplants, however. Japanese eggplants are sufficiently vigorous not to require hybridization.

If you are gardening without sufficient irrigation, solanacae will adapt to these conditions, as they did in homestead gardens before the advent of electric pumps and piped, pressurized irrigation water.

Eggplants

Eggplants are the most sensitive of any solanacae to cold soils and chilly air;

otherwise they are very hardy.

They need rich soil to be productive, and one cup of cottonseed meal worked in under each transplant helps greatly. The eggplant bed also is a good place to deposit extra chicken or rabbit manure—both types are much richer than most other manures. Success with eggplants is extremely unlikely very far north of Portland or along the coast unless they are grown in a cloche or greenhouse.

Culture

Start the seedlings indoors under lights about eight weeks before the last frost. Make two furrows about a half inch deep in a small nursery tray and sow the seed fairly thickly. Keep them growing indoors at regular room temperatures until they have developed the first real leaves. Do not thin them unless the seedlings are grossly overcrowded. About two weeks after sowing, transfer the trays to a cold frame tight enough to maintain a forty-degree temperature regardless of outside conditions. It should not be much warmer, however, or the seedlings will not harden off well. You can expect a proportion of the seedlings to die within a few days of being put outdoors. If it is a mild spring, this will not happen, but certainly all the seedlings will go into shock and stop all growth for a few weeks. When growth resumes, select the most vigorous seedlings and transplant them into individual three- or four-inch diameter peat pots, keeping them in the shade for two or three days after transplanting to lessen the demand on injured root systems. Grow the seedlings in the cold frame until their roots begin to extend out through the pot's bottom in large numbers. This should not happen until after things are quite warmed up outside. Transplanting eggplants into chilly soils—and chilly to an eggplant would be warm to any other vegetable except melons—sets them back badly, as do nights below forty degrees. A black plastic or tarpaper mulch set over their growing bed a few weeks before transplanting will warm the soil considerably. Black mulch is particularly useful with transplants purchased from a garden store. The seedlings can be set in through holes cut into the mulch, and the mulch can be left in place all summer. In more marginal areas, such as coastal valleys, higher elevations, and north of Portland, attempting to grow eggplants with any hope of success demands the use of black mulch. Even in areas where it is not required, the extra soil heat accelerates growth and maturity. Transplant twenty-four inches apart in rows twenty-four inches apart.

Garden Planning

A healthy plant will produce five or six large fruits in a season. Japanese types produce fifteen to twenty fruits each. Because they are slow-growing for the first four or five weeks after transplanting, the eggplant bed is a good spot to sow a quick crop of radishes that will be picked before the eggplants need all the space.

Insects and Diseases

Eggplants usually have no problems with insects or diseases.

Water

Eggplants are very demanding of all nutrients, heat, light, and water. It would be foolish to try to grow them where there is a shortage of any of these, particularly water.

Harvest

Pick the fruits when they are slightly immature, when they have just stopped enlarging and their skins are shiny and thin.

Saving Seed

Eggplants are almost completely self-pollinated, but an occasional extraordinarily energetic bee does effect cross-pollination. Purity can be ensured by a fifty-foot separation between varieties, especially if there is a tall crop like sweet corn between them. If you have only a small garden and want to save seed, you will be able to grow only one, or at most two, varieties.

The seeds mature after the fruits have reached full size. You can pick a fruit and let it stand at room temperature for a week or two. This ensures that the seeds are fully ripe. Then crush the fruit into a mass of pulp and seeds, and wash the seeds free of the pulp. Finally, dry the seeds completely at room temperature.

Varieties

Dusky Hybrid (TS, BUR, STK) is the best adapted large-fruit variety. *Do not grow Black Beauty*, which will only mature in the warmest of summers. Early Black Egg (JSS, TS) is a Japanese open-pollinated nonhybrid eggplant that makes a pear-sized fruit and is earlier than Dusky. The Japanese eggplants are all earlier and more vigorous than European varieties, but their fruits usually are cucumber- or zucchini-shaped with very thin skins—very good for stir-frying. Japanese types also have purple stems and leaves. Sometimes garden stores sell Morden Midget, which is satisfactory.

Peppers

Climatic variation makes quite a difference when raising peppers west of the Cascades. South of Roseburg, Oregon, almost any variety will do all right. In the Willamette Valley, early types are required. Washingtonians around Puget Sound and north of there have a bad time with peppers due to lack of heat, as do gardeners along the coast. Many gardeners there give up trying or use cloches all summer.

I find that hot peppers are better adapted to cool conditions than bell types are. The small sweet peppers are only a little earlier than bells. This suits me fine, because hot peppers are a vital part of my diet—much to my wife's chagrin. I cannot get enough of them for pickles and kimchi (a Korean sauerkraut made with Chinese cabbage and peppers).

Culture

Sow the seed indoors about eight weeks before your usual last frost. Here, that is about the first of April. Pepper seed is particularly sensitive to cold soils, and it needs a stable seventy degrees for several days or it will not germinate well. Once the seedlings have their first set of true leaves, move them out into the cold frame if it is warm enough to be sure the seedlings will be kept above forty degrees at night. It should not keep them much warmer than the minimum necessary to ensure their survival. In a few weeks, some seedlings will have begun to grow faster than the rest—these are the ones you want to use. Transplant the selected seedlings into individual peat pots three or four inches in diameter and keep them in shade for two days to ease the shock on the damaged root systems. Peppers grow very slowly, if at all, in cold soils, so transplant them as late as possible. Wait until they are just beginning to become rootbound. Their growing bed must be rich and especially well supplied with nitrogen for the first six weeks after transplanting so they make vigorous vegetative growth. Well-manured, rich garden soil is sufficient for their later growth, but a healthy addition of blood meal at transplanting is very useful. I use about a half cup per plant, side-dressed. Set them out at least twelve inches apart in rows at least eighteen inches apart. Black mulch (plastic or tar-paper) is very helpful if set out over the bed two weeks before transplanting. The warmer soil greatly increases growth in June.

Garden Planning
Bell types usually produce six to ten nice peppers per plant. Small-fruited types make dozens. The smaller the fruit, the larger the yield. I find that a dozen hot-pepper plants provides sufficient supply even for me.

Insects and Diseases
Insects and diseases are rarely a problem.

Water
Peppers are able to tolerate drought fairly well, although they will not set fruit if they are too dry. Using black mulch greatly reduces their water requirement. A small bed of peppers could be nursed along on a little household waste-water. I know I would include some hot-pepper plants in any garden, no matter how short my water supply.

Harvest
Many bell types will ripen and change from green to red if you let them, acquiring a sweeter taste in the process. This is also true of hot peppers. If hot peppers have not ripened before the frost, hang the entire plant upside down indoors, and the peppers will turn red and dry simultaneously.

Saving Seed
The procedure for saving seed is very similar to that for eggplants, except that the seed is ripe when the pepper is ripe. Remove the seed and dry completely at room temperature.

Varieties
Peppers are quite variable. Strains bearing the same varietal name from different seedsmen may perform quite differently. This is because each company grows its seed under different conditions and is thereby selecting that strain to perform well where that selection is taking place. The maritime Northwest is at the extreme limit of the pepper's ability to adapt, and we need strains selected for chilly conditions and short seasons. The peppers that Stokes says are early are generally early enough. The rest of the peppers in their massive catalog are too late. Johnny's peppers are all fine, as are Territorial's. These three companies and Harris all sell Staddon's Select—the best bell pepper for home gardeners in marginal areas. The usual Yolo Wonder or Cal Wonder peppers everyone seems to buy in the nursery are among the most likely varieties to fail to produce in a chilly summer. Early Jalapeño (TS, JSS) is very reliable. So is Hungarian Wax, from just about any company. Cayenne Long Thins and Red Chile do particularly well. I think Territorial has the best strains—but then, I decided which strains they were going to sell. Italian Sweet (TS) is the first pepper to fruit.

Potatoes
Putting potatoes in with the other solanacae is not done only as a sop to the

trained botanist out there who would cringe if I classified them as anything else. Potatoes also have soil requirements similar to those for peppers, tomatoes, and eggplants. They are much more cold tolerant, however, making them the basic food supply for many people living in chilly places like the maritime Northwest. Potatoes make their optimum growth under moderate temperatures and seem to dislike anything over eighty degrees. They seem happiest when the air is about sixty degrees, or even fifty-five. Potatoes prefer soil not heavily limed, with a fairly low pH (5.5–6.0). I find, however, that they will tolerate higher pH very nicely without much trace of the dreaded potato scab threatened by most authorities if you dare to grow them where any lime has been used for several years. Potatoes like lots of nutrients and are very demanding of soil, particularly its potassium. This makes them a natural cash crop because our soils have great reserves of potassium. They do not cure as well in our damp falls, however, as they do in dry areas like eastern Oregon and Idaho, so we do not grow them commercially west of the Cascades. I suspect growers could do well with them if they tried the early potato market.

Culture

Potatoes do best in light soils like loams and sands. Heavy clays do not leave the tubers enough room to expand properly. If you have a heavy clay garden, grow potatoes on top of the soil with five or six inches of mulch on top. The tubers will form between the soil and the mulch. If the tubers begin to show through the mulch, toss more on them. Otherwise, plant the potatoes at least four inches deep and at least twelve inches apart in the row, and make the rows at least eighteen inches apart. Potatoes are not started from "seed," but from other potatoes called "seed potatoes." Large seed potatoes should be cut up—but make sure each chunk contains at least two or three eyes. Let the cuts heal in a bright cool area inside the house for two weeks or so before planting. This healing prevents the seed potatoes from rotting in the soil and eliminates any need to treat them with fungicide. I prefer to pick through the seed potato bag and find tiny ones that do not need cutting. The small uncut seed potatoes never rot and always germinate 100 percent.

Sow early potatoes during March. They will tolerate light frosts, and should the vines be killed back by a good hard freeze, the plant merely puts up more greenery. Storage potatoes are grown later to mature later so they will sprout later and keep longer—hopefully until the next spring or later. Start storage potatoes in early June. (If necessary, they will still make an acceptable yield if planted as late as mid-July.)

All potatoes tend to form tubers on the surface. This is undesirable, because these surface roots are exposed to light and turn green. The green color is evidence of a poisonous substance. The poison is supposedly rendered harmless by cooking, but I think green potatoes always taste bitter. To prevent this, hill up a little soil around the base of the plants as they grow, or sprinkle mulch several times. This covers the surface tubers.

Garden Planning

Three or four early potato plants should keep a potato lover supplied from June to October. In my clayey loam I get four or five pounds of potatoes per plant. Lighter soils would yield more. You can figure about the same harvest for late potatoes.

Insects and Diseases

Garden books are all full of worrisome data about flea beetles and nematodes attacking and ruining potatoes. Well, I have seen a few (but fewer each year as my soil improves). So what? Over 85 percent of my potatoes usually are quite good eating and taste many times better than anything from the market. Some potato diseases, however, are no laughing matter. To protect against these, use certified seed potatoes from a garden store.

Water

Potatoes are quite demanding of water. Early crops easily can be grown to maturity on field moisture, however, and the drying out of the soil in July will coincide perfectly with the harvest. I suspect that in pioneer times, when there was no electric pump and no pressurized irrigation, the summer potato patch got much of the kitchen wash water. Few crops are more worth irrigating. Growing them under mulch almost eliminates the need for water, even with a late crop—if we get over an inch of rain every month.

Harvest

Begin using early potatoes in June, once the blossoms start to form. Dig up a plant at a time as you need more potatoes.

Withhold water from late potatoes for a month before harvest. This is not always possible, as the harvest is usually in middle to late September, and you cannot prevent rain. Dig the potatoes after the tops have completely yellowed. Leave them in the sun for a few hours to dry and put them into a cool place for storage all winter. If the soil was well dried out before digging, the skins will be toughened up and well cured. The potatoes will store well. If the skins were not dried out, they will not keep well at all. That is why the late-potato growing regions are on the other side of the mountains.

Saving Seed

There is no reason not to save seed for your own potato crop. Save the small potatoes for "seed" and eat the big ones. If you did not bring in disease with the original seed, it is unlikely that it will ever appear. You also should feel free to borrow seed potatoes from some old-timer nearby who might have a far better and tastier home garden strain than what is available from the garden store.

Varieties

Start with certified seed. Good varieties are Netted Gem, Norgold, Russet, Red Pontiac, Nordland, and Red LaSoda. And, as mentioned above, ask your neighbors if they have any special potato strains. There is nothing tastier than a German Fingerling or a Purple Potato.

Tomatoes

When they have passed the transplanting stage, tomatoes grow fairly well even in poor soil. Getting all their fruit to ripen is another matter, however, and many maritime Northwest gardeners complain about green tomatoes. So there are two difficult stages in raising tomatoes—getting the seedlings to become vigorous plants and getting those plants to ripen their fruit. Read on!

Culture

Although they will survive and even fruit a bit on poor soil, tomatoes prefer rich garden soil, so do not stint on their bed's preparation. Then about six weeks before the usual last frost, sow your seeds in small flats or nursery trays. Plant them about a half inch deep, fairly thickly, in rows about two inches apart. I usually start one five- or six-inch-long row of seedlings for each variety. Each row usually will result in five or six nice plants, and the rest of the fifty or so seedlings that come up are not used or die during hardening off. Keep the flats under Gro-Lux lamps or in a bright window, and keep the soil moist until the seedlings do germinate. Maintain as warm a temperature as possible in the flat, as the seeds do not germinate well below sixty-five degrees, and they prefer seventy. A Gro-Lux fixture automatically will maintain sufficient warmth. Within a few days of germination the seedlings will be standing up strongly. At this time, move them out to the cold frame. Keep a close eye on the frame and the weather prediction. Any night that frost threatens, cover the frame with a thick blanket to hold in the heat. Many of the seedlings will die during the first week in the frame. After a few weeks, a few of the seedlings will begin to grow again. Take these out and transplant them into individual peat pots, keeping them in the shade for a few days to allow damaged roots to recover. Try to use a three- or four-inch pot for each plant so there will be no rush to set them out into the garden. The selected seedlings will grow vigorously in the cold frame from this point until you transplant them. If the pots are not becoming too rootbound, delaying transplanting until two weeks after the usual last frost date allows the soil to warm up more and results in much less shock. A black plastic or tarpaper mulch over their bed for a few weeks before setting the plants out will warm the soil and result in much more vigorous early growth, but it is not absolutely necessary except in very cool areas. Holes are cut in the mulch and the plants set into the holes. Tomatoes adapt equally well to row and bed growing. Transplant the seedlings about three feet apart in rows at least four feet apart.

Tomatoes have either determinate or indeterminate growth habits. Indeterminate means that the vines keep growing vigorously all summer and must be staked up or they are likely to be eight feet in diameter by summer's end. Determinate tomato plants tend to limit their growth and set more fruit on smaller vines. Determinate types usually are earlier to mature, so we usually grow those west of the Cascades. Some varieties are much smaller than the average and can use closer planting. Some varieties, such as indeterminate cherry tomatoes, are very large, and a four-foot spacing in the rows, with the rows five feet apart, is helpful for them—but who would want *rows* of cherry tomatoes?

There is no reason to stake up a plant unless the fruits are lying on the ground, which invites rot and slug damage. It is rarely necessary to stake up determinate tomatoes, as most support their fruit off the ground. Some people prune indeterminate tomato vines. The idea is to remove all side branches and shoots and leave the plant with only one or two long vines trained up a stake or fence. The vines are planted much closer together when staked and pruned—eighteen inches apart in the row is standard for gardeners who waste their time doing this. Pruning limits the amount of fruit set per plant and causes these few fruit to become very large. If you do any of this, tie the plants with wide, soft strips of cloth to avoid abrading the stems. Do not tie them too tightly, as the stems will continue to enlarge. A simpler method to hold the vines off the ground is good for both determinate and indeterminate types. Instead of tying the vines to poles, make a growing cage of reinforcing wire (the kind that is like fencing) rolled into two-foot cylinders about four feet tall. The cages are set over the plants after they are set out, and the vines are guided up the wire. Wire cages also can be turned into giant hotcaps by surrounding them with greenhouse plastic.

Garden Planning

I grow one or two Early Cherry plants so I have some fruit as early as possible. I also put in one regular, indeterminate cherry tomato that provides salad tomatoes throughout the entire summer. I do not think a family of four could keep up with one vigorous Small Cherry after mid-August. I find that three or four vines will keep the two of us in slicing tomatoes. If you make tomato sauce or can tomatoes, I suggest you grow varieties intended for this use. For serious food preservation, start with a dozen plants this year and see how it goes.

Insects and Diseases

Flea beetles are notorious for attacking newly transplanted seedlings. I find that properly hardened off, unshocked transplants are ignored by them. Should flea beetles be a plague, use rotenone every two or three days until the seedlings have come out of shock and are growing again. Side-dressing blood meal reduces transplanting shock. Tomato horn worms (big, horrible green things with large horns on their heads) can denude entire branches in a single day. Dipel handles them beautifully, as do birds or handpicking. Dipel also handles tomato fruit-worms, but I have never seen them around Lorane nor heard of anyone having trouble with them.

Assorted diseases plague tomatoes, but the most common problems are leaf curl and blossom-end rot. These are not actually diseases at all but simply the result of fluctuating soil moisture. If large amounts of water are added to very dry soil, the plants respond by curling their leaves, and the blossom-ends of the fruits often rot. These problems can be prevented by maintaining a steady level of moisture—which will happen automatically if you understand and use the information in the chapter on watering. The many assorted wilts and diseases tomatoes are prone to are greatly limited by rich soil. Most home garden varieties are strongly resistant anyway. Should a plant be diseased, pull it out immediately, and do not compost it but burn it or take it to the dump. If slugs disfigure too many of your tomatoes, stake up the vines to eliminate hiding places.

Water

Tomatoes adapt well to limited water supplies. If thickly mulched in mid-June after the soil has warmed up well, they will manage to grow on field moisture (unless you have a sandy soil) until mid-August. If it does not rain and the soil dries out entirely, all that will happen is that the dying vines will mature all their fruit! If there is enough moisture to keep them going, the vines will set all summer and leave you buckets of green fruit after the frost. Non-irrigated vines will be smaller and less productive but are still an asset.

Harvest

Around the first of September, most tomato vines are covered with green tomatoes, and the vines are continuing to set more fruit. Three things can be done to encourage these green tomatoes to ripen. One is to plant the correct variety in the first place. The second is to stop all watering around mid-July. This puts the vine under water stress after a few weeks. If it does not rain, the drying soil will force the dying plant to ripen all its fruit. Cutting off water in mid-August also will work if September turns out to be a very dry month. A more painstaking method is to begin handpicking all the new flower clusters starting about the first of September. An even more painstaking (and more effective) strategy is to remove all small tomatoes at this time. A final solution is to learn to love dilled green tomato pickles.

Green tomatoes left on the vine after the first frost has touched them also can be ripened easily. Harvest all fully developed green fruits and store them in a cool (not cold) room in buckets. Over the course of the next six weeks, all the fruit will ripen. Some people wrap the tomatoes in newspaper to hasten the ripening by holding in a gas the fruit emits. (This same gas ripens bananas.) But green tomatoes will ripen up fast enough—and faster than you can use them—simply sitting in buckets. You have to sort through the buckets every few days and segregate the ones that have started ripening, or they may ripen and rot at the bottom of the bucket.

Saving Seed

When growing transplants, stress the living daylights out of the seedlings, let them drop over and die and damp-off, select the best survivors to put out in the garden, and then save seeds from those that are earliest and make the nicest tomatoes. Allow some fruit on the selected plants to get completely ripe. Tomatoes do not cross-pollinate, so no isolation between different varieties is necessary. Scoop out the pulp from the tomato and allow it to ferment at room temperature in a bowl for three or four days. The seed will settle to the bottom of the bowl, and the pulp will rise to the top. Remove the seed, wash it well, and dry completely at room temperature.

Varieties

Oregon State University has been studying tomato varieties seriously for over five years. They have found that only a very limited number of tomato varieties can be grown in the maritime Northwest. People along the coast and around Puget Sound are the most limited, while gardeners south of Roseburg have an easy time of it. This is because tomatoes, like peppers and eggplants, are responsive to heat, and heat is one thing we have little of in summer. Eastern favorites like beefsteaks cannot be grown reliably. If you are a recent immigrant, forget your old favorites and start over.

There are some varieties you can count on. All the seed companies I recommend have one or several of these. For early production grow New Yorker, Willamette (developed by Oregon State University), Fantastic, Early Girl, Early Cascades, Spring Set, and Jet Star. Fantastic is the only indeterminate tomato on this list. Johnny's sells a line of highly determinate Sub Arctics that are very good for coastal gardeners, though they do not taste much like tomatoes. Some local nurseries sell one called IPB, but I cannot see why people around the Sound like it so much. It is early—there is no disputing that—but it has little of what I consider a good tomato taste or texture. Heinz 1350 and 1370 are fine, acid, determinate canning tomatoes and quite as prolific and early as any. Cherry tomatoes generally are earlier than the big-fruited ones, but I do not recommend Sweet 100 (except from Roseburg south). Territorial sells an Early Cherry that is highly determinate, has a heavy fruit set, and ripens several weeks earlier than anything except the Sub Arctics and IPB—and tastes the way a good tomato should. The only earlier ones I have seen are some experimental lines being developed by Jim Baggett, the plant breeder at Oregon State. San Marzano, a determinate variety, seems to be the best paste tomato for this area, though it fails in cool summers. I am researching an earlier and equally tasty variety. Yellow subacid types do not do well here, but Sunray is the best of them.

Legumes

Legumes are a prolific source of free nitrate fertilizer, and while adding considerable amounts of mineralized nitrogen to their growing bed, they also feed you. A healthy legume crop adds enough soil nitrate to grow a fine crop of any heavily feeding vegetable such as sweet corn or eggplants.

Only lustily growing legumes will fix very much nitrogen. To get abundant growth, the gardener need supply no nitrogen at all, because legumes are totally self-sufficient. They are heavy feeders on potassium, however, and especially phosphorus. There is an old farmer's adage about this that says: "Feed your phosphate to your clover, and then feed the clover to your corn, and you can't go wrong." This is the truth. Heavy use of rock phosphate or bone meal before planting legumes makes a world of difference, both to them and the following crop. Legumes also tend to prefer fairly neutral soil.

Since half the actual plant material is underground in the root system, pulling out legumes still leaves lots of humus and most of the nitrogen that has been fixed. Legume vegetation is so rich in nitrogen that it heats up rapidly in the compost pile. I have come to consider fresh bean, pea, or clover vegetation as the equal of horse manure as far as composting behavior goes.

If you doubt the value of legumes, try this experiment. Plant half of a raised bed in peas early in spring. Plant the other half in any other early crop. When the peas are through, pull up and compost all the vegetation from the entire bed and plant the whole bed to one type of vegetable—say overwintered onions. Observe the difference in growth between the half where the peas were and the other side.

Bush Beans

Bush beans were developed for canneries and other commercial purposes in which an intensive harvest period saves money. Bush beans do not require trellising, and modern types can be machine harvested. Their taste has been improved to the point that some are almost as good as pole beans. Because bush types produce intensively for a short time, they are usually planted two or three times during the beginning of the frost-free growing season. The result is that as one planting peaks in production and starts to decline, another is a few weeks behind it, ready to take up the slack. Some home-garden-only varieties have retained the longer, more gradual maturation of pole types.

Culture

Beans like warm soils and will not germinate if temperatures are below sixty degrees. Instead, the seed rots. And even a sixty-degree soil is not really warm enough to make the seedlings feel welcomed. Shocked seedlings do not grow for several weeks. Standing there with only two puny leaves, waiting for more warmth, the seedlings are defenseless against cucumber beetles. These hungry critters chew the leaves up so rapidly that the seedlings can be ruined. If the soil temperature had been a bit higher (and the soil reasonably rich), the seedlings would easily have outgrown the beetles' damage. I always try to outguess the weather and make sure I plant the seed just at the beginning of a week or longer spell of warm, sunny weather. Generally, the later they are planted and the warmer the soil temperature is, the better the seedlings do. Once off to a good start, no other trouble is to be expected when growing bush beans, except for keeping them picked at harvest time. Sow them every two weeks from mid-May until the first of July. Space the seeds two to three inches apart in rows at least twelve inches apart, and bury the seeds about an inch deep. Thin when well established (which means when they are outgrowing their predators) to about six inches apart in the row.

Garden Planning

If overwintered or spring crops are mature soon enough, follow them with bush beans. The beans themselves will probably be harvested in time to permit the transplanting of late or overwintered cauliflower or overwintered onions, and certainly in time for a bed of winter spinach or corn salad. Five to ten feet of bush beans will keep an adult in fresh beans for three weeks or so and then taper off. Ten feet of row will make one or two quarts of canned beans three or four times before the bushes are exhausted.

Insects and Diseases

Cucumber beetles do serious damage to nongrowing seedlings. If cucumber beetles are eating the leaves faster than new growth is being put on, spray rotenone or handpick the bugs. Once the plants are growing fast, beetles rarely do more than minor damage and can be ignored. Beans are sensitive to several diseases, most of which are spread by the grower who touches wet plants. Wait until the sun has dried off the morning dew before handling bean plants. Most new types of bush beans are disease resistant.

Water

Clayey, humusy soils will hold enough moisture to mature a small crop of bush beans if they are planted fairly early. Soil dryness does limit production greatly, however. Mulching will help if applied after the soil has warmed up enough to provoke lusty growth (usually mid-June). Spacing out the beans more (eighteen inches between rows) also will help in dry situations.

Harvest

Keeping the plants well picked will extend the harvest for several weeks and increase the overall yield. And, as mentioned above, make sure the plants are dry before harvesting them.

Saving Seed

Crosses between varieties of beans rarely happen naturally, so isolation is unnecessary. It is a good idea, however, to save seed from as large a number of individual plants as possible. Note at least the first ten plants to set beans that are good specimens. You might want to select for straight, fleshy, tender pods. Flag these selected plants with plastic tape or brightly colored yarn. Let the first pods on each flagged plant swell up and develop mature seed. After the seeded pods are dried out, pick them and allow them to dry fully indoors. Then rub out the seeds and store them. If you want more seeds than this, let the entire flagged plant go to seed.

Varieties

The best canning variety of green snap beans is Blue Lake (TS, BUR, STK, HAR). These make large plants that are very slow to get seedy, and their harvest is concentrated. White Half Runner (TS, BUR, JSS) is an old-timey variety that exhibits all the "bad" traits bred out of modern beans. It vines a bit but does not climb much. I think Half Runners have the fine flavor of pole types. Seeds from Half Runners swell up rapidly (another bad trait) and make excellent shell beans or dry beans that cook like navies. Blue Lakes, on the other hand, never develop a string and are so slow to develop seed that seedsmen do not like to grow it. Another excellent green snap bean is Tendercrop (HAR, BUR, STK). For wax types, Earliwax (TS) is a very fine canner, making a concentrated set. Eastern Butterwax (TS) is the most tender, sweetest bush bean I know of and has a very long harvest period. Oregon State University also recommends Wade, Topcrop, Tendergreen, Puregold, Earligold, Goldenrod, and Kinghorn Wax. No bush variety has ever done poorly in our trials, so feel free to experiment with any type that catches your fancy in a seed catalog. I do advise against using bush types that "hold their pods up in the center in a way suitable for machine harvest." These types are not bred for taste but for profit and convenience. A good bush bean should be a pleasure to munch on raw right in the garden.

Pole Beans

Pole types are much more prolific yielders than bush beans but are slower to mature. They have an extended harvest period and do not need to be planted more than one time. Their taste is far superior to that of most bush types, and there is no pole variety we have not relished uncooked. Pole beans are the true bean-lovers choice—and mine, too.

Culture

Beans are beans. If you can grow bush types, pole varieties offer nothing novel to be handled, except that they must climb something. Their support must be at least seven feet above the ground. Pioneers used rough fir poles about two inches in diameter at the top, with the smaller end put into the ground. The poles are set eighteen to twenty-four inches apart in rows at least three feet apart, and four or five seeds are planted at the base of each. Once the seeds are well established, they are thinned down so that each pole has only two or three plants growing up it. Pole beans also grow up fences, and some gardeners erect a trellis made of string zigzagged up and down between two stout wires. The wires are stretched tautly between end posts. The bottom wire runs a few inches above ground, the top is elevated six or seven feet. The zigzags of string are six to eight inches apart, and one seed is sown every five or six inches down the trellis. Sow pole beans about a week after the last frost date. At Lorane, we plant them about the first of June.

Garden Planning

I find that about fifteen feet of fence will keep two adults well supplied with fresh beans. If you intend to can you will need a much larger planting. I usually grow several varieties, and each one is a taste treat.

Insects and Diseases

Pole beans have the same insect and disease problems as bush beans.

Water

Since they grow slowly, pole beans will rarely succeed without irrigation, unless we get at least three inches of rain in both July and August. They could use even more water than that.

Harvest

Proceed as for bush beans.

Saving Seed

Follow the procedure described for bush beans.

Varieties

Blue Lake Pole is the canner's bean par excellence. They are not bad raw, either. Kentucky Wonder is the original home-garden bean that has been the standard of good flavor for generations. Romano is a flat-podded bean with a fine, unusual flavor. Romanos also have large, round, attractive seeds that make fine shell beans and dry beans. Kentucky Wonders also make very good shelling beans. Blue Lakes have been bred for very slow seed development. A few of the other old varieties around would also probably do very well. All the seed companies generally carry several types of pole beans.

Fava Beans

Known to some people as horse beans and to the English as broad beans, fava beans actually are not beans at all but vetches. The plant cultures like a pea, and it also is useful as a green manure crop.

Culture

Except along the coast, plant favas from February to the end of March. The coast allows for overwintering favas planted in October, since it does not experience severe low temperatures. This makes them mature much earlier. Overwintering can be attempted in interior areas, but until someone offers varieties bred for overwintering, many fall plantings will fail. Sow the seeds 1½ inches deep and 5 inches apart in rows at least 12 inches apart. Thinning is unnecessary. If they are being grown for green manure, plant more seed—about 3 inches apart in rows 6 inches apart.

Garden Planning

Five feet of row will provide a meal for two people about every ten days from mid-May until the first of July if planted in spring. Even if you grow favas as a green manure, there still will be a few beans to eat before you pull the plants in May.

Insects and Diseases

Insects and diseases are not a problem.

Water

Fava beans can grow entirely on natural rainfall and would make an excellent field crop for the self-sufficient homestead. Being able to plant them in fall for overwintering is a big advantage. This would make favas into an edible green manure or seed crop. The beans mature and dry out at the same time the soil does in summer.

Harvest

The beans are shelled and eaten green like limas. They also can be allowed to dry out in the pod and, after harvesting, can be saved for making bean soup and stews. The pods themselves can be used like snap beans if they are picked very young—well before the beans themselves begin to fill the pod. Some people are allergic to fava beans *if they are uncooked.* It is a good idea to go at them very cautiously at first if you eat them raw.

Saving Seed

Like beans and peas, favas are self-fertile and require no isolation should you have more than one variety growing. For a small supply of seed, individual pods can be allowed to develop fully and then be picked when they are fairly well dried out. After further indoor drying, they may be threshed by hand and the seed put into storage. If they are being grown on a larger scale for dry beans, allow the entire crop to field dry, and thresh out the beans. One good way to accomplish the laborious chore of hand threshing is to bang a handful of plants against the sides of an open fifty-five-gallon oil drum. This knocks out the seeds, and they fall to the bottom of the drum. If you want to improve your strain, select plants for early production, extended production into hot weather, and uniform bean size.

Varieties

Windsor (long pod) usually is the only variety available (TS, BUR, STK, HAR). Windsor was developed in Europe for spring planting and is best adapted to continental climatic areas in the States. Overwintered varieties should also be sold west of the Cascades. Territorial Seed Company is conducting trials with over-wintered beans, and should they prove suitable, will offer them for sale in coming years. Windsor will usually overwinter in milder areas such as those along the coast.

Lima Beans

Limas are not recommended for growing west of the Cascades. Occasionally, I meet a gardener who takes exception to this statement. I suspect that when a gardener succeeds at growing limas, the location is very favorable, having slightly warmer than normal temperatures. Such a location might be found on the south side of a white-painted building, where the beans are grown right against the wall, so that they receive extra radiated heat at night and brighter light during the day. If you insist on trying limas, your best chance will come with either Fordhook 242 (bush) or King of the Garden (pole). Their culture is like that for other beans, but limas are more intolerant of cool nights. There is a bean that some people call "Oregon lima." It is really not a lima at all, though the seed resembles one. It is actually in the same family as the old runner beans grown for shelling. Sometimes old-timers have a strain of Oregon lima available for the asking.

Okra and black-eyed peas fall into the same category as lima beans, which is unfortunate for those of us who like them. The best substitute for lima beans in maritime Northwest gardens is soybeans.

Soybeans

Soybeans have a very high nutritive value and taste good when eaten fresh like shell beans. Their culture is nearly trouble-free if proper varieties are chosen.

Culture

Soybeans are heat-loving beans that are fairly tolerant of cool nights. The seed will not germinate in cold soils, so there is no sense in planting them before the soil is above sixty degrees. The first of June is about right at Lorane. It is very helpful to have second-guessed the weather and planted the seed just before a long, sunny, hot spell really heats up the soil. Sow the seed in rows at least twelve inches apart, the seeds about one inch deep and about an inch or two apart in the row.

Soybean sprouts are not very vigorous and will not push through a hard crust. The seed bed should be worked to a finer consistency than most other beans demand. There is no need to thin the beans unless they stand closer than one inch apart.

Garden Planning
There is little reason to grow many plants for fresh eating, since soybeans are highly uniform in rate of maturation. Three or four feet of row probably will keep a soybean fancier happy for about ten days. The fresh beans will be harvested by late August, making their bed a fine place for late cauliflower or other brassicas.

Insects and Diseases
Soybeans usually do not have problems with insects and diseases.

Water
If soil warms up early enough in May to be sure of germination by the first of June, there probably is sufficient field moisture in any humusy, clayey soil to support growth to full maturity (dry, sproutable beans). If it should rain in July or August, the harvest will be much larger, but even in a year that provided very little rain after 20 June and none after 9 July, my beans matured. When grown in dry conditions the beans should be spaced out farther—rows eighteen inches apart and the established plants at least four inches apart in the row.

Harvest
Harvest as shell beans when most of the pods are full. Pull an entire plant, strip off the pods, and steam them briefly for no more than five minutes. If steamed too long the pods turn to mush and hinder shelling. Shell them by hand. The Japanese lightly salt the steamed pods and slip the beans out between their teeth, eating soybeans as we eat popcorn. For dry beans, allow them to mature fully in the field, which will take three or four weeks longer. When most of the seeds are fully dried out, cut the plants, stack them up under cover to complete their drying, and thresh out the seed.

Saving Seed
Saving seed is described under Harvesting.

Varieties
Beware of untested varieties. Soybeans start to flower when days have shortened sufficiently, and that point varies according to the latitude in which the bean is bred to grow. There are seven specific day-length areas in the United States alone, and only beans bred for the northernmost area respond properly to our mix of day lengths. Fiskeby (JSS, STK) has rather small seeds but is abundant and early. Envy (JSS, TS) has fine large seeds and is the one we grow at Lorane as an irrigationless field bean. Frostbeater (BUR) also is very good. Other types of soybeans developed mainly for oil or for processing purposes might not please a gardener if eaten as shell beans.

Field Beans
Growing field beans (dry types) is possible on a small scale west of the Cascades. Irregularities in fall weather make field drying uncertain and so prohibit large scale commercial bean growing. The gardener or homesteader, however, can

dry the crop under cover if necessary.

Culture

Culturing is the same as for bush beans, but planting is done in rows up to twenty-four inches apart—although this varies greatly according to the varieties. All field beans grown commercially at this time are bush types, although some get viney, like White Half Runners (snap beans). The more viney the bush is, the more space it needs. A small bush type like Soldier, grown with irrigation, can have as little as twelve inches between the rows.

Garden Planning

I suggest you put in only a small row of field beans if you have never grown them—not because you cannot grow them easily, but because you may not enjoy all the effort necessary to thresh and clean them at harvest. If you do like growing them, they can be used to rebuild beds where demanding crops were grown the previous year. Very early types like Soldier can be followed by transplanted brassicas early in September or by spinach or lettuce.

Insects and Diseases

Insect and disease problems are the same as those for bush beans.

Water

Dry beans are better grown in field conditions than in a small garden because you will want to be able to withhold water as soon as ripening begins. Otherwise the plants will be too slow to dry out. If you find yourself waiting too late in the season to harvest, the fall rains may complicate things still further. If you do grow them in a garden, try to put them in a spot that does not have to be watered after early August. Early types do fine without irrigation in clayey, humusy soils. If there is no irrigation water, grow the rows rather far apart and space the plants out a bit to give them more root room. One good irrigationless system for small-scale bean growing would be to plant the field in crimson clover in October. Then in early May—or late April in warmer areas—cut the clover with a scythe and rake it into windrows about three feet apart. Then, with a tiller or by hand, work up seed beds between each windrow of drying clover hay. Plant beans. In June, after the beans are growing vigorously, rake the hay under the bean plants for mulch.

Harvest

Back east, when most of the plant's leaves have fallen and the pods are dry, the beans are pulled out by the roots and the seeds separated by hand threshing. West of the Cascades, the procedure is to pull the plants out by the roots when they are fairly well dried out, after many of the leaves have fallen, and right after the weather report states that it is going to rain for several days. Then stack the damp plants up inside where lots of air can move through them. When the plants are well dried, thresh them. This can be done in several ways. Either shell the pods individually by hand, holding several plants by the roots and banging them back and forth inside a barrel or metal trashcan, or beat small piles of plants with a flail. Store the well-dried beans in a cool, dry place. Putting them in a jar may reduce germination if the beans are meant for sprouting or for a seed crop. If, upon inspection during storage, you find dust or bean particles accumulating in the bottom of the container, you have living bean weevils at work. Put the beans into the freezing compartment of your refrigerator for twenty-four hours to kill off the weevils.

Saving Seed

Select ten or more of the best plants on the grounds of general appearance and yield, as well as early maturity, and flag them with bright plastic ties or yarn. Harvest these separately for your seed crop. The more plants that go to make up the seed crop, the better.

Varieties

You can grow any beans that are now in your cupboard or for sale in your supermarket or health food store. With our wet harvest seasons, however, it is best to grow the earliest varieties, such as Soldier (TS, JSS). Johnny's makes a specialty of dry beans and has many other interesting varieties. Many heirloom beans are floating around the Northwest, and perhaps one of the older gardeners in your area has a strain that is well adapted to the area. Most people growing beans like this are uncertain of the correct varietal name. Some of these strains may have been in their families for centuries. A few of these types of beans are sent to us each year by helpful gardeners, so someday Territorial Seed Company may offer heirloom bean varieties.

Crimson Clover and Other Green Manures

There are numerous clovers that have great use in various soil rotation schemes. The best one for garden use is crimson clover. It is an annual and a large plant, producing an abundance of biomass. White clovers and Dutch clovers are small, low-growing perennials. Using one of these by mistake can establish quite a "weed" situation.

Culture

Sow crimson clover any time from late September through October. Early plantings "take" better if there is sufficient moisture. The seeds can be scattered among standing crops if the crops have not been harvested yet and are not intended to overwinter. Broadcast the seed at a rate of about a quarter pound per hundred square feet of bed. This is a much heavier sowing rate than is used in field plantings, but it ensures complete coverage, and it will not hurt anything if the seedlings are crowded. If you can, rake the seed into the soil very shallowly. Austrian field peas are sown the same way at the same times, at a rate of about two pounds per hundred square feet.

Garden Planning

Any bed that is not going to overwinter a crop or that does not have root crops still in it should be planted in legume green manures.

Insects and Diseases

Insects and diseases are not a problem.

Water

Green manure crops grow on rainfall.

Harvest

Pull out all the vegetation any time from March until flowers begin to form on the clover, or when the first set of peas begins to fill out on the vines of the Austrian field peas. Do not allow it to make seed if you are using it as green manure, because once seed formation starts, the nitrogen value of the vegetation begins to decline. Compost the vegetation or allow it to dry in the paths like hay, and use it as summertime mulch.

Saving Seed

If you wish to, allow a portion of a bed to mature seed and dry out. Since it will probably be exposed to overhead irrigation, harvest as soon as the stalks are fairly browned off, and dry fully in the sun. Thresh out the seeds and store them.

Varieties

I know of none. Crimson clover is crimson clover. Austrian field peas are Austrian field peas.

Peas

Peas are a great crop for our region, but many gardeners have been very disappointed trying to grow them. It seems that if you do not get peas planted early enough, they will wilt and quit producing almost before they get started. This problem has been solved with newer varieties of enation-resistant peas. For homesteaders, field peas should be the basic staple legume since they have no difficulty maturing on field moisture and produce abundantly.

Culture

Plant varieties nonresistant to enation as early in spring as the soil can be prepared. They must be in by the first of April, or you are not going to be happy with the crop. Enation will begin wilting the vines in June. Using raised beds with compostable green manures allows peas to be planted any time you are willing to experience the weather. I think the first of March is the earliest good date to plant, because February plantings seem to rot in the ground. Enation-resistant varieties can be planted all summer, although the best peas will come from plantings made before the first of May. Plant the seeds thickly, about one inch deep and one inch apart in the rows, and have the rows at least sixteen inches apart. Dwarf varieties do best planted in twin rows. The two rows support each other and keep the vines off the ground without the need to use a trellis or low pea-fence. Climbing types need a fence or trellis. Do not thin the plants; peas like to grow thickly.

Garden Planning

It takes about a twenty foot row of peas to satisfy me during May and June. Just me. It takes another fifteen feet for my wife, but she is a small eater. This is only what we require for fresh table consumption. When we used to freeze peas, we planted sixty to one hundred row-feet more. Growing lots of peas, especially the very early round-seeded types (which are for pea soup), is a good way to grow a green manure crop that adds considerable nitrogen. The peas will be picked and gone by the time your fall garden is ready to start going in.

Insects and Diseases

Insects rarely do significant damage to peas. Enation is another matter. Pea enation is a kind of viral disease that causes a wilted vine and a warty appearance on the pods. Enation is transmitted by insects, and there is no way to keep it out of your garden. The disease rapidly ends production of nonresistant varieties when it strikes, and it usually appears in middle to late June. Originally developed by

Oregon State University, enation-resistant varieties make it possible to plant peas all summer. The pea plants still do best, however, when peas are being matured during the months of May, June, and July. The sunlight is strongest then, and the vines are able to make much more food and sugar to sweeten up the seeds.

Water

All the basic pea varieties grow on rainfall in the early summer. They may take considerable irrigation if planted after 15 April, however, because the soil begins to dry out too much during their seed set and ripening period. Field peas will grow very well on field moisture, and mature their crop naturally as the soil dries out.

Harvest

Pick fresh peas when the pods have just filled but before the seeds are getting tough and dry. Keeping the vines picked will extend the harvest somewhat. Cut field peas when the vines are dying and brown. The peas will be rattling around in the pods when it is the correct time. Threshing and storage is similar to dealing with field beans. Peas are much more likely to be harvested dry, maturing as they do at the end of our rainfall period, rather than the beginning of it as beans do. The peas can be used whole for pea soup, but if they are split by running them through a grain mill (steel-burr type) they will cook more quickly.

Saving Seed

Follow the instructions for field beans.

Varieties

The most flavorful of the old freezing and canning varieties are Little Marvel, Dark Green Perfection, and all of the Laxtons. All the seed companies have one or all of them, except Territorial, which only carries enation-resistant varieties. Another good freezer pea is Lincoln (HAR). Enation-resistant freezer types include Aurora (TS), Corvallis, Knight, and Maestro (TS, BUR). Aurora and Corvallis were Oregon State University developments. Feel free to experiment with any kind of peas, as long as you plant early. Only grow enation-resistant varieties if you plant after mid-April. The best edible-pod type is Oregon Sugar Pod—another Oregon State enation-resistant development. Most seed companies sell it. Sugar Snaps, which are the favorite of many gardeners, are not enation-resistant and are not a dwarf pea. They require both early planting and a trellis or fence, but the extra trouble is well worth it. Everyone sells Sugar Snaps. Alaska peas are smooth-seeded types to use for making soups. They are extremely early, prolific, and easy to grow. Alaskas are the ones to try to grow by the tenth acre if you are trying for real food self-sufficiency. Alaskas can be purchased from a seed company (JSS), or from your market or health food store if unsplit. There are both green and yellow types of Alaska peas.

Miscellaneous Legumes

I have experimented with growing other legume crops west of the Cascades and want to point out that it is possible to grow them. Lentils culture like peas, although they are not quite as frost hardy. The best planting date seems to be the first of April. Apparently there are different varieties, but it is not possible to know which variety you are getting when you get a pound of seed from your local market. Garbanzo beans also are a pea but seem to mature rather late. I would not plant them until mid-April or the first of May. They matured for me in non-irrigated plantings under field crop conditions.

Mung beans are not suited to our climate and belong in the same category as limas and black-eyed peas. Adzuke beans do not do particularly well either. Do not forget that your favorite snap beans have seeds, too, and some of these may be interesting eating.

Greens

There is no botanical classification called "greens." The vegetables I classify in this group actually are members of many different families of plants. I categorize them this way because they share patterns of growth and behavior.

Nutrient requirements of plants change as they go through their growth stages. I think of these stages as the seedling, vegetative, and seed formation stages. This classification system works for me. During the seedling stage, plants require abundant potash and phosphorus and very little nitrogen. During the vegetative stage the plants will use great amounts of nitrogen _if_ it is available. They respond to nitrogen by making more growth. During seed formation, which starts with flowering and ends with mature seed, the plants need additional potash and phosphorus and very little nitrogen. Overly abundant nitrogen at the time plants are flowering tends to limit fruit set and provoke unwanted vegetative growth.

Greens are plants that have been bred to rush into the vegetative growth stage shortly after germination, and they are picked before they leave it. All greens were bred to make abundant, succulent vegetation. They need lots of soil moisture because the greens have limited root systems. I suspect that root growth has been sacrificed by plant breeders "training" greens to make more vegetative growth.

Greens respond wonderfully to nitrogen fertilizers. Rich organic soil generally will supply enough nitrogen for fairly good vegetative growth—after it has warmed up thoroughly. Using strong stuff such as chicken manure, cottonseed meal, or fish meal in the bed is very helpful. In early spring, nitrogen supplements are needed if large succulent leaves are to be harvested. I use large quantities of blood meal on spring greens, and if I could not afford to use this expensive organic material, I would substitute urea. Unless your soil has been almost overdosed with chicken manure or cottonseed meal, nitrogen fertilizer applied at almost any time of the year will result in lusher, more attractive plants. I use small amounts of blood meal as a side-dressing with some summer greens if I want to provoke a growth spurt. It is poor practice to use nitrogen fertilizers on fall greens or other fall crops, because the rapid growth induced by nitrogen is soft and tends to die easily in cold spells.

If greens are allowed to grow too slowly, their vegetation becomes the opposite of soft—indigestible. The slower the growth is, the more woody the plant becomes and the poorer the flavor will be. Make sure there is sufficient nitrogen in your soil to permit continuous, rapid growth of greens. If it stops, side-dress the plants with a quick-releasing fertilizer.

Celery
You will have better luck growing celery if you consider it a fall crop rather than a midsummer one. If planted out too early, weather fluctuations and cold nights cause celery to bolt and begin seed formation. If you buy nursery transplants,

I advise you to purchase them as late as possible—even mid-June. Celery will mature even if directly seeded as late as 30 June.

Culture

I used to recommend that the seeds be sown indoors after mid-March, but I am coming to think that directly seeding outdoors after mid-May would be a better idea. This late planting date avoids the trouble of transplanting and also avoids the cool nights, thus eliminating early bolting. Celery is frost hardy, so early spring frosts will not harm the seedling, but the vegetable determines the correct time to make seed by counting up the number of hours that temperatures are below fifty-five degrees. When enough hours have accumulated, the plants bolt. If you want to start celery early, keep its temperature above fifty-five and try to delay transplanting until the weather has settled as much as possible. Celery seedlings are very slow growing, so a mid-March sowing indoors will be ready to transplant about the first of June. Whether sowing indoors or out, plant the seed very shallowly and keep it moist until germination occurs—which may be two weeks. Transplant the seedlings at least twelve inches apart in rows at least eighteen inches apart, or gradually thin out directly seeded plantings to the same spacing. Celery is capable of using prodigious amounts of nitrogen, and its roots are very close to the plant, so side-dressings must almost touch the stem to be effective. If celery does not grow rapidly, it gets stringy.

Garden Planning

A half dozen plants will keep the two of us in all the stalks we can use.

Insects and Diseases

Celery rarely has insect or disease problems.

Water

Celery requires a lot of water and must be treated very gently during the hottest parts of the summer. Its small root system is not capable of extracting enough moisture from dry soils to enable it to make rapid growth. And if it does not grow rapidly, it is almost inedible.

Harvest

Cut off single stalks from the outside of the plant as they are needed. If the winter is not too hard, celery will stand until spring, allowing light pickings for soups and salads. Even if celery should bolt, the small leaves and stems still can be eaten.

Saving Seed

Celery is a biennial, flowering in its second year unless cold weather makes it bolt prematurely in midsummer. Early bolting in the first year is not useful for seed production, both because you do not want to select for early bolting and because the seed is unlikely to mature. Celery crosses easily with other varieties of celery and celeriac, so isolate varieties by at least 200 feet for fair purity. Celery must overwinter, and the easiest way to accomplish this is to leave it in the garden and hope for moderate winter temperatures. The next spring, if it has survived, celery will put up seed stalks, make small white flowers, and form seed that matures in summer. The seed detaches from the flower easily, so use care in harvesting. Dry the heads indoors on newspaper or cloth to catch the seed that otherwise would fall out and be lost. If your area is too cold to overwinter celery reliably, relax and take a philosophical attitude about it. Remember that the seed is long lasting and that you need to have only one mild winter out of five or six to make enough seed to last you for fifteen years. Before the last batch of seed loses too much germination potential, a new crop will overwinter and resupply your celery seed jar. Select plants on the basis of long, firm, tender stalks, which have less tendency to be stringy.

Varieties

Everyone carries Utah 5270, which is the standard celery grown in America. Burpee has their own similar strains. Other types, such as yellow, golden, or self-blanching will also do well.

Celeriac

Celeriac is a type of celery grown for its large tender roots. These have a mild celery taste and can be used like potatoes. Grow celeriac exactly as you do celery, but thin them to eight inches apart and make the rows twelve inches apart. Celeriac also has a high water requirement. Mature roots will keep through much of the early winter and may stay in good condition until spring. Most seed companies sell Prague, which tends to be knobby. Europeans have made selections for smooth roots, making a greater percentage of the plant edible. They also have worked to eliminate the discoloration the roots sometimes have when cooked. I recommend any variety of celeriac.

Corn Salad

The herb corn salad is actually a European weed that would come up in the cornfields after harvest. The Europeans call any small grain "corn"; what we call "corn" they call "maize." The weeds made good salad greens and were completely winter hardy, so they were bred to increase leaf size and flavor. If it is allowed to go to seed in your garden in spring after planting in fall, corn salad will establish itself as a natural edible "weed."

Culture

The seed will not germinate until soil temperatures have dropped considerably from their August peak. Around the first of September (and as late as mid-October), sow the seed thickly in rows at least twelve inches apart, or broadcast the seed for a green manure crop. Bury the seed about a half inch deep. Thinning is unnecessary.

Garden Planning

Corn salad makes a fine edible green manure crop following the demise of frost-sensitive summer annuals. It makes abundant vegetation and leaves the soil in very nice condition the following spring. It can be pulled out of the soil in spring, leaving no clumps or root balls to interfere with making up a seed bed. For salad uses, only ten feet of row per adult will be an adequate supply. If sown in early September, it will be pickable by November. If sown later, it may not make much food for you until early March.

Insects and Diseases
Corn salad generally does not have insect or disease problems.

Water
In nonirrigated fields, corn salad can be sown after the fall rains have restored the level of field moisture. In a nonirrigated garden, a little hand-carried water could get a nice bed to germinate early enough to make a fine fall salad crop.

Harvest
Pick individual outer leaves as needed once they are full-size.

Saving Seed
Corn salad will begin making seed in spring. As flower formation begins, the taste gets spicy, but the leaves still are good. Even undeveloped flowers are good to eat. The seed will mature in late spring and begin dropping to the earth as it ripens. A sheet of cardboard under the plants can catch this falling seed. Collect it before you water the garden or before it rains, and dry it fully indoors before storing it away.

Varieties
Several strains have been named in Europe, but the differences are insignificant. Corn salad is available from Stokes, Territorial, and Harris.

Endive
Most people think endive is a sort of lettuce, but it is not. Lettuce is a slightly frost-hardy annual. Endive is a very hardy perennial. Although it is commercially grown in summer, endive is much improved by some stiff frosts, getting much sweeter and becoming an excellent salad green.

Culture
Plant the seed in rich ground that has not been overstimulated with nitrogen fertilizers. If the soil is poor, dig a five-inch-deep furrow, sprinkle about one pound of blood meal (or urea) per fifteen feet of row, fill in the furrow until there is only a small dip remaining, and sow the seed in the dip. This puts the nitrogen right under the seedlings and makes sure the plants get a big boost during the month of August. Seedling growth is greatly stimulated, but the nitrogen level drops off rapidly as the plant enlarges and prevents it from becoming too soft. During the last half of July or early August, sow the seed thinly about a half inch deep in rows at least eighteen inches apart, and thin later to about twelve inches apart in the row.

Garden Planning
Plant more endive than you think you will need. It gets quite tasty in October and November and may last until the Christmas salad even in very harsh areas. Twenty feet of row are enough for the two of us. Endive follows peas very nicely. In a garden of limited size, it could be raised in nursery beds or bedding plant trays and transplanted out in early September after the early sweet corn has been harvested. If there is really a space shortage, start endive as late as the first of September in a nursery bed, and transplant it out in October. Certainly the frosts will have come by then, opening up many vacancies. Endive started late still will

be productive though much smaller. Do not use any nitrogen fertilizer if you are starting the plants late, because they will not have sufficient time to harden off.

Insects and Diseases

Insects and diseases are not a problem for endive.

Water

Endive is well worth growing, even in situations where water is limited. Raising it as transplants and starting it late makes it possible to stretch irrigation water to the limit. In a wet year, there may be enough rain by mid-August to start it directly seeded, and you might need to water the seed row only a few times.

Harvest

I suggest you do not cut entire heads but pick individual outer leaves as they are needed. The blanched leaves in the center are more tender and sweeter and may induce you to cut entire plants.

Saving Seed

Hope for a mild winter. If the endive survives past mid-February, you can be certain of a seed crop. Select the nicest surviving plants—and do not limit it to too few. Endive is mostly self-pollinated, so different varieties require no isolation. For purity of the type the finest seedsmen try for, an isolation of a few hundred feet between varieties is called for. The plants will put up a seed stalk, flowers will open, and the seed will ripen. When half the seed heads have feathered out (the seeds are like dandelions), cut the stalk and hang it up to dry. Then shake the heads inside a drum or paper bag to dislodge the seed. If the seed crop is important and your location regularly has cold winters below eighteen degrees, the plants can be over-wintered under cloches.

Varieties

Two basic types of endive are sold. The Ruffics are green throughout, lacy and frilly like salad-bowl lettuce. The Batavians are similar to bibb lettuce, with thick, juicy, blanched inner leaves. We prefer the Batavian types, which are sometimes called escarole. There is enough commercial interest in endive for seedsmen in this country to be quite careful with their endive strains. You can buy any variety with confidence, as long as you have confidence in the seedsman. Endives from Europe seem more likely to be cold hardy. Stokes has a European Batavian that should be better than most.

Lettuce

Lettuce is a moderately hardy green that can be grown from spring to fall. Loose-leaf types are the easiest to grow, but many gardeners prefer iceberg types. These require much higher levels of nitrogen to head out properly.

Culture

Lettuce requires moderately rich garden soil. Extra nitrogen increases succulence and speeds growth, but ordinary garden soil will grow acceptable leaf lettuce without extra nutrients. To grow good head lettuce, work some blood meal into the planting row when seeding the crop, and side-dress the row several times as the plants develop. After the first of April, sow the seeds outdoors a half inch deep, thinly, in rows at least twelve inches apart. Thin loose leafs to about eight inches apart and heading types to about sixteen inches apart. It is essential that head lettuce varieties be thinned early, or they will not head well. Head lettuce can be sown until 15 July. Loose-leaf types can be sown until 15 August and still make large enough heads before frost ends their lives. If sown after 15 August, the heads will be smaller than you want.

Garden Planning

We like to have three to four kinds of loose leaf lettuce. Only small quantities of each are needed, and four feet of row will be plenty for each type. I like to sow lettuce three times in the season so that I have a continuous harvest. The first sowing is in early spring. Another made about the first of June will come in as the spring planting starts to go to seed. The last sowing should be close to the first of August. Heading types must be planted every two weeks or so if a relatively continuous supply is desired. You know how many heads you need in a two-week period. I would grow about 50 percent more than that, because even with the best strains of lettuce a large proportion of the plants fail to head out properly.

Insects and Diseases

Insects and diseases are rarely a problem, particularly if you buy mosaic-tested seed. Mosaic is a lettuce disease that can ruin whole plantings and is transplanted to new areas with the seed itself. Mosaic-tested seed comes from fields free or almost free of the disease, costs somewhat more than other seed and is marked with an "MT" or "MI" (mosaic indexed). Not all varieties come indexed, but all the head types do, and so do some loose leafs. You might be able to use any kind of lettuce seed for many years, without ever seeing mosaic ruin the plants, and then again, you might not. I would suggest that if you see a company offering seed that has been indexed, you buy from them.

Water

Only spring lettuce will grow on rainfall. If late plantings are desired, be prepared to irrigate them. The last planting can be started on rainfall in a wet summer or can be sown in a nursery bed and transplanted out sometime in September.

Harvest

Head lettuce will stand for a week or so in the field before it begins to go bad. A planting will produce a harvest for about two weeks' time. Loose-leaf types are better harvested by picking off the large outer leaves than by cutting the entire head. Doing it this way permits a small number of plants to supply an enormous number of leaves. The supermarket sells a whole head because they have no other way to do it.

Saving Seed

Lettuce is an annual. It rarely cross-pollinates, and little or no isolation between varieties is required. The seed forms in late summer from a very early spring planting. Commercial production is done in California, where the season is very long and the plants have no difficulty maturing seed before season's end. You may have to start lettuce indoors in February and transplant it out in late March to enable the seed to mature by fall. Select the best plants from your earliest planting to make seed. Allow the stalk to mature and become feathered out like a dandelion flower. Then cut the stalk and allow it to dry indoors under cover. Shake the head into a bag or drum to collect the seed. If you are growing crisp-head seed, cut the top of the head in an X pattern about two inches deep with a sharp knife. This allows the seed stalk to emerge through the head.

Varieties

Just about any loose-leaf type will do very well in Oregon. Each has a different configuration and taste. Experiment and choose what you like. I have found that the best adapted and most resilient type of bibb lettuce is Buttercrunch. With crisp heads there is a big difference in varieties, and you must be quite choosy. The two best are Ithaca (TS, JSS, STK, HAR) and Calmar (TS). Calmar tolerates summer's heat a little better than Ithaca, and heat toleration might be the deciding factor between heading and failure for gardeners south of Roseburg—or during a really hot spell. I grow Ithaca in spring and switch to Calmar about mid-May. There are also cold-hardy heading types that have been bred to mature in fall and allow planting after mid-July. These are strictly of European origin, however, and the only one available in the United States at this time is Winter Density (JSS). I am studying winter lettuce and hope that other varieties soon will be available west of the Cascades.

Mustard

Mustard grows very well at either cool end of the season. A few Chinese types even are able to handle summer's long days without going to seed. We find mustard vital in spring. Without mustard greens, we would not have stir-fries of mustard, collard flowers, overwintered broccoli, sweet white overwintered onions, winter spinach, and radishes (both tops and bottoms).

Culture

Mustard needs rich soil with extra nitrogen added if you want large, succulent leaves in springtime. Fall-planted mustard will grow adequately in ordinary rich garden soil. Sow the seed when the crocuses begin to pop out of the ground. I have seen volunteers come up in early January and actually survive six-degree lows, but they are set back so badly by this kind of environment that seeds planted in early March become bigger plants much sooner than the earliest volunteers. Plant the seed about a half inch deep in rows about eighteen inches apart, and space the seed so about one seed is placed every half inch along the furrow. This dense stand of seedlings will mostly feed the flea beetles, so you will not have to thin too much. When the plants are growing rapidly, thin them to about two inches apart in the row. Then, when this gets crowded, thin again to four inches apart. These thinnings will be large enough to eat, and in early springtime, you will be grateful for them. Finally, thin the plants to about eight inches apart. I would not plant most types of mustard from mid-April to late summer, because they will bolt before they have grown much. For the fall garden, plant mustard again from mid-August to mid-September. The spring planting should be well fertilized, either with blood meal or by using chicken manure in the planting bed before you sow seeds.

Garden Planning

If you have not eaten mustard greens before, plant about four feet of row and try them out. The two of us need about twenty-five feet of row to keep ourselves supplied in early spring. I replant a few summer mustard plants to use when I get in the mood for stir-fry—maybe four feet of row in all. I put in a nice big patch again in late summer. Try to have the greens follow a legume.

Insects and Diseases

You could fight the flea beetles with rotenone when they seem to be destroying your seedlings, or you could plant enough seeds in rich enough soil so that the beetles only do some natural selection for you.

Water

Spring mustards grow on natural rainfall. If a dry August delays planting, sowing the seed after the September rains still will work but produces smaller plants and lower yield.

Harvest

Pick off the large outer leaves as needed. When the plants go to seed, do not pull them up, simply smile to yourself as you contemplate the tastiest part of the harvest. Mustard flowers are delicious, and the more of them you pick, the more the plant makes. Eventually you will tire of them when sweeter fare comes in.

Saving Seed

Mustard puts up a seed stalk late in spring and goes into its flowering cycle for several months. It is a relative of the brassicas but will not cross-pollinate readily with other cabbage family members. It will, however, cross easily with other mustards. Isolate flowering varieties by at least 200 feet for fair purity and by 1,000 feet or more for good purity. Since the seed lasts for seven years or so, you could maintain several strains by letting only one go to seed each year. Mizuna should be grown as a fall plant and selected for its ability to tolerate cold weather and survive until spring. Select all varieties for slow bolting. It might be possible to plant all mustard varieties in the fall and from the few survivors select out more winter-hardy strains. Then you would not face the likelihood of losing your fall mustard crop to fifteen-degree temperatures. The seed stalks resemble those on cabbage, and the seed should be handled like that of any brassica.

Varieties

All mustards grow well west of the Cascades. Flowering is triggered by day length, and most mustards flower in May, regardless of when they were planted. Some varieties are slower to flower than others, and this improved trait is indicated by appending to their name the words "long standing." Chinese Pac Choi (bok choy)—at least some strains of it—is so bolt resistant that it can be planted anytime in spring, summer, or fall (TS, JSS). Even if it is provoked into flowering, it first will have attained a very large size. A strain of Pac Choi called Le Choi has much more succulent stalks than other strains, but it is not frost hardy and bolts easily (BUR). All kinds of Pac Choi have stalks so mild that they can be used as celery. The American mustards such as Tendergreen, Mustard Spinach, and Southern Giant Curled Long Standing are quite beautiful plants and seem to be perfect examples of the plant breeder's art. Mizuna (TS, JSS) is a Japanese mustard bred for overwintered production. It is exceptionally cold hardy for a mustard and sometimes makes it over to spring west of the Cascades. Mizuna is mild enough to be used as a salad green.

Parsley

Many people think you must buy seedlings and transplant parsley. This is not true if you can sow it fairly early outside.

Culture

Parsley likes rich soil with lots of nitrogen but will grow all right on anything it has. The seeds are slow to germinate (there is an old saying that "you have to wait for the seed to go down to the devil and come back before it sprouts")—three weeks is usual. They must stay damp during this time. This condition usually is met if the seeds are planted outdoors before the first of May. I start them as early as the first of March. Sow the seed fairly thinly a half inch deep in rows at least eight inches apart. Thinning is not necessary, but if you do thin them to about four inches apart the final plants will be better developed. If you want to make heavy cuttings and have rapid regrowth afterwards, side-dress the plants with blood meal or chicken manure whenever the growth slows.

Garden Planning

Four feet of row should keep any family in parsley. Put the plants in somewhere that will not have to be bothered for an entire year, since one spring's planting will produce until next spring.

Insects and Diseases

Insects and diseases are not a problem.

Water

Parsley has a large carrotlike root that will hold considerable moisture. If you are growing parsley on nonirrigated land, a little mulch, and a side-dressing of water once a month will keep a small bed alive. It will not grow much after things get dry until the rains come again. If you have to, you can start parsley in late summer, but you must pay very careful attention to the moisture content of the seed bed—if it dries out, the planting will fail.

Harvest

Cut individual stems as needed. Parsley is winter hardy and survives most winters west of the Cascades, going to seed the following spring.

Saving Seed

Parsley cross-pollinates readily, so if you are trying to grow more than one variety at a time for seed, isolate them by over a thousand feet. This should not be a problem, however, because one variety is all anyone really needs. The seed stalks are similar to onion flowers. When they mature, cut the heads, dry the seed heads fully indoors, and thresh out the seed.

Varieties

There are two basic kinds of parsley—curly and plain. The plain types are more strongly flavored and better for seasonings. Since all varieties are grown as biennials, they are all quite winter hardy. All are well adapted to our area. This is a good vegetable to experiment with, because the curly types have been bred to the highest possible standards of beauty. Each is a masterpiece of the plant breeder's art. If you are in an area of severe winter temperatures, you might want to experiment with varieties, looking for increased ability to handle temperatures under ten degrees.

Spinach

Spinach is a natural crop for our gardens. Long cool periods at either end of the season make large, tasty plants. Spinach is remarkably cold hardy and forms a large part of the winter salad supply at our house.

Culture

Spinach is highly responsive to increasing day length. Once the days have reached the triggering duration, the plant goes to seed on the first hot day. Breeding has increased the tolerance of spinach for long days, so some varieties will grow longer into spring before bolting than others. Once the days are shortening up, spinach is much less likely to bolt, and by late summer, it can be planted with the certainty that it will not bolt until the following spring. Sow the fall and winter crop during August. The earlier it is planted in August, the larger the leaves will get before they *almost* stop growing for the winter.

Spinach requires rich garden soil with abundant nitrogen. If deprived of nitrogen, spring spinach will grow very slowly, and the leaves will tend to be bitter and tough. Fall crops do best if given a less stimulating soil. It is helpful to side-dress fall crops once with a quick-acting form of nitrogen, such as blood meal, shortly after planting. This provokes rapid growth for about one month, and then the plants settle down and harden up for winter. Plant the spring crop early in April. If you cannot get at your garden or miss the planting date, grow one of the later-bolting varieties, which may be started as late as the end of April. After it has overwintered, spinach should be side-dressed monthly until it bolts to get the maximum harvest. Preparing the spring seed bed with chicken manure will eliminate the need to side-dress. Plant the seeds about a half inch deep and about one inch apart, in rows at least twelve inches apart. Thin later to about three inches apart.

Garden Planning

We find that a twenty-foot row of spring spinach gives us enough greens for salads and occasional cooking. If you prefer cooked spinach and rarely use it in salads, double the amount of plants, because they cook down quite a bit. I always plant more for the fall. During winter, the plants grow very slowly and a much larger area is needed to keep us in salads. Fifty feet of row handles my wife and me from October to early May. The overwintered spinach bolts then, and the spring-planted spinach just begins to come on at the same time. The spring planting carries us into June, and by then there are lots of other greens. I do not try to grow spinach into July, or even late June. When it bolts, it bolts. Since it is being so heavily demanding on the soil, spinach is best planted following a legume. This is easy enough in spring if you use a crimson clover green manure. I prefer to follow the overwintered crop with bush beans if possible, or with roots if enough bean beds are already planned.

Insects and Diseases

Insects and diseases are not a problem.

Water

If you are gardening with limited water, the fall crop could be started after rains have restored field moisture to some extent. This late start means a crop in spring, with very small plants overwintering. An earlier start will give you a crop in fall, winter, and spring.

Harvest

Since you are not shipping your spinach to the supermarket, there is no reason to cut off the entire plant. Snip off the large outer leaves as needed, and the plant will go on making new ones until it bolts. The bolting will not be influenced by how much you pick the plants. Once bolting begins the flavor deteriorates and leaves stop forming. Bolting ends the harvest within a week.

Saving Seed

When bolting begins, remove the smaller, stunted plants. These are males, which make male flowers only. There are also females and bisexual plants. After the males have bolted, the females and bisexual plants will begin to bolt. Remove the first 15 or 20 percent of these, too, since early bolting is an undesirable trait. After pollination the seed stalks ripen unevenly, and harvest can be delayed until the stalks are brown. Cut off the seed stalks and dry fully indoors. Thresh out seed between your palms. Spinach pollen is carried long distances by wind, so grow only one variety for seed in any one year.

Varieties

Two varieties are basic to the home-garden spinach patch. One is Winter Bloomsdale (called Cold Hardy Savoy by Stokes). The other is Bloomsdale Long Standing, used in spring. All the seed companies have one or both. Bloomsdale spinaches are highly savoyed (crinkled), juicy, and sweet. Canneries do not like them because it is more difficult to wash the leaves when they are savoyed. Seed companies have bred numerous hybrid smooth-leaved varieties for this market. Most are relatively flavorless and have a higher fiber content than Bloomsdale, so processing does not cook them down as much. Until I have investigated these hybrids more extensively, I do not recommend any, because the thirty or so types I have tasted are highly unsuitable for home garden use. Most are bitter or cardboardy. America is a savoyed variety a little later to bolt than Bloomsdale Long Standing (STK). Giant Noble is a nice garden spinach with smooth leaves and also is a very slow bolter.

Swiss Chard

Chard is a member of the beet family grown for its large and tasty greens. The leaves cook like spinach and may be used in salads. The stalks are somewhat like celery and add a nice crunchy texture. Chard is frost hardy and will stand through mild winters until it bolts in spring. It will grow well in soils of only moderate fertility, but rich soil and nitrogen fertilizer are necessary for heavy production and rapid regrowth after cutting.

Culture

Make your annual sowing sometime between April and June, whenever it is convenient. Sow eight to twelve seeds per foot, a half inch deep, in rows at least eighteen inches apart. Thin the seedlings when they are well established to about ten inches apart in the row. Eat the thinnings. Harvest begins about sixty days after sowing and continues for nearly one year unless the plants freeze out.

Garden Planning

Ten feet of row should keep all but the largest families supplied with chard for at least nine months. It is probably a good idea to put chard off in a corner or to plant it in the same bed in which you grow parsley and leeks. Both are in the ground nearly the same amount of time chard is. If you do not eat cooked greens frequently, one or two plants probably will be enough. Chard is a very beautiful plant, growing three feet tall, with highly savoyed, bright leaves. It is an excellent candidate for growing in a decorative border bed in place of flowers.

Insects and Diseases

Insects and diseases usually are not a problem. Sometimes cucumber beetles will make a hash of seedlings. If this has happened, enrich the bed and replant. The beetles will not destroy a stand of vigorous seedlings. Since with beet family members many plants come up from a single seed, you should not mind if the beetles do some thinning for you. Cutworms will make big holes in the leaves during summer. These are best ignored, since the holes do not reduce the palatability of the leaves one iota.

Water

Chard has a very deep root system and is somewhat drought resistant.

Harvesting

Cut the large outer leaves as they are needed. The inner leaves will continue to form. If you find that the plants are not supplying you with enough greens, side-dress them well with blood meal and water. If the winter temperatures stay above fifteen degrees, you can be fairly confident of having chard to eat until it bolts in spring.

Saving Seed

Chard is a member of the beet family, and it will cross readily with other beets. Allow as many plants as possible to participate in the seed-making process, and rogue only for very undesirable traits. See "Beets" for detailed information on saving seed.

Varieties

The essential difference between varieties is in appearance. Flavor variations are slight. All varieties seem to be well adapted to our area except for some European types that do not handle midsummer heat very well.

Brassicas

The brassica family is the group of vegetables best adapted for the maritime Northwest. The family includes kale, kohlrabi, rutabagas, cabbages, cauliflower, broccoli, Brussels sprouts, collard greens, and Chinese cabbage. Mustards are close relatives. Plant breeders think that all these vegetables originally derived from a few types of wild cabbages found in places with climates similar to ours, such as the coast of England. The brassica family has a wide genetic potential. Any tendency the family has can easily and rapidly be exaggerated by breeding. Thus, a stem can be thickened into a kohlrabi or turnip or rutabaga; a flower can be enlarged into a broccoli or a cauliflower; a terminal bud becomes a cabbage; side buds become Brussels sprouts. To demonstrate that this had been the course of development, plant breeders took some wild cabbages and, within a few generations, developed elementary cabbages, root crops, and flowering crops.

Brassicas are very cold hardy, produce large quantities of food for the space they occupy, and grow fairly well on soils relatively low in available phosphorus.

They do require a nearly neutral pH which can be created by liming. Brassicas are unusual in their high demand for calcium. Even in fairly neutral soils (which are quite rare in our region), additional lime causes marked improvement in their growth. Winter rains wash out an average of 500 pounds of calcium from each acre each year. This amounts to about 12 pounds per thousand square feet. If your soil has not been limed for years, 50 pounds per thousand square feet of garden would not be too much, even if the pH did not need adjusting. Brassicas that are suffering from calcium deficiency are among the most pathetic plants I have seen.

Brassicas host the cabbage fly's larvae. These maggots cripple or destroy brassicas. The fly's preferences and the plant's inherent root vigor seem to be the factors that determine the effect of the maggots. Cauliflowers are very sensitive and are often ruined in early spring. Chinese cabbage is devastated in fall. The old rule still applies, however—vigorously growing plants have healthy root systems and are not severely damaged by nibbling. I have found that high levels of available phosphorus in the soil, sufficient calcium, and general good tilth seem to greatly limit maggot damage. For a complete discussion of maggots see the chapter on "Insects and Other Pests."

Brassicas also are troubled by a disease called clubroot. All of them can get it, but it affects each vegetable differently. Clubroot is a soil-borne fungus that infects the root, causing grotesque swellings that inhibit the root's efficiency. Healthy soil can be infected from purchased bedding plants, from composts made from infected plants, and from the gardener's feet and tools. Once clubroot is in the soil, it can be eliminated only by ceasing to grow all brassicas. Eventually the disease dies out from lack of a host plant to support it, but this takes about seven years. Growing brassicas on a four-year rotation in infected soils is one way of limiting the effects.

I have not heard of much trouble with clubroot in Oregon, but I have heard of many people troubled with it in Washington. Laurence Hill's book (see "Further Reading") deals with this disease in detail. Washington State and Oregon State University Extension Services have fact sheets about clubroot (EM 4205) that are free for the asking. If your plants mysteriously wilt or are dwarfed, and upon inspection you find the roots are swollen and knobby, you should get the extension data and take care not to spread the disease. Do not compost infected plants, but burn them or take them to the dump. Nondisinfected tools, and even your shoes, can spread the organism from infected soil to healthy soil.

Brassicas differ in their response to high nitrogen levels, but in general it is similar to that for any other greens. Spring-planted brassicas require abundant nitrogen. Summer plantings for summer and early fall harvest can benefit greatly from the addition of nitrogen. Varieties that mature in late fall or during the winter or that overwinter are better off without too much stimulation, which can produce soft growth. Overwintered brassicas are greatly benefited by generous side-dressings of nitrogen in early spring (February or March).

Many kinds of brassicas adapt well to transplanting, especially those that are sown in spring. Although all brassicas are frost hardy, the seedlings are not nearly as resilient as more mature plants. Once the period of hard frosts is over—usually around mid-April in Lorane—brassicas can be directly seeded outdoors. They still can be raised as transplants from May to August, if you wish, by starting them in a nursery bed and moving them to the growing bed when they are about four inches tall. The family characteristically has seedlings that vary widely in vigor. To compensate for this, I always sow the seed rather thickly and thin later. There will not be as much thinning as you might think, because an insect called the flea beetle loves above all things the seedlings of the brassica family. If the mature plant will

be a small one, such as kohlrabi, I sow the row thickly and thin after the beetles
have had their chance to eat the less vigorous seedlings. If the mature plant will be
a large one, such as cabbage or broccoli, I plant a clump of ten or so seeds on the
desired final spacing and thin to the best single plant. If the beetles ruin an entire
planting, the soil was too infertile.

Brassicas vary in cold hardiness. Some types are frost hardy, some are freeze
hardy. Brassicas form the heart of the winter garden and should be the central
plants in any coastal garden all summer. Where fruiting plants like tomatoes will
not make it because of lack of warmth, brassicas will thrive.

Hybridization of brassicas generally results in increased uniformity and not
much increase in vigor. Uniformity is not what a gardener wants in the family, and
hybrid seeds should be avoided as a needless expense.

To grow brassica seed, the same basic procedure is used regardless of the type.
Most brassicas are biennials, meaning that they must overwinter and make their
seed in the second year of growth. They are all pollen-exchanging plants, so a large
number of plants are needed, unless you wish to risk the consequences of inbreeding. I would not save seeds unless at least ten plants participated in the pollen
swap. This will result in enough seed to last a gardener nearly ten years, and ten
years is about the maximum storage life under usual home conditions. To prevent
cross-pollination with other types of brassicas, a minimum isolation of 200 feet is
required, with a tall crop like corn in between. Seedsmen, desiring high purity, use
2,000 feet for isolation.

Late in the spring of their second year, the plants put up a seed stalk covered
with small yellow flowers. The bees will work these over very heavily. Little pods
form where each pollinated flower was, and each pod will contain at least six seeds.
As the summer progresses, the plant makes fewer and fewer flowers, and eventually the seed pods start to dry out. When they are fully dry, harvest the plants, stack
them up on a clean white sheet or newspapers, and allow them to dry completely.
Then walk around on the dry stalks, beat them with a stick, or rub them between
your hands. Most of the seed eventually will be lying on the sheet or newspapers.
Lift up the straw and compost it. Allow the seeds to dry fully and store them. If
you want to clean out the chaff it can be winnowed or screened, but I see no reason
for a gardener to try to produce perfectly cleaned seed.

Broccoli

Broccoli is one of the easiest of garden vegetables to grow. It is very hardy and
will provide continuous crops from early March until late fall. It will grow in soils
of only moderate fertility, but to get really big heads like those sold in supermarkets, very high levels of nitrogen are required throughout the entire growth
period. Hybrid varieties also are necessary for growing giant heads, because they
have been bred for making a large central head at the expense of later side shoots.
(In other words, they produce a one-time harvest.) Size is not everything,
however, and smaller plants with smaller flowerettes still will be tasty and will
yield for a long time.

Culture

In spring, start broccoli about the first of February for transplanting out about
mid-March. (See the section on cabbage for instructions on raising seedlings.)
It will not hurt the seedlings to spend at least two weeks hardening off in the cold
frame before transplanting. Set the seedlings out at least eighteen inches

apart in rows at least eighteen inches apart, and place hotcaps over them. The caps do two things: they protect the seedlings from chilly weather, inducing more rapid early growth, and they keep maggots away from the plants for three weeks or so after transplanting. After the caps have been outgrown, the seedlings have such vigorous root systems that maggot infestation rarely ruins them. Side-dress the plants with blood meal or chicken manure at this time. If you missed getting an early start, I suggest you wait until April before starting new seedlings. Broccoli can be directly seeded any time after the first of May and before the end of July. Sow the seed a half inch deep in clumps eighteen inches apart in all directions. After the first of May, it can also be started in a nursery bed and transplanted later. The more nitrogen you give the plants (within limits), the larger the flowerettes will be. Stimulating later plantings too much will result in softer plants that cannot take cold weather very well. Well-hardened broccoli usually is productive until December. A type of broccoli that has been bred for overwintering is planted in mid-July or thereabouts. Overwintered broccoli should not be given any fertilizer because it must be quite hard. As soon as growth resumes in early spring, however, the plants should be side-dressed abundantly.

Garden Planning

Five or six plants keep the two of us well supplied with fresh broccoli. We do not can or freeze any because we can have fresh flowers from early March until December. I start a half dozen plants in spring, another half dozen in midsummer for fall and winter harvest, and another half dozen at the same time for over-wintering. I often start radishes between the clumps of seedlings, because radishes are harvested before the broccoli needs the space.

Insects and Diseases

Maggots rarely damage large plants in spring, or the fall or overwintered crop. You do have to fight for the spring planting. If maggots are a serious pest at any other time of the year, I suggest you investigate your soil improvement practices. Cabbage worms do not seem to like broccoli very much, but if you find them on the plants, spraying with Dipel will be an excellent control. Sprayed plants never seem to have worms in the flowers. Aphids occasionally will roost on the plants, and they prefer the succulent flowers to any other location. They are hard to wash out, and I can offer no consolation. I ignore them if there are only a few. If infestation is severe, I suggest cutting the plant back severely, side-dressing it heavily, and making it produce a whole new batch of flowers. By the time these are developing, the aphid population probably will be much smaller.

Water

Spring-transplanted broccoli will mature a fine crop without irrigation. Mulch in early June will extend the harvest period, as will slightly increased spacing—say twenty-four inches in all directions. Overwintered broccoli can be started later than mid-July in a nursery bed and set out sometime in September. Even a mid-August sowing will produce a large enough plant to overwinter. The fall crop can also be started late but is less likely to make a big yield.

Harvest

Cut the central heads when the individual flowers start to separate. Garden varieties make many delicious side shoots, which come on after the central head is cut. To encourage the production of side shoots, side-dress the plant when the main flower is cut and side-dress it again anytime growth slows down. One planting can be encouraged to produce an abundance of large flowers for five or six months if the ground is kept fertile. If it is not, the plants will produce an abundance of small flowers that will be somewhat woody and unpalatable. To encourage the production of larger side shoots, harvest by picking off the entire stem all the way back to the main stalk. Overwintered broccoli only produces side shoots but does so abundantly for several months. If you do not keep the side shoots cut, the plant will begin to flower and set seed and will become almost inedible.

Saving Seed
To get a mature seed crop, broccoli must be started before June or else overwintered. Since fall types will not reliably overwinter, they probably cannot be grown for seed in the maritime Northwest except in the mildest areas along the coast. Perhaps fall strains could be improved by attempting to overwinter them year after year and selecting those plants that survived. Early and overwintered types are easy to grow for seed. The part we eat actually is an unopened flower. Left on the plant, it will open, form a yellow flower, and make seed. Select only dark-colored, crisp, large-headed plants with tight buds. Also select plants that make the nicest side shoots. The central heads and the first crop of side shoots may be eaten, allowing a very carefully considered selection. When you are tired of cutting the flowers, let the selected plants make seed. Overwintered broccoli can be harvested until you are tired of it and then allowed to make seed. This should begin by May or June.

Varieties
For spring planting, De Cicco (TS, JSS, BUR) is very nice. It also will grow in fall. There are numerous hybrids that make larger, more uniform central flowers. These are good for someone who wants to can or freeze broccoli, since they provide a large, concentrated harvest. For hybrids, Green Duke, Green Comet, Premium Crop, or Gem are all fine. For the fall crop, Waltham 29 (HAR, JSS, TS, BUR, STK) makes larger flowers than De Cicco. For overwintering, grow Purple Sprouting Early (TS), which is imported from England. It makes masses of purple side shoots starting very early in spring.

Brussels Sprouts
If the only ones you have tasted come from the supermarket, you may not like Brussels sprouts. Commercial crops are grown almost exclusively in California. Unfortunately, the climate in the Salinas Valley is very mild in winter. The sprouts never experience a severe frost there, so they remain rather bitter. The same thing happens to Oregon-grown sprouts when they are harvested before the end of October. Once the weather has stiffened up a bit and frozen the sprouts on the stalk a couple of times, they get sweet as sugar. The only way to enjoy this is to grow your own. Fortunately, this is not difficult.

Culture
Brussels sprouts like good rich "cabbage soil." That means that it has been well limed, the pH is above 6.0, and there is a steady supply of nutrients and water. Additionally, sprouts seem to prefer stiff soils—those that are heavy and clayey—but they will do well anywhere. Sprouts do better when not overstimulated by fertilizer. In other words, give them good garden soil but no more.

There are two basic times to plant sprouts. Both early and late varieties can be planted at the same time—in late spring. Early varieties can also be started in summer, resulting in a later harvest from early strains. The later the sprouts mature, the easier they are to grow and the better they taste. Sow early and late varieties directly in the garden between mid-May and mid-June. Plant ten or so seeds in a clump, a half inch deep. Space the clumps about twenty-four inches on all sides. See which seedling is the strongest when they are about three inches tall, and thin out the others. Do not plant any earlier than this because you do not want the sprouts maturing in hot weather. Early types can be started all during June and even until mid-July, giving later and later harvests. Late types should be started before mid-June, because they are very slow growing. As the plants grow tall, it is helpful to pick off the lower leaves. This provokes enlargement of the sprouts and also causes taller growth. Do not trim too many leaves—always permit at least ten or twelve to remain on the top. As the plant grows, remove a few leaves off the bottom from time to time.

Garden Planning

My wife and I are not great lovers of cooked food—even when it is something as tasty as cooked Brussels sprouts. We also do not find them first-rate fare when eaten raw, so what we grow is probably less than the "average" need. Some families might not find that fifty plants were too many. I grow a dozen plants—six earlies and six lates. One helpful technique when growing sprouts is to sow crimson clover in their growing bed after the weather cools down, about late September. The clover will not interfere with the sprouts at all until March—when they are through producing anyway. Then the clover takes over and makes a green manure crop that enriches the bed.

Insects and Diseases

Planting in May avoids the cabbage fly. The plants have vigorous roots, and maggots rarely will do any visible damage. If aphids go after your sprouts, you will have to peel off half the crop before cooking it. The solution to aphids is to grow later varieties so there are no large sprouts during the aphid season for the aphids to ruin. Cabbage worms rarely do major damage. Spray them with Dipel if they are eating too many new leaves.

Water

Sprouts need an abundant water supply all summer. If you are trying to deal with a very limited supply, I suggest you grow early varieties planted as late as possible (even as late as mid-July) in a nursery bed and transplant them out when they demand it. This should give you a November to February harvest.

Harvest

Snap off or cut off individual sprouts as they form; the first ones will be at the base of the stem. The harvest should continue for several months. Do not forget to continue picking off the lower leaves as the plant grows. Commercial growers need hybrid varieties that have a very concentrated maturation. Otherwise, picking costs are so high that they make no profit. To encourage uniformity, growers pinch off the growing tip of the plant three to four weeks before harvest. Doing this prevents further vertical growth and the formation of new sprouts and forces the enlargement of those already formed. Do not do this unless you can or freeze the sprouts and want a highly concentrated picking. After all the sprouts are harvested, the plants make another batch of smaller, more open, flowerlike sprouts. These are delicious and are good for stir-fries.

Saving Seed

Sprouts are among the hardiest of brassicas, and they overwinter most years without protection. In colder areas of Europe the plants are carefully dug up in late fall, overwintered in a cellar (with the sprouts still on the plants), and planted back out in early spring to make seed. Select the seed-making plants for large, clean, firm, compact sprouts with a nice green color. You also might select for sweeter plants with longer harvesting periods, which is just what commercial seedsmen do not want.

Varieties

Jade Cross E is the best early hybrid generally available (JSS, HAR, BUR, STK). It is an early maturer, making sprouts from mid-August to late October. Stokes also has a hybrid called Lunet, which is quite nice. Early Dwarf Danish (JSS, TS) is a very short, open-pollinated type my wife and I like very much. Other seed companies offer Catskill or Long Island Improved, which are early, open-pollinated types of no particular distinction. Commercial production has gone almost entirely to hybrids, so there is no interest in the old open-pollinated types except at Johnny's and Territorial. Late maturing types can only grow in California and the maritime Northwest, so they are unavailable to gardeners at this time except through Territorial. Their Roodnerf Late Supreme harvests from November to late February. I am researching late, midseason, and early types and hope more good open-pollinated varieties will be available to gardeners west of the Cascades. I think the late ones hold great commercial potential for small farmers in the milder areas of the maritime Northwest, such as coastal valleys and banana belts around the Umpqua Valley and near Portland.

Cabbage

Cabbages are one of the best vegetables for the Pacific Northwest. They produce more food per square foot than any other crop except some roots, and they are easy to grow.

Culture

There are four basic types of cabbage. Growing the wrong type at the wrong time is a frequent reason for gardening failures. Early types were bred for starting indoors and transplanting out. This is done because cabbage seedlings are not sufficiently cold hardy to take the heavy frosts of spring. Early types are sown in February for transplanting in early to mid-March. Midseason types also can be started indoors late in March for transplanting out in late April or early May. When starting cabbage family seedlings, sow the seeds in nursery trays about ½ inch deep. Make two furrows in the tray and put in two or three seeds per inch. Grow them indoors—or better, move them out to the cold frame after they have gotten their first true leaves. Many seedlings may die from damping-off diseases. This is all right. After the stand is well established, thin the tray so that each seedling has a space about 1½ inches square.

Transplant early varieties under hotcaps. Using these miniature greenhouses is more important than you might think: if you do not use hotcaps, the transplants will be badly set back by flea beetles, and maggots will carry off the majority of them. After the seedlings have been out for three or four weeks, they should be outgrowing the caps. Remove them and, if you really need every cabbage, mulch each seedling with sawdust to protect against the maggots. Otherwise you are going to lose a percentage of the crop. Transplant midseason cabbages as late in May as possible to avoid the tail end of the maggot infestation. Spacings vary on cabbages, but most early types are small, so they need only about an eighteen-by-eighteen-inch area. Midseason types need about twenty-four by twenty-four inches. Once the weather has warmed up and the cabbages are growing rapidly, side-dressing them with a strong source of nitrogen will cause them to make bigger heads.

Transplanted early and midseason cabbages will mature from June until the end of August. If you want cabbages to mature in September, directly seed midseason types in early May. Sow a clump of seeds about a half inch deep with about a twenty-four-by-twenty-four-inch spacing. Thin each clump to the best single seedling after they are well established. Side-dress this planting also. Fall and overwintering cabbages mature from late September through the next June, depending on what type you grow and when you plant. They are best directly seeded. Plant late varieties in mid-June. Overwintered varieties are best planted around mid-September. Late varieties are large cabbages and should be spaced twenty-four by twenty-four inches or even thirty by thirty. Overwintered types are small like the early varieties and need only an eighteen-by-eighteen-inch spacing. Plant them as you would directly seeded midseason types. If the late crop is intended to be harvested after mid-October, stop side-dressing it by mid-August, or the final heads will be soft and will freeze out easily. Overwintered types should be grown slowly to be very hard by fall and should be fertilized heavily around March, when they begin to grow rapidly.

Other things can be done with cabbage. For example, early varieties, which are rapidly maturing types, can be planted in summer and harvested in fall. Late cabbages probably can be grown as midseason types. Midseason varieties will make late maturations if planted in July. Sticking to the right time slot for the right variety, however, is a way to ensure a more certain harvest. For example, early varieties have a tendency to burst in hot weather. If they mature too late in June, or in July, they are likely to split before you realize they are ready to harvest. Midseason types have been bred to like the heat of midsummer maturation. Lates are very slow growing and seem to increase their growth rapidly once things cool down in late August.

Garden Planning

I like to put in about a dozen early cabbages and a dozen midseason types and then directly seed another half dozen midseason types. I grow several varieties with different maturation dates to get a continuous harvest from June through September. Then in mid-June I directly seed about two dozen late cabbages. This keeps us going from October until January, and if it is an easy winter, into February. Then there is a cabbage famine until the overwintered crop comes in (if it manages to survive—cabbages will not take temperatures below twelve degrees or so, and Lorane sometimes gets colder than that). This starts in late March and lasts about one month. I use several varieties of lates to spread out the harvest, but at this time I use only one overwintered type. I am doing research and hope to find other varieties that mature in April, May, and even early June, all from a September planting.

Insects and Diseases

Flea beetles make hash of cabbage seedlings but always seem to leave enough to establish a good stand. Do not fight them. If you feel that the beetles must be sprayed, also find out why you have such slow-growing seedlings. Root maggots are a plague to early cabbages, but use of hotcaps and mulching with sawdust after the caps are off will ensure a good crop. Cabbage worms bother midseason and late types but are easily controlled with Dipel or can even be handpicked if necessary. Slugs do no harm in my garden, even though I find many resting in the outer leaves of the later cabbages.

Water

Early varieties mature on rainfall, but midseason and late types need abundant irrigation. If you are short of water, you should try for a fall sauerkraut harvest by starting earlies—particularly Golden Acre types—in late July or very early August in a nursery bed. Then transplant them out when the rains start or when their size demands it. Early varieties are not well adapted to field holding in a headed state in fall, however, and would not stand for long without rotting. Overwintered cabbages, started in September, are a natural for the nursery bed and later transplanting. They, too, mature on rainfall.

Harvest

Some people are offended by certain things about organically grown cabbages: slugs, earwigs, and earthworms. All will nestle in the outer leaves of the head. There is no difficulty in removing them. Simply peel off the first few layers of the head, and all the bugs will come off with them. Once you are well into the head, you can be sure there will be no surprise fauna in your flora. The bugs and worms do no harm, incidentally.

Cabbages have to be harvested before they burst. As the inside enlarges, the outer leaves get more and more woody and less able to stretch. Eventually, the expanding inside splits the outer leaves. If the head should burst before you harvest it, it is still quite usable. Midseason types are less prone to bursting than early varieties but still have to be cut when they demand it. When the head is really tight, it is ready. Some varieties can stand without bursting for an entire month after maturation; some will not last two weeks. To prevent mature late cabbages from bursting, twist the entire cabbage in the ground about forty-five degrees. This breaks enough roots that water uptake and growth are slowed. If you do this to early or midseason types, the plant is likely to wilt. Very early types that overwinter have a tendency to bolt, since they are being grown in the same way that seed crops are raised. Overwintered cabbages have been bred not to bolt easily—they are long-standing types—but eventually the seed stalk will emerge. Harvest before that happens. Sometimes early types (particularly Wakefields) will bolt, too, even though they have not overwintered.

Saving Seed

Mount Vernon, Washington, and areas of the Willamette Valley have many acres devoted to cabbage seed production. Inexpensive seed is commercially produced much as overwintered cabbage is grown. All varieties (early, midseason, and late) are directly seeded in late summer and grow to be small plants that have not headed up by the time cold weather stops their growth. These open plants overwinter nicely without rotting because water does not get trapped in the leaves. In spring they start putting up seed stalks without forming heads. A few varieties (especially Wakefields) do head up and must have an X cut in the top about two inches deep so that the seed stalk can emerge. The liability of this easy method of growing seed is that mature heads do not develop, so the variety cannot be selected for desired traits and rogued for unwanted ones. Home gardeners should not use this method except with cabbages intended for overwintered production. I would select overwintered cabbages for variable maturity, tight heads, and slow bolting. All first-class cabbage seed (and the seed used to sow the fields growing inexpensive seed) is grown by a different method. Full-size heads are grown in fall and overwintered, which allows for selection. The mature heads are dug out in fall, roots and all. The large outer leaves are cut off, and a method of overwintering is chosen. One method is to store the plants in a root cellar, much as any nineteenth-century farm family did. In spring, they can be replanted so that the heads rest on the soil. The heads are then cut with an X and allowed to produce seed. Another method is to immediately replant the heads in a trench after cutting off the large leaves and hill up a few inches of soil over the heads. This soil is removed in spring, the heads are cut with an X, and the seed is grown. To produce seed of early and midseason types, grow them so they mature in fall. Select for solid, heavy heads with small midveins and for variable maturity. Sauerkraut cabbages may be better selected for uniform maturity. Overwintering mature cabbage is an involved procedure but one you should attempt at least once to familiarize yourself with the entire life cycle of the cabbage plant.

Varieties

Any seed catalog presents an almost bewildering assortment of cabbages, but it can be easily simplified. The gardener can eliminate all hybrid varieties from consideration. Hybridization of cabbages results in little or no increase in size or vigor; it only gives them uniformity in growth, appearance, and maturity. Almost any type of cabbage will do well in our region if it is grown in its proper maturity period. Cabbages have been developed to be large or small, red or green, and savoyed; to have thick leaves or thin. Most taste excellent when fresh. Stokes specializes in cabbages and has a very large selection. For early planting I recommend Jersey Wakefield types, including Greyhound (TS), and Golden Acre strains. Johnny's has some interesting Golden Acre strains; some of them make good midseason cabbages and resist bursting (the seed catalog will let you know of this because burst-resistant strains are something to be proud of). Copenhagen Market, Early Dutch Flat, Meteor, Red Acre, Baby Early, and Libra are only a few of the fine midseason types. For late cabbages, Danish Ballhead and its variants, such as Penn State Ballhead, are fine sauerkraut cabbages. Mammoth Red Rock and Meteor make large red heads and stand a long time without rotting. Chieftain Savoy is an excellent savoyed cabbage that makes a fine slaw. January King (TS) will not head up until Christmas and sometimes will field-keep until February. I believe that what are sold as "storage" types are for growing in colder regions where the heads freeze solid in the field. They do not necessarily make good fieldkeepers west of the Cascades. If you want overwintered cabbage, only Territorial sells them at this time. Some people have had success overwintering Jersey Wakefield.

Chinese Cabbage

Chinese cabbage is a relative of the mustard family and, like them, bolts on long day length. It has traditionally been a fall crop, but bolt-resistant hybrids allow you to grow it from late spring on. It is not an easy crop, because the cabbage fly seems to prefer Chinese cabbage above all other food. It also requires rich soil to form nice heads.

Culture

Plant early types from 10 May through mid-July and fall types from mid-July to mid-August. Do not transplant, because Chinese cabbage has long taproots that would usually be ruined. A generous application of cottonseed meal or chicken manure to the soil before sowing is very helpful. Sow the seed in furrows a half inch deep, with the rows at least eighteen inches apart. Thin the seedlings gradually so that the mature plants stand about eighteen inches apart. Side-dressing liberally with blood meal or chicken manure when the plants are about four inches in diameter also is very beneficial.

Garden Planning

Early varieties will not field-keep for long. Late varieties will, but the longer they stand, the more likely it becomes that maggots will ruin them. Unless you like kimchi (Korean sauerkraut), do not plant too many at any one time.

Insects and Diseases

Slugs like to roost in the leaves but can be washed out as the head is cleaned. They do not do any damage. Root maggots attack in an unusual way: instead of invading the roots, they prefer the base of the stems and sometimes even farther up. Undermining the stalks, they cause rotting, and the plant collapses, totally worthless. Early plantings that mature in August—before the maggot resurgence in fall—are not bothered much at all. A few late varieties seem to be able to tolerate maggots, producing nice heads despite them. The damage usually is confined to the lower inch of stem and can be trimmed off. Because I am a fanatic kimchi fancier, Chinese cabbage is the only vegetable that tempts me to break my vow of strict organic growing and spray Diazinon (a chemical insecticide that kills maggots and flies). Instead, I make twice-weekly sprayings of rotenone on my fall crop, beginning when the plants first have some size on them and are beginning to head. I think that rotenone kills the flies and prevents egg-laying. Someday I will make a screen house to put over the entire bed.

Water

Chinese cabbage demands a great deal of water. A very early or very late sowing might mature well on field moisture.

Harvest

Cut off the head at the base, strip off the outer leaves and slugs, and make sure there are no slugs in the tight inner leaves. Early types will stand a week or so in a mature state before bolting. Late types will stand for months if the maggots do not find them. They are not nearly as hardy as ball-head cabbages—twenty degrees may be the lower limit for Chinese cabbage. They should all be harvested before they freeze out.

Saving Seed

I have not found any reliable open-pollinated strains, so I do not recommend saving seed.

Varieties

The old open-pollinated Michilli and Wong Bok types do not do very well. Wong Boks are too easily ruined by maggots and bolt quickly if grown in summer. Use Spring A-1 (TS, JSS) or Springtime (STK) for early planting. Stokes sells Summertime, which makes a larger head than A-1 but cannot be planted until late June. For late varieties, grow Wintertime (STK) or China King (TS, JSS). Matsushima (JSS) is an open-pollinated fall type that can tolerate maggots to some extent, but not nearly as well as China King. In our trials, nearly 50 percent of Matsushimas were lost to maggots, while only one in six of Wintertime and China King were lost.

Cauliflower

I am prouder of my cauliflowers than of any other vegetable I grow. They are not easy! Any time a cauliflower has its growth checked, from seedling to maturity, it is very unlikely to make a good head thereafter. Raising your own transplants in spring or directly seeding them in the garden after April is the only way to ensure that they make steady, continuous growth. A long cloudy spell can check greenhouse seedlings, and you will never know it when you purchase them. Transplants that are rootbound have also been checked, so inspect the trays before purchasing.

Culture

Start early cauliflowers indoors from the first of March through April. I would suggest growing them indoors until they have a good set of leaves before moving them to the cold frame. If it is a chilly spring, keep them in the house under artificial light. It is not a bad idea to start a new tray of cauliflower seedlings every two weeks. Then if one planting grows poorly, you can discard it in favor of a later planting. You are better off waiting until late April to plant, because the weather will have settled some, and by the time these seedlings are ready to go outside, the maggots will have declined. Transplant all varieties of cauliflower in spaces twenty-four by twenty-four inches. From the first of May through July, cauliflower is best directly seeded by dropping a clump of seed in each spot and covering them a half inch deep. After the insects have finished working over the seedlings, thin to the best single plant. If you have a small garden, you may want to start cauliflowers in a nursery bed. This can be done without much liability, but do be very careful about transplanting shock, because overly shocked transplants may not make good curds. All cauliflowers that are going to mature before really chilly weather sets in should be planted in rich soil that has been well fertilized with chicken manure, cottonseed meal, or fish meal. When the plants are about eight inches tall, side-dress them well with a generous dose of blood meal or chicken manure. What you are trying to accomplish is the creation of a very large plant before it decides to make a curd. When curd formation begins, the plant takes all its surplus energy and puts it into swelling up the flower. The bigger the leaves, the more sunlight and energy the plant can trap, so the more food it can make and the larger the flower gets. Cauliflowers intended to overwinter should not have any fertilizer added to their soil. These varieties have much more time to grow and get large on poorer soil. Overwintered types should be heavily side-dressed very early in spring.

Garden Planning

Cauliflower tends to be quite uniform in maturity date and does not keep well in the field after the curds are ready to be cut. In fact, curds usually go from nothing to fully formed in about one week. Planting a few plants every few weeks is a better idea than a large bed that overwhelms you.

Insects and Diseases

Cauliflowers tend to have delicate roots, and maggots make a mess of early transplants. If you are setting them out in April or early May, put sawdust around the stems to keep the flies off the soil. Individual hotcaps made of window screen are used by some gardeners who are really serious about having cauliflowers to pick in June or early July and who sincerely believe in organic practices. During the balance of the season maggots should not do noticeable damage. If they do, something is wrong with the vigor of those seedlings. Check your soil improvement to see where you have been getting lazy if this happens.

Cabbage worms can make a nasty-looking trail across the curd that can be trimmed off easily. If the air is thick with their little white butterfly parents, spraying Dipel might not be a bad preventative measure. Sometimes earwigs like to roost in the curds. They actually are looking for aphids to eat and should be commended for their concern as you carefully pick them out and release them back into the garden. Do not be frightened of earwigs, no matter how dangerous they may look. I have heard that they can bite, but I have never done anything but admire them, and none has ever done anything but try to get away from me.

Water

Spring transplants mature on rainfall. Cauliflower is a very demanding crop, however, and I would not even consider growing them during summer if I had to be miserly with my water. A large nursery bed could be planted in early August and held until mid-September before transplanting for overwintering.

Harvest

The curds swell up quickly once formation starts. As soon as you see this happening, tie up the inner leaves with thick string. Sometimes, being lazy, I break over an inner leaf or two to shade the curd. This blanching keeps the curd white instead of yellowish green. Even when you do not blanch it, the curd still tastes fine. When the curd has reached its maximum size, it immediately begins to separate out. This is called "getting ricey." You should cut the curd just before this happens. Very late plantings may head out in midwinter. If the weather is mild (not hard frost) at this time, the curds will be excellent. If the temperatures stay continuously below thirty-two degrees during the time curds are forming, the quality will be very low. Growing for midwinter harvest is very chancy, unless you are in a mild-winter area such as a coastal valley. I always take the chance, because usually some of the flowers will be excellent. (To get very late cauliflowers, attempt planting late types in August or grow special strains bred for this purpose and used in Europe, where they do not have a southern California to supply them.)

Saving Seed

After the curd separates and gets ricey, the seed stalks begin to emerge, and the plant behaves like any other brassica. Because our climate is too severe to successfully overwinter most strains of cauliflower, I suggest you save seed only from overwintering strains or from very early strains that behave like annuals.

Varieties

For planting in early spring, use Early Snowball (STK), Snow Crown (JSS, HAR, BUR, STK), or Alpha (TS). All will do well. For May and June sowing, it is better to switch to Dominant (JSS), Raket (TS), or Snow King (BUR). For planting from July through mid-August, grow Snowball Y (STK), Burpeeana (BUR), or White Top (TS, STK). These will mature from September through November, depending on their date of sowing. For overwintered harvest in spring, grow

Armado April (TS). Other fall and overwintered varieties mature from November to February. I have been testing them, and they soon may be available to gardeners in the maritime Northwest.

Collards

Some gardeners do not grow collards because they misunderstand what part of the plant they are supposed to eat. Collards are usually grown to produce winter greens. These are tough, mustardy, and have to be cooked a long time, usually with some meat stock for flavor. There are better things to come from this plant, however, if you only wait until early spring to start harvesting.

Culture

Collards need the same rich soil as any brassica. Plant thinly in mid-July about a half inch deep in rows about twenty-four inches apart. Thin to at least twelve inches apart in the row.

Garden Planning

A dozen plants will produce all the spring "broccoli" you will want.

Insects and Diseases

Insects and diseases are not a problem.

Water

Start collards late if you are short of water. This will reduce the winter greens crop, but will not particularly affect the spring flower crop.

Harvest

Eat the leaves all winter if you are desperate for greens. Let the plants overwinter and begin to flower in very early spring. Pick the flowers as if they were small broccoli. A good side-dressing at this time will increase the number of flowers and their size. You should be able to pick them well into June. Collards make the garden in a very cold year, because they will overwinter when everything else dies.

Saving Seed

Seed-saving procedures generally are the same as those for any other cabbage family member. When you are tired of eating the flowers, let them open up and set seed. I would select my plants for the size of their flowers and gradually change the plant into a green-sprouting broccoli, similar to the Purple Sprouting broccoli from England.

Varieties

Use Vates. Everyone has it. Do not use Georgia, which is less cold hardy than Vates is.

Kale

If more people had tasted good home-grown kale after cold weather had frozen it a couple of times, more people would be eating it. The supermarket product comes from California and generally is very inferior.

Culture

Do not make the soil too rich, as the fast growth is too soft to handle winter. Sow seeds about the first of August. Two weeks on either side of this date still will produce a nice crop of kale, but I think earlier sowing would be better than later, giving a larger fall harvest. Plant thinly a half inch deep, in rows at least twenty-four inches apart. After the seedlings are well established, thin them to about eighteen inches apart. You could eat the thinnings, but kale tastes better after really cold weather has set in.

Garden Planning

Ten to fifteen feet of row generally will be enough unless you like to eat large amounts of cooked kale during the winter. Certainly it is enough to find out what you think of this vegetable.

Insects and Diseases

Kale normally does not suffer from insect or disease problems.

Water

Plant kale late if you are short of water, or use a nursery bed and transplant.

Harvest

One of the hardiest of brassicas, kale will stand through most winters. Picking it fairly heavily in October (even if you do not need the leaves to eat) stimulates new growth that can then be picked through the winter. This new growth will be milder in flavor and less coarse. Snip fresh leaves as needed from the outside lower leaves.

Saving Seed

When spring comes, kale goes to seed just as any other brassica does. I would select for sweet flavor and for winter regrowth.

Varieties

All types of kale are quite cold hardy. I think the main differences are in the plant's growth habits. One group of kale has large leaves that grow from a central point near the ground, like Swiss chard. These are usually called Siberian kales. The other type grows from a central stalk and is usually called Scotch. A very large type of coarse kale is called Thousand Headed. Although it is used commercially for animal feed, some gardeners really like it for food. Both Siberians and Scotches vary in height, size, and flavor. As a general rule, Siberians are milder and make better salad greens, but there is no guarantee, because every seed company in this country has a different strain of kale, even if they call it by the same name as that of another company. Only Johnny's and Territorial seem to have any real interest in kale. Johnny's has a couple of varieties from Denmark.

Kohlrabi

Kohlrabi is a member of the cabbage family that produces an edible "bulb" above the ground. It is mild and sweet eaten raw, and it can be cooked. Kohlrabi is hardy and is seldom troubled by anything except hot weather, which makes it get woody and mustardy.

Culture

Sow the seeds thinly about a half inch deep in rows at least twelve inches apart. Spread out the spring planting during the entire month of April. May plantings will mature in hot weather south of Portland but will probably do well farther north. When they are well established, thin to about three inches apart in the row. At this time a side-dressing of chicken manure or blood meal will make them grow rapidly and produce sweeter and juicier bulbs. For a fall crop, sow kohlrabi in late July or early August. Do not side-dress the crop, as you want this one to be slow growing. Fall-sown kohlrabi has less tendency to become woody and may stand far into December, especially if planted late.

Garden Planning

Because a sowing matures quite rapidly and fairly uniformly in spring, only a few feet of row should be planted at any one time. Staggered plantings about ten days apart are the best way. The fall crop should be larger, as one sowing, or possibly two, will probably last until the crop freezes out. Kohlrabi is hardy to about fifteen degrees.

Insects and Diseases

I have seen maggots in kohlrabi roots during spring, but they never seem to limit the crop very much.

Water

Spring-sown kohlrabi matures without irrigation. If you are short of water, sow when the late summer's rains have increased the moisture sufficiently. If this is not too late in summer, you will still have a crop.

Harvest

It is very important to harvest spring kohlrabi when the bulbs are small. They will get larger than tennis balls, but by that time they are very poor eating. To eat tender, sweet bulbs, harvest when they are less than two inches in diameter (radish-size bulbs can be stir-fried with the leaves left on). Fall kohlrabi is not as touchy about size.

Saving Seed

Kohlrabi behaves like any other cabbage family member. If overwintered, it makes seed the following year. For seed, grow as a fall crop and hope it makes it over the winter. (Hilling up soil over the bulbs increases their chances of survival.) It will bolt the following spring. I would select for the location of the leaves, which should be attached to the top of the bulb and make as small a crown as possible, round shape, and variable maturity. I would like also to select for flavor, but I cannot figure out a way to do this without destroying the plant.

Varieties

The green types generally are more delicate and better textured than the purples. Johnny's has some superior Danish varieties. In this country, the vegetable is strictly a home garden item, so it receives little attention. The Japanese recently began to hybridize kohlrabi, and they are producing hybrid seed that is offered by several seed companies in the United States. The seed is quite expensive. Hybrid seed features the dubious advantage of more uniform maturity. It also shows a reduced tendency toward woodiness, which truly is an advantage.

Rutabagas

I plant a large bed of rutabagas for in-the-ground storage through much of the winter. If the ground does not freeze, they will keep through the winter until early spring. These plants are a result of an accidental cross between a cabbage and a turnip. Because they originated in Sweden, they are often called Swedes or Swedish turnips. Supermarket rutabagas are not particularly tasty, so it is not surprising that many people do not like them. There are, however, good varieties that are sweet and tender enough to be eaten like potatoes or radishes.

Culture

Rutabagas need fairly rich soil, but they should not be overly stimulated. Plant the seeds about mid-July; if you sow later, they will be smaller but equally good. Sow thinly about a half inch deep in rows at least twenty-four inches apart. When the row is well established, thin them to about eight inches apart in the row.

Garden Planning

Try five to ten feet of row if you have never liked rutabagas before.

Insects and Diseases

Some people's rutabaga crops are bothered by cabbage maggots. Mine never has been, and if it were, I could think of no organic solution to the problem. I have had slugs chew up the outer skin of the root, but they rarely get in deep enough to do any serious damage. We just trim off those parts they have gotten into.

Water

I would not ever try to transplant a rutabaga. If you have to, start them later. If sown in July, they generally get to about eight inches in diameter by the time chill stops their growth in late October or early November. If sown the first of September, they might get to be only four inches across. Thin them accordingly.

Harvest

Harvest as needed. If the ground freezes regularly at your location, mulch well with straw in December and cover the straw with a plastic sheet to prevent it from becoming compacted and losing its insulating ability.

Saving Seed

After overwintering, rutabagas go to seed. For the finest production, it is best to carefully dig the mature roots in autumn, select the finest ones for seed production, and either store them in a cellar or plant them back out and cover them with straw and plastic. In either case, trim the tops back to about two inches above the crowns. If you do dig them and replant either immediately or next spring, set them into the earth as deep as the crown, about one foot apart in rows about twenty-four inches apart.

Varieties

American Purple Top is the usual one found in supermarkets. If you like those, grow it. Laurentians are better-selected strains. The one we like and I have grown for many years is Altasweet (TS, STK). This one is the gardener's variety. It does not have the toughness to stand bouncing around in trucks and will not keep until next July in a cellar, but it certainly tastes good!

Roots

Numerous vegetables produce edible roots. These plants have no close botanical relationship to each other. I put them into one "cultural group" because there are many similarities in cultural practice when growing them.

First of all, roots are very sensitive to soil tilth. The basic growth pattern is to put out a taproot (or, in the case of potatoes, a feeder root) and then fill it up with stored food. If the soil is soft, the taproot grows straight. If the soil remains soft, the root will swell up evenly, producing a shapely and tasty carrot or parsnip or beet. Some roots will not develop at all if the ground is too hard. Such sensitivity to soil compaction makes root crops a natural for raised-bed growing. Even in those years when I was experimenting with mulch gardening or with row crop methods, I still made raised beds for my root crops.

Roots are plants that are adapted to making vegetative growth in relatively poor soils. If you see a lot of wild carrot (Queen Anne's lace) in a field, you can be certain it is a poor piece of land. Roots use a different strategy than greens or fruiting plants. Instead of making a large array of leaves capable of seed production from the *current* light, water, and nutrients, root crops slowly store up food during an entire year or season, and then overwinter. The next season the plant draws on this supply of underground food to make flowers and seeds. Most root crops are biennials. Roots should not be encouraged to make too much vegetative growth. In other words, limit the nitrogen in their beds. But all roots will be bigger and sweeter in soils with abundant phosphorus and potassium.

Creating the soil they prefer is not always simple. It must be soft, and the only way to really soften up soil is by incorporating manures or composts. These contain considerable amounts of nitrogen, and if too much nitrogen is present in the soil, the roots become hairy, or fork, or are tough, or simply do not develop well at all. The solution is to prepare the root bed a year in advance and grow something there that uses the nitrogen. The following year the soil will still work up to a very light consistency without further manuring.

Another touchy thing about roots is thinning. If you want beautiful roots, the seedlings must be carefully thinned. First of all, the roots must not be bumping into each other, which will deform them. Second, the tops have to gather light, and if there is overcompetition, root size suffers. Some varieties of carrots have such variability in seedling vigor that thinning is not necessary—the more vigorous ones crowd out the weaker ones.

Roots require large quantities of water to be succulent, sweet, and large. Careful attention to irrigation is necesary, unless they are growing at a time of year when rainfall is abundant. I generally locate my roots in parts of the garden where the irrigation pattern puts the most water.

Hybridization of roots seems to increase uniformity but not particularly to affect vigor. Open-pollinated strains do quite nicely in the garden.

Beets

Beets will grow fairly well in almost any soil but prefer rich gardens. Taking time to improve their bed will often triple the yield, but you could till up almost any old pasture, plant it to beets, and get something back. Beets do best when the air temperatures are moderate, since they dislike both very chilly and very hot weather. Cold spells or temporarily dry soil results in zoning (white rings) but these do not affect the flavor or texture.

Culture

Extremely soft soil is less crucial for beets than for other root vegetables, because the roots develop on the soil's surface. If only the top few inches of soil has good tilth, the seeds germinate and grow well. Beet seeds germinate in soils warmer than forty-five degrees, and the seedlings are frost hardy, but I find that it is better to wait until the weather has settled a bit before planting. Patience is rewarded by more vigorous seedlings that do not succumb to insect attack, and those very early plantings do not mature much sooner than those made a month later anyway. Sow spring beets from April to the end of May. Plant one seed per inch, ½ inch deep in rows at least 10 inches apart. Each seed is actually a fruit containing several embryos, most of which will sprout. When the plants are 3 or 4 inches tall, thin carefully to about 3 inches apart. Unless they are carefully thinned, you will get many small, misshapen roots. The thinnings can be eaten as pot greens or used in salads. If you wish, two thinnings can be made—the first only to 1 inch apart in the row, and the second made when these small plants have roots about the size of radishes. Tiny beets are a delicacy when steamed with the tops attached. When planting a fall crop, sow the seeds from mid-July until mid-August. Later sowings than this will result in small beets. Sow about eight seeds per foot, ¾ inch deep in rows at least 16 inches apart. Grow winter varieties, which make larger plants. Thin when the seedlings are well established to about 6 inches apart in the row.

Garden Planning

Ten feet of row provides the two of us with all the beets we need from mid-May until the end of summer. For fall, I plant twenty or thirty feet of winter beets, which are mature enough to eat by the end of September and will stand through the entire winter until spring.

Insects and Diseases

Cucumber beetles will chew on spring seedlings. If the seedlings also are in shock from too many frosts and chilly days, the beetles eat them down faster than they are growing. Planting a little later than the earliest possible date avoids this situation and does not delay the first harvest by more than a few days.

Water

Spring-planted beets will mature on rainfall. If water is short, sow the fall crop late. Instead of getting to be eight inches in diameter, the roots will only get to the size of ordinary supermarket beets, so thin accordingly.

Harvest

Mature beets will stand a long time in the ground if it is kept watered. Once the really hot weather comes, however, some varieties tend to become woody. Detroits are the best adapted to hot temperatures. Winter beets will stand in the field unmolested, unless the ground freezes. If this happens, they rot after the thaw. Covering the roots with a few inches of straw and then a sheet of plastic sometime in late November is a cheap insurance policy, guaranteeing that the crop will be harvestable until the beets resume spring growth. Beet greens are very edible and can be used raw in salads or steamed.

Saving Seed

Beets are biennials, making seed stalks the year after they form a root. The pollen is very light and readily wind-carries. Isolations of at least a mile are used when commercial crops are grown. Beets also cross-pollinate with chard. Since the seed lasts many years, a different variety could be allowed to produce seed each year, solving the isolation problem. For seed, all beets are planted as a fall crop. Overwinter the beets under mulch and plastic after selecting for smooth, round roots with good greens and a small crown area. If you wish, the beets could be carefully dug and the taproot inspected, selecting for a fine root that does not result in much loss when it is trimmed off. If you dig the crop before selection, trim the leaves before replanting. Another desirable trait would be continued root formation in fall, allowing later plantings. It might also be possible to make some correlation between the taste of the greens and the sweetness of the root. In spring, the beets resume growth and put up a seed stalk that flowers, forms seed, and dries during the summer. Harvest the stalks when most of the seed is dry and brown. Strip off the seed by hand and store it.

Varieties

Early Wonder types (sometimes called Crosby's Egyptian) are the quickest maturing beets for early spring planting. Ruby Queen is a fine canner's beet—it is big, smooth, round, and red, with little or no zoning and a fine taproot. Plant Ruby Queens after the first of April. Detroits tolerate heat without becoming woody or zoning as badly as other strains do, so they are the ones I leave standing during July and August to be harvested as needed. All the seed companies carry these standard varieties. Stokes offers many of the other types available. Their catalog can positively baffle you with possibilities. But I do not think anything will do any better than the old standards. There also are some fine novelty beets that you should feel free to experiment with—almost any variety will be successful in fairly good soil. For winter beets, the best bet is Winterkeepers or Lutz. There is not much difference between them, and most companies have one or the other.

Carrots

If moles have not yet learned to eat them, carrots are an easy crop to grow. Even fairly poor soil will grow fine crops *if* you take the trouble to make a deep, fine bed. A soil rich in phosphorus and potassium will grow a more abundant crop. A well-manured bed from the previous year is the best spot. Fresh manure or the use of too much fertilizer makes the roots split, get hairy, and fork.

Culture

The whole key to good production is soil preparation. For many varieties, it is very helpful to reduce eight inches of top soil to powder, although short types will do fairly well in heavier soils that are not as well worked. The soil should contain enough humus to remain in a very loose condition for about eight weeks after tilling—sufficient time for the bulk of root development. Then as long as the taproot does not encounter high concentrations of nitrogen, it will not fork. Soil to be worked up into a good carrot bed must be damp but not too wet. The rule about testing soil for moisture before tilling applies doubly for the carrot bed. You could get away with tilling when the soil is a bit on the wet side for any other crop. Most people are too eager to plant carrots and are then disappointed when their cloddy ground will not make smooth, straight roots. You must wait. In my clay-loam garden, I need at least ten days that are dry and somewhat sunny before the soil is ready. Often I have to wait until middle or late May. In a wet spring, I will plant a small, early carrot bed but withhold starting the main summer patch until conditions are right. Preparing the carrot bed is the last use I still have for my roto-tiller—though I could do it by hand. Hand preparation is labor, except in sandy soil, because the soil must be chopped up deeply and finely.

Carrots can be planted from April until August. Make the last planting a good winter variety and they will last until spring. Sow the seed thinly a half inch deep in rows at least six inches apart. Carrot sprouts are puny and will not push through a hard crust on the soil's surface. Working some fine manure or compost into the surface inch of the bed will greatly enhance germination without making splits or forks. This small amount of manure will not cause them to get hairy either. Once the seedlings are well established, careful thinning gives much more uniformly large roots.

Garden Planning

It takes about fifty feet of row to keep up with our appetites from June through September. I plant another seventy-five to one hundred row-feet in mid-summer for fall and winter use. Carrots are about the most prolific food producer I know of. A hundred-square-foot bed (five feet by twenty feet) can support forty five-foot rows, or two hundred row-feet. This will produce bushels. Carrots do well following a crop of greens or brassicas that have taken much of the nitrogen from the soil.

Insects and Diseases

Carrot maggots and wireworms burrow into carrots, causing rotting and leaving the carrots with a bad flavor. Handling maggots is fully discussed in the "Insects and Other Pests" chapter. I have no consolation to offer for wireworms. It is generally thought that as humus percentage goes up, wireworms go down. If damage to carrots is severe, in-the-ground storage might not be possible, and some kind of root cellar storage will have to be resorted to for the fall crop.

Water

Spring-planted carrots will mature on rainfall but will not last long in dessicated soils. The fall crop can be planted late if you are short of water, but the result is smaller carrots. I am experimenting with some varieties of winter carrots from Europe that are reported to have more frost-hardy tops. These might continue enlarging their roots longer into the fall than the usual varieties.

Harvest

Winter carrots store in the soil if it is well drained and protected from freezing. Planting them in raised beds will solve minor drainage problems. A straw mulch about two inches thick prevents freezing in a cold snap and, in addition, makes the carrots cleaner at harvest. Covering the mulch with a sheet of plastic increases the protection. The carrots eventually will begin to go to seed in the spring, ending the harvest.

Saving Seed

Carrots are biennials. Their flowers are cross-pollinated by many kinds of insects. The main umbrella-shaped flower is followed by numerous secondary flowers. Varieties must be isolated from other types and from wild carrots (Queen Anne's lace) by at least a thousand feet. Wild-carrot intercrossing will give a small, whitish root that lacks sweetness. Plant the seed crop in midsummer so they mature in late September. Carefully dig the crop up and examine the roots. Select the ones with strongly anchored tops, good color, shape, and smell (sweetness can be gauged by the odor). Immediately replant these about twelve inches apart in rows at least thirty inches apart or, in a raised bed, about eighteen inches apart in both directions. Plant at least twenty roots. Mulch them well after the tops die back and cover them with clear plastic. In early spring, remove the mulch and let them go to seed. The selected roots could also be overwintered in a cellar and planted out in early March. The seed matures unevenly, so harvest the flowers when the main head is fully ripe, or cut off individual heads as they mature. It is best to allow the flowers to dry fully under cover. Thresh out the seed by hand.

Varieties

Almost any kind of carrot will do all right. Chantenays are good for clayey soil and overwinter pretty well. Danvers are longer than Chantenay types and are not as fat, but they are fairly fibrous. Nantes types have the best flavor (if it is a good strain). For the best winter carrots you need a high fiber content to avoid splitting in the ground. Scarlet Keeper (JSS) and Caramba (TS) are both European varieties developed for wintering over. Imperator types are foul beasties sold in supermarkets and are long, thin, and pretty—and taste like cardboard. Hybrid carrots tend to be more uniform, but this is more important to a farmer than to a gardener. Different strains of the same kind of carrot are highly variable, so test them until you find one that you really like the taste of. Good carrots are sweet.

Parsnips

The parsnip is a hardy member of the carrot family. It is seldom bothered by anything except moles during the winter, and it produces reliably.

Culture

Growing parsnips is very similar to growing carrots. Parsnips are even more sensitive to manures and strong soils in contact with their taproots, and their bed needs to be worked even deeper than the carrot patch. Parsnips usually are over twelve inches long, so the bed must be worked at least that deep. Till up or spade the bed twelve to sixteen inches deep. Sow the seed from the end of May until late July—the timing is not critical. The later you plant, the smaller the roots will be at harvest time. Parsnips could be sown as late as mid-August and still make carrot-sized roots. Parsnip seed germinates poorly, so make the surface inch of soil at least 50 percent compost or manure. Plant about a half inch deep with the seeds about a half inch apart in rows at least twelve inches apart. Thin carefully when well established to about three inches apart in the row if you sowed early. Later sowings may be grown closer together.

Garden Planning

Unless you like parsnips better than potatoes, ten row-feet will be more than enough. Parsnips are a good crop to follow spring greens or early cabbage.

Insects and Diseases

Insects and diseases are not a problem.

Water

If you are short on water, start them late.

Harvest

The flavor of the roots is sweeter after the tops have been touched by hard frosts. Dig parsnips anytime from October to spring. The roots naturally bury themselves under an inch or so of soil, which is usually sufficient protection against slight ground freezing. If you find that parsnips rot in your area after a severe cold snap, mulch them a bit next year, or hill up some soil over the rows in November.

Saving Seed

Harvest the remaining parsnips in early spring while they are still dormant, and select for shape, quality, and overwintering ability. Replant the selected roots about two feet apart each way and allow them to resume spring regrowth. Cross-pollination is done by insects, so if you are growing more than one variety, separate them by at least a thousand feet. The seed tends to fall from the flowers very easily, so harvest promptly and finish the drying indoors before threshing.

Varieties

All seed companies sell parsnips, and any of the varieties should do well.

Radishes

Although radishes technically are a brassica, I class them with root crops because they have no use for the rich soils that brassicas prefer. Radishes can be grown almost anytime. With some knowledge and a little luck, you will have a considerable portion of them when the maggots are finished. Radishes are particularly valuable in early spring, when very little else will grow. Large crops can be matured in less than six weeks before mid-April and in about three weeks in summer.

Culture

Although they do better in moderately fertile garden soil, radishes will successfully mature almost anywhere. Sow the seeds about a half inch deep and about a half inch apart in rows about eight inches apart. Thin them to over one inch apart after the flea beetles have stopped chewing them back faster than they seem to be growing.

Garden Planning

Radishes make a good temporary crop. Put some in wherever a widely spaced vegetable is being sown or transplanted. Because they mature fairly uniformly, sowing a few feet of row every week or so is a good practice.

Insects and Diseases

Root maggots really like radishes. "Insects and Other Pests" chapter details how to handle this pest.

Water

Radishes need abundant water. If you are short, do not plant them after early June. Resume planting after the rains come for a fall crop. I find, however, that it is very difficult to grow them maggot-free in the fall.

Harvest

Pick radishes promptly, before they become pithy, split, or get hot. Maggots tend to find them, too. There are two parts of the plant most people do not realize can be eaten. One is the tops, which make nice greens in early spring stir-fries. The other is the immature seed pods. If allowed to produce seed, a few radishes can keep your salads spiced up with juicy pods all summer.

Saving Seed

Radishes are annuals and make seed the year you sow them, except for the Chinese and Japanese varieties. Separate varieties by at least a thousand feet to prevent cross-pollination. For European types, carefully dig the roots, select those with the nicest, reddest roots and smallish crowns, and carefully replant those selected radishes about twelve inches apart. Prune off the largest leaves to lessen the transplanting shock, and allow them to continue growing. Seed stalks are produced, and the pods that emerge from yellowish or whitish flowers look and act like cabbage seed pods. If the maggots will let you grow Asian radishes, dig them in the fall and store in a root cellar. Replant them out in spring after selection.

Varieties

I can remember how bewildered I was at the large number of varieties in the Stokes catalog. I still am not familiar with all of them. Champions are the most valuable radish to maritime Northwest gardeners since they are the best adapted to very cool spring weather. I plant them around the first of March, and they mature in about forty days. Since the maggots are not in force until late April, I get a large and much needed crop before the fly shows up. The last few to be harvested generally get a little maggoty. When this happens, the greens still are usable. No other radish I have tested does so well in spring. I do not like fighting, so I do not plant another crop until mid-May. Then for my summer crop I grow Cherry Belle, Scarlet Globe, or Red Prince. Chinese and Japanese radishes and other winter-storage types such as Black Spanish should be sown to mature before mid-September if possible, because that is when the maggots become really thick again. Some gardeners, however, maintain that fall crops can be grown without difficulty.

Turnips

Turnips grow like large radishes, and sometimes the maggots will leave you most of them.

Culture

Sow from April until August. Turnip culture is similar to that for radishes or rutabagas. Sow the seed a half inch deep and a half inch apart in rows at least twelve inches apart. Thin to about two inches apart when the seedlings are well established. If you like turnip greens, do not thin; pick the greens when they are small and tender.

Garden Planning

Five to ten feet of row should be sufficient.

Insects and Diseases

The cabbage fly likes turnips as much as or more than radishes. See the

"Insects and Other Pests" chapter for complete pest-handling details.

Water

Turnips demand a lot of water, but a spring crop can be grown on field moisture. Do not grow them in dry soils in summer. You might try an early fall sowing.

Harvest

Pick them small. They are sweeter then than when they get larger, and they also are less likely to have maggots.

Saving Seed

Seed production is the same as that for rutabagas. Turnips are less cold hardy, however, and require mulching and plastic to overwinter successfully. Plant the seed crop for a fall maturity, and select for a small crown and fine taproot.

Varieties

Purple Top (Milan) is the standard American variety, and it is fine. Shogoin is primarily for greens. Hybrid Asian turnips are larger, better tasting, and more vigorous than the old open-pollinated types.

Curcubits

Curcubits are annual vining plants that make fruits. The family includes cucumbers, melons, and squashes. All curcubits are frost sensitive and are poorly adapted to our cool soils and damp, chilly days. The most vigorous group, squashes, do fairly well here. Cucumbers manage, but melons have a very hard time and should be reserved for the warmer areas of the maritime Northwest. Hybridization of curcubits results in greater vigor. Hybrids are probably the best choice in many instances, particularly for melons.

The whole family is especially sensitive to cool, damp conditions in the seedling stage. Being slow to plant or transplant them does more to produce a timely harvest than rushing does. The more stabilized the weather has become and the warmer the soil is, the fewer seedlings will be lost to diseases and the more vigorous the resultant plants will be.

All curcubits have similar fertilization needs. The family has a peculiar maturation pattern—it never ceases making vegetative growth. During its continual expansion, fruit is set and ripened, and seeds are matured. Curcubits need an abundance of plant nutrients through their entire life cycle. The vines are hard to side-dress because the root system does not extend out nearly as far as the vines do. The only way to produce sustained growth is to fertilize their bed with a large quantity of slow-releasing fertilizer like cottonseed meal or chicken manure. This eliminates all need to side-dress. Ten pounds of cottonseed meal per hundred square feet of growing bed is about right. Fifty to sixty pounds of chicken manure would do the job as well. This is double the usual recommended amount, but the family members are very heavy feeders. It is best to locate most of this fertilizer directly under the transplant.

All curcubits make separate male and female flowers. The difference is very easy to recognize: female flowers are attached to an ovary that looks like an immature fruit. Cross-pollination is required for the ovary to be fertilized and to expand into a mature fruit. Unpollinated ovaries wither and fall off. If there are no bees visiting your plants (they usually do so in the morning), you will have to pollinate by hand, or they will not set fruit. This is done by collecting pollen from male flowers on a small artist's brush and applying it to the inner parts of the female flower.

If you are trying to grow prize-winning watermelons or Hubbard squashes, simply removing all female flowers except the first one or two to be pollinated will force the plant to put everything it has into that single fruit. It becomes very large and much more flavorful.

Cucumbers

Cucumbers are a tropical or semitropical desert plant. Like melons to some degree, they become susceptible to all sorts of fungus diseases when experiencing cool, damp conditions. The ideal habitat for them would be dry, hot air and continuously damp soil such as might be found at the edge of a desert stream.

Culture

The most vital time for cucumbers to have ideal growing conditions is when they are seedlings. This does not mesh well with our climate. The month of June, when they are planted, often has overcast, dewy, chilly mornings that warm up slowly, if at all. If you are starting the vines directly from seed, the longer you can keep yourself from planting, the more likely the seedlings will survive the sowing. Should your first planting not germinate, do not get angry with the seedsman. It will probably mean that your soil was too cold and the seedlings died from disease before they even emerged into the light. Keep planting seeds until a planting takes. I wait until 10 June, and some years plantings have not taken until 1 July. This still gives sufficient season to mature more cucumbers than you will ever care to eat, pickle, and try to give away. If you want earlier production, start the plants indoors in individual peat pots. Cucumbers do not transplant easily, so do not use a container they have to be cut out of. Start them a couple of weeks before the usual last frost in your area. Grow the plants indoors in a warm part of the house under Gro-Lux lamps. After they are up and growing well, move the seedlings out to the cold frame if you have one. This early hardening off makes a difference in their vigor at transplanting. Keep them in the frame until they are outgrowing the pots before transplanting out. If directly sown, plant the seeds in clumps of four to six, three feet apart, in rows at least four feet apart. After the clump is up and growing well, thin to the best one or two plants per clump. If transplanting, set out individual plants two feet apart in rows at least four feet apart. Many kinds of cucumbers still will climb a trellis or fence as their wild relatives can. Burpless cukes (Japanese types) are better grown so they can climb. The fruits hang out straighter this way. Cucumbers also like growing into partial shade, such as that found at the south end of the corn patch.

Garden Planning

One or two plants will keep you in fresh cucumbers. A few more will make buckets of pickles.

Insects and Diseases

Assorted mildews nestle on the leaves toward the end of the year and in a wet summer may do so all summer. The mildews can kill the plant or cripple it enough to limit fruit production. Nothing can be done about this except to grow resistant varieties and to avoid overhead watering in a wet year.

Water

Cucumbers are heavy users of water and should not even be attempted unless you can keep them well supplied. A mulch put down after the soil has warmed up enough to provoke rapid growth can help. Do not mulch too early, or the chilly soil will not warm up enough to suit them. Using a black plastic mulch over their bed helps greatly, and it can be put on before the plants are set out. In a water-short situation, starting them as transplants gets the crop in early, when there is likely to be moisture in the soil.

Harvest

Keeping the vines picked continues the production of new cucumbers. Allowing them to yellow and ripen fully on the vines tends to limit future fruit set. Even if you have no use for them at present, harvest large cukes whenever you see them. They make fine compost or chicken feed.

Saving Seed

Cucumbers do not cross with other members of the curcubit family. Honey bees must pollinate the flower for a cucumber to be produced. Isolate your seed patch at least a quarter mile from other varieties if you want purity. For fair quality seed, a 200-foot isolation with a tall crop in between is sufficient. The seed-saving gardener is probably going to grow only one type. I find that pickling cukes are not necessary for making good pickles. Larger types can be harvested smaller if you want small pickles, or big ones can be sliced up when served. I am happy growing only one variety—particularly a Japanese one. Because cross-pollination is required, grow many plants so they do not inbreed. Then select the best plants and allow several fruits to fully mature on each. Do this fairly early in the season. The fruit is ripe when it turns yellow or golden. Cut the cucumber in half lengthwise and scoop out the seeds and pulp. Put this in a bowl and leave it at room temperature for several days, stirring it once daily. After three to six days, fermentation will be complete, and the pulp will have liquefied. The light, unlikely-to-germinate seeds will float to the top. Pour these off and remove the good seeds from the bottom. Wash the seeds thoroughly until they do not feel slippery any longer. Spread the seeds out on a piece of newspaper to dry. If it is warm and sunny, do this outdoors. Keep the drying temperatures below 100 degrees, and dry completely.

Varieties

There are numerous hybrid cucumbers, which have some advantage for coastal and Puget Sound gardeners. Gemini (STK, HAR) is one. Many of the burpless types also are hybrids, but Suyo Long (JSS) is not. I prefer burpless cukes strictly on the basis of flavor. Marketmore types are the best supermarket-type cuke for our region. SMR 58 is the best pickler and is highly disease-resistant. Many gardeners like Lemon cukes for their mild taste. I would not depend on other varieties because many types tend to throw bitter fruit, and the ones listed here rarely do in our climate. Any variety of Japanese cucumber is unlikely to be bitter, however.

Melons

Melons are even more adapted than cucumbers to warm soils, hot days, cool nights, and dry air. Watermelons need warm nights. Fogs, heavy dews, and cloudy, damp conditions induce many diseases and slow growth. Lack of summer heat greatly retards ripening. June conditions in this area almost prevent early seedling growth in many years. Yet melons can be raised here, at least as far north as Portland. Oregon State University has been intensively studying the growth of melons. At their trials, only a few types perform really reliably. Most of these are standard muskmelon varieties. I am investigating European and Japanese cantaloupes in the hope that I will find some early enough and disease-resistant enough to be counted on in cooler summers. It is much easier to grow melons from Roseburg south to the California border.

Culture

Melons prefer a light, sandy soil and require full sun all day. Dolomite lime is helpful at a rate of about ten pounds per hundred feet of row or hundred square feet of bed, even if the soil already has almost neutral pH. Dolomite contains magnesium, a plant nutrient that helps increase sugar content. The use of fertilizer to provide an abundance of nutrients throughout the life of the vine is also useful. North of Roseburg, black mulch is *required,* and it is helpful even in the warmer southern valleys. Black mulch increases soil temperature and the air temperature close to the plants during the day. A long row of black plastic about three feet wide is anchored with soil along its edges, and the melons are transplanted into the center of the plastic every two feet. Melons can be grown with overhead sprinkling, but a drip line under the mulch is better, especially in damp summers, because it promotes drier conditions on top of the mulch. Sow the seeds indoors about the first of May. Plant two or three seeds in each three- or four-inch individual pot. South of Roseburg, you might plant a week to ten days earlier. Thin the pots to the best single plant after the seedlings are well established. Grow the seedlings under dry, warm conditions, such as those under Gro-Lux lamps, until they have developed at least one true leaf and are growing vigorously. If you have a cold frame, transfer them to it. Keep the plants in the frame or under lights until they are getting slightly potbound. Using four-inch pots is not a bad idea because this lets you delay transplanting another week. Try not to set out the melons until after 1 June. The tenth of June would be even better. The longer you can treat the seedlings to warm nights in the frame or the house, the more likely they are to continue growing after transplanting. This is especially true for watermelons. Unless the summer is very warm, our watermelon crop usually fails at Lorane, though they do better in the Willamette Valley.

Garden Planning

A bed that overwintered crimson clover is the best site for the melon patch. Because the vines travel great distances, plan on their overtopping the bed you have given them and spreading out into the paths. Growing several varieties is a good idea, because this tends to spread out the harvest.

Insects and Diseases

Several fungus and mildew diseases attack melons, particularly under the cool conditions of June and September. Growing resistant varieties helps greatly.

Water

Melons require large amounts of water all summer.

Harvest

Each type of melon has a different indicator of ripening. I think a ripe smell is the best indicator for cantaloupes and muskmelons. With cantaloupes, when cracks circle the stem where it joins the fruit and the stem begins to look shriveled, it will separate easily and "slip the fruit." This also indicates maturity. Watermelons are harder to read. Some people can thump the melon and know by the sound, but it takes experience.

I have found, particularly in the case of watermelons, that thinning the vine to one or two fruits produces larger fruits that ripen more quickly. All melons must be vine-ripened, since they will get no sweeter after harvest. This is why home-grown melons usually are better than those from the market, because really ripe melons do not ship well.

Saving Seed

Cantaloupes, muskmelons, and watermelons are all different species and do not cross-pollinate. Muskmelons have netted skins; cantaloupes (generally from Europe or Japan) do not. Varieties of the same species will cross readily, however, and need at least 200 feet of isolation to preserve a fair amount of purity. The seed is ripe when the melon is. Scoop out the seed and the pulp around it, place it in a bowl, and allow it to ferment for a few days. This separates the seed from the thin layer of pulp surrounding it. Stir a few times daily. When the fermentation is over, the good seed will be at the bottom of the container, the pulp and light, nonviable seed will be floating on top. Remove the good seed and wash it thoroughly, then dry it completely at room temperature.

Varieties

There are many varieties that will produce in a good year. Many people swear by these. If you are a gardener with a favorite melon, continue to grow it. Some of these "sworn by" varieties are not ordinary muskmelons but exotic types of cantaloupes. I am not familiar with all of them. Oregon State University has looked extensively at melon growing, feeling that it holds potential for small farmers. After studying their years of testing, I have concluded that only two melon varieties can be counted on in good and bad years: Harper Hybrid (TS, STK) and Iroquois (TS, STK). Iroquois is open-pollinated, though it has somewhat lower yields than Harper Hybrid. For watermelons, Crimson Sweet (BUR, HAR, STK), Sugar Baby (TS, JSS, BUR), and Sweet Meat II Hybrid (TS) perform as well as watermelons can.

Squashes

All squash varieties (including pumpkins) grow basically the same way. The bush varieties actually are still a vine plant but have been bred for shortness of the interstem. This compacts the vine so much the plant appears to be a bush. Squashes are one of the more successful garden vegetables, because they will tolerate all sorts of bad conditions and still make some crop.

Culture

All squashes do much better on rich garden soil with adequate moisture. The seeds can be directly sown or started as transplants. I do not see much point to starting transplants in an effort to obtain earlier production. Summer squashes are so prolific that we quickly tire of eating them—so why rush the harvest by a few weeks? Even when directly seeded, summer squashes will be producing heavily by late July. Winter squashes and pumpkins will make a much earlier yield, too, but early yield is not desirable. Winter squashes go into storage when the frosts come and are better when they mature in late September rather than in late August. Only a zucchini fanatic or someone who wants to win a prize for a Hubbard squash at the state fair should consider starting transplants. If you do raise them, the procedure is the same as for cucumbers. Sow the seeds outdoors after the last frost date in your area. Like other curcubits, squashes need warm soils to germinate well, but they are more tolerant of less than optimum conditions than either melons or cucumbers. At Lorane we sow them around the first of June. Plant five or six seeds in a clump, about one inch deep, and space the clumps four feet by four feet for summer types and at least six feet by six feet for winter types and pumpkins. When the seedlings are up, thin to the best one or two plants per clump. A hotcap placed over the seed hastens germination. Should the seed not be up within a week, assume that the cool soil has caused it to rot, and plant again.

Garden Planning

One summer squash plant per person will more than do it, unless you like to preserve summer squashes. I would suggest that you plant a different variety for each person in the family and enjoy the slight differences in flavor. Do not grow too many zucchinis. One or two plants probably will be enough. Come mid-August, you will not be able to give away the bucketfuls that a half dozen plants will produce every other day. Winter squashes vary in production, both by the variety and by the summer's weather. I have found that a couple of good vines keep the two of us supplied until early spring. Squashes can be heavy users of nitrogen, so if possible give them a bed that overwintered crimson clover, and certainly follow them with a clover green manure crop.

Insects and Diseases

Squashes can get mildews and are also very sensitive to various damping-offs and seedling diseases. These are mostly induced by too cool soils at planting time. Squash seed almost never fails to germinate (in the technical sense seedsmen use when referring to the percentage of germination), but it often does fail to make it to the surface before diseases kill the seedlings. Waiting for the beginning of a warm, sunny spell of weather before sowing the seed ensures success.

Water

Squashes, like other curcubits, demand abundant soil moisture. If they are mulched after they are established, summer types often can be carried into August with little or no irrigation. If you are short of water and want to grow winter types, dig a hole about three feet in diameter and about two feet deep, and fill it half-full of pure compost. Then top it off with soil. The compost makes a spongelike reservoir for the plant. Then after the seedlings are up and growing, mulch around them for about three feet in all directions. This works very well, even if you have plenty of irrigation. I make squash holes the lazy way. I dig them in the winter and fill them up with kitchen garbage. When they are nearly full, I hill the soil up over the garbage. By planting time, the garbage has composted, and the soil has settled back down. Five gallons of water each week will keep a squash vine with a reservoir under it going all summer.

Harvest

For better summer squashes, keep the plants picked clean. Do not allow the fruit to go unharvested. Chickens, livestock, and compost piles all like giant zucchinis. For better winter squashes, pinch off all new female flowers and any small squashes that have not come close to enlarging, starting about one month before the first expected frost. We do this about the first of September at Lorane. Pruning like this forces the vine to finish maturing the fruit already set and gives them more flavor. When the stems are shriveled, or after the frosts wither the vine, cut the stems about one inch above the fruit. Cure them in the sun—if there is any—for about ten days, covering the squashes at night to keep the dew and frost off. If it is rainy, put them in a warm room for five days to cure and then store at forty-five to sixty degrees with good air circulation. The trick to long storage is dry, hard skins. Sponging the skins with a disinfecting bleach solution after curing will prevent molds from forming and add several months to keeping time. We store ours in a large, cool closet in a back room, and they keep until March.

Saving Seed

Knowing which kinds of squash cross with which is a little complicated, but at least they will not cross with cucumbers or melons. Squashes are all bee-pollinated and commercially require at least a quarter mile of isolation. For the garden, this can be reduced to as little as 300 or 400 feet. If you are about to save your own seed, there should not be another garden too close. For the practical gardener, this means you cannot be raising seed from more than one variety of squash in each pollination group. (Squash variety crossing is highly undesirable, because many times the result is quite inedible.) All the winter varieties, with the exception of butternuts, are in one group—*C. maxima*. Included are buttercup, Hubbard, delicious, banana, and most of the other large, hard-shelled squashes. The summer varieties such as zucchini and the acorns, all pumpkins, and some novelty types such as Lady Godiva, Spaghetti, and Delicata, are in a group called *C. pepo*. All members of *C. pepo* cross easily with each other. Butternuts are in their own group—*C. moschata*. A fourth group contains the cushaw types. *C. maxima* and *C. moschata* ripen their seeds when the squash is ripe. Summer squashes (*C. pepo*) have not yet ripened seeds at the stage we eat the fruit. Zucchinis and other summer squashes have to be left on the vine to become a yard long and develop a good, hard, thick skin approaching that of a pumpkin before the seeds are ripe. To collect the seeds, cut the fruit in half, scoop out the seeds, and remove as much pulp as possible from the seed. After drying the seed at room temperature, separate as much pulp as you can, and store.

Varieties

There are lots of varieties and you can grow about any you wish. A few are a bit slow to mature in our region and will not work very well in cooler locations and sometimes in cool, rainy summers even in the Willamette. Avoid scalloped or Patty Pan types. Scallopini Hybrid (which just about all seedsmen sell), however, is more vigorous than Patty Pan and much earlier. Another problem squash is butternut. It tends to be too late for gardeners around Puget Sound and near the coast. There are now some early butternut hybrids and two new open-pollinated early varieties called Ponca and Patriot that are much better for us than the old Waltham Butternut.

Alliums

In this group are found onions, leeks, and garlic. They are all quite winter hardy and are excellently suited to our climate.

Almost all alliums are highly photoperiodic. This means that the photoperiod—the duration of light versus dark—determines their growth. Alliums have built-in clocks that measure the season by remembering how long the nights are. When the duration is correct, the plant makes a bulb and goes dormant or else flowers and makes seed. Growing an onion variety properly adapted to photoperiods such as those found at about forty-five degrees latitude is essential.

All alliums are naturally biennial. They bulb in their first year and then use that store of food to get through the winter and to flower the next spring. Unlike roots, however, they do not bulb gradually, but rapidly, within a month or so after the photoperiod has demanded it. To get large bulbs, it is necessary to encourage the growth of large tops first, so that when bulbing starts the plant can put a great deal of food into it. Once the bulb is formed, the top usually withers and goes dormant. The bulb acts exactly like a flower bulb, overwinters, and sprouts the following spring. High levels of fertility are essential during the time the plant is making leaves.

In continental climates, onions have to be stored in fall to last until the next summer's scallions come on. This is hard to do in the maritime Northwest, because rarely can we cure the skins of our onions well enough to prevent sprouting during the winter. Fortunately, our mild climate allows a harvest of alliums year-round. The cycle starts with harvesting scallions in July, sweet Spanish onions in August, storage onions in September, leeks from October to April, overwintered scallions in March through May, and overwintered bulb onions in June.

Alliums have the nice trait of transplanting easily. This means that slow-growing types like leeks and sweet Spanish onions can be started indoors and grown in a cold frame for months, then set out after the weather has settled down a bit. If this could not be done easily, the harvest would be mostly small plants and tiny bulbs.

Hybrid onions are more uniform and somewhat more vigorous. For garden purposes, however, variation in size is not critical and is actually somewhat helpful. There are no hybrid leeks at present.

Garlic

A summer harvest of garlic will keep for months, so growing your own is a very simple alternative to buying it fresh. The delicious sweet smell of freshly harvested garlic drying in the house is a treat to be looked forward to each year.

Culture

Break a head of garlic into separate cloves and plant them root side down, one inch deep. Do this in late September or early October. Grow the plants in rows at least twelve inches apart, three to four inches apart in the row. In spring, side-dressing the plants with organic fertilizer will make nicer bulbs at maturity.

Garden Planning

The bulbs will not mature until midsummer, so put them in places that do not have to be tilled in spring. Five to ten feet of row will certainly overwhelm most families with garlic. Follow the harvest with a fall crop.

Insects and Diseases

Insects and diseases are not a problem. In fact, garlic is reputed to deter insects from neighboring plants. Garlic cloves blended into a slurry and sprayed kill insects in many gardens.

Water

Garlics will grow and mature without any irrigation.

Harvest

The behavior of garlics varies somewhat at maturity. Some types put up a seed stalk, and when it is mature, the bulbs are. (The seeds are not usually viable.) Others will brown off and fall over like onions. Either way, this usually is happening by July. Dig the bulbs and leave the tops attached. Hang them in the sun to dry for about a week, then clip the tops and store them.

Saving Seed

Use the largest cloves for planting the next year's crop. Doing this results in more vigorous seedlings and larger bulbs the following summer. Varieties do not cross-pollinate.

Varieties

The best garlic varieties are not found in seed catalogs or supermarkets but in Italian or Greek specialty stores. One unusual kind, called Elephant Garlic, is grown by many local gardeners who would probably be delighted to give you a clove or two for the asking. Elephant Garlic can be recognized by the large bluish seed balls that stand over five feet tall in July. Its bulbs are three or four times the size of regular types.

Leeks

This valuable vegetable is not easy to start, but once established it grows like a weed. The trouble leeks take is well worth it, because winter leeks are so frost hardy that they will supply you with fresh "onions" all winter and into the spring, no matter how cold it gets. Leek soup, leeks in salads, leeks in cooking—they are all delicious.

Culture

Leeks have to be sown indoors sometime before the first of March, since the seedlings will not stand outside conditions at this time of year. Transplanting the seedlings is very picky and painstaking, but it must be done. The bedding soil used for the transplants must separate easily without forming lumps at transplanting time. I recommend the addition of some sphagnum moss to your garden soil to keep it light and loose. Plant two rows of seedlings in a small tray (keep the rows about 1½ inches apart). The seeds are sown about ½ inch deep, and after germination the stand should be thinned to about ½ inch apart in the row. Leek seedlings are vigorous and fairly hardy if given a little protection from the weather, so move them out to the cold frame as soon as it is necessary to make more space indoors. They will make faster growth, however, under the Gro-Lux lamps. It is helpful to keep the tops trimmed so the seedlings do not get over 3 inches tall. This makes stockier plants with better-developed root systems and a better chance of standing transplanting.

Sometime in May, the urge to transplant the seedlings will come over you, but do not let this urge overcome your good sense. Set them out only after the garden has dried out enough to work up a very fine seed bed—almost as good as needed for growing carrots. I like to plant leeks in a row up the edge of my garden, where they are out of the way during their long growth period. The leek row is one of the few places I still use my old rototiller, although it is a job that could be done with hand tools. Make the soil quite fine at least ten inches deep. After it is well tilled up, dig a trench about six to eight inches deep and about the width of a combination shovel. Stack the soil up neatly on one side of the trench. Then, using a garden rake and a lot of patience, remove the clods from the bottom and sides of the trench until there is an inch of very fine soil on the bottom. Then, sitting by the trench, transplant working backwards. The leeks can go in with an almost bare root. If the bedding soil is fine enough and humusy enough, the leeks separate from the tray with a considerable root system intact. Spread the root system out and lay the leek on its side in the bottom of the trench. Cover the roots with about a half inch of soil scraped up from the bottom or off the sides of the trench and press the fine soil down firmly on the roots. Then gently stand the plant upright and press a little soil around the back of the base to hold it. Leeks are most efficiently planted in two staggered rows about four inches apart down the bottom of the trench.

Water the seedlings gently to get the soil particles in close contact with the root hairs, then sprinkle the entire row with organic fertilizer. Ten feet of row can use two or three pounds of cottonseed or fish meal or about ten pounds of composted chicken manure. Avoid fresh chicken manure because it may burn the seedlings. If it is hot and sunny, water the new transplants daily for about a week. After that, they are on their own and almost indestructible. Because transplanting is so fussy, I have tried directly seeding leeks as early as the first of May in a trench and thinning them later, but leeks grown this way are no larger than ordinary scallions by fall. To blanch the stems and thus create more edible material, gradually rake the soil back into the trench as the plants grow taller.

Garden Planning

Leeks are going to be in the ground for nearly one year—and longer if a seed crop is contemplated. Locate them where this will not interfere with other garden activities. Twenty feet of row will keep the two of us fairly well supplied until spring.

Insects and Diseases

Leeks generally do not have insect or disease problems.

Water

Leeks require abundant water all summer.

Harvest

In late fall the leeks will be over one inch in diameter, and many will be double that. They are ready to dig. Start at one end of the row and harvest them as needed until March or even later. No protection is needed to overwinter them. Sometime in spring they will put up seed stalks. Once this begins, the harvest is over.

Saving Seed

Allow some of the nicest looking specimens to survive and make seed. They will automatically be selected for cold hardiness. The balloon-shaped flowers will eventually show the black seeds they contain. Cut the stems off and allow the flowers to dry fully for several weeks on a tray inside. Then rub the heads between your hands until the seeds drop out. Leeks cross-pollinate and require at least a hundred feet of isolation. Allow at least ten plants to make seed to reduce the danger of inbreeding.

Varieties

Giant Musselburgh is the standard American winter leek and is offered by most seed companies. Musselburghs are large—often over two inches in diameter at the base—and slightly bulbous. The flavor of all winter leek varieties is quite similar. The Europeans are very fussy about the appearance of their leeks. It gets to be a matter of "taste" as to which is the prettiest. Territorial likes Catalina from a Dutch seedsman. Johnny's likes Siegfried from a Danish company. Stokes has a couple of nice ones called Elephant and Unique, but beware of purchasing their autumn leek, which is not very winter hardy. Burpee sells their own strain, Broad London. Harris has Electra and also sells an autumn leek. Only a devoted leek fancier will want to grow autumn leeks, because there are a lot of onions ready at the same time. Autumn leeks are juicier and sweeter than the fibrous winter leeks, however.

Onions

Four kinds of onions are grown from seed. Storage types are sown in late spring and mature in late summer. If well dried and cured, they will keep until spring. They are pungent. Sweet Spanish types are sown in early spring and harvested in summer. They are slower growing than storage types and in our climate should be started like leeks are and transplanted out. If directly seeded, they will make rather small bulbs. Sweet onions do not keep very long in storage. Overwintered onions are planted in late summer; the following spring they can be harvested as scallions or allowed to make bulbs. Overwintered onions usually are sweet types and lack the pungent preservative found in storage onions. Usually they will last from their June harvest until fall. Scallions are a quick crop and can be planted several times in the season. Any onion can be used as a scallion if harvested before bulbing begins, but the sweet types are better flavored. Some scallions have been bred not to bulb at all, no matter how large they get. Some are multipliers, meaning that they form new plants in clusters as they age. Eventually there is a whole clump of scallions attached at the base—much as for chives or shallots. Onion sets are mature onions grown under very crowded conditions. When replanted in spring, they sprout vigorously and make scallions in less than a month. If allowed to mature, the bulbs have a tendency to split or bolt. Onions grown from sets usually are poor keepers. Sets do have the advantage of being able to germinate in poor soils in which onion seeds would fail. This has caused many gardeners to feel that sets are easy to grow and onions from seed almost impossible This is not true. Once germinated, there is not any difference in maturity time, and both make onions of about the same size.

Culture

Sow storage onions in early May. Plant the seed thinly about a half inch deep in rows at least twelve inches apart. Thin when well established to about three or four inches apart in the row. Sow sweet types indoors in early March and grow them exactly like leek seedlings, transplanting them out in May on the same spacing you use for mature storage types. Sweets also can be directly seeded in mid-April but will not make bulbs nearly as large. Push the onions into the most rapid growth possible so that large bulbs are formed. The bed should be well fertilized before planting, and side-dressings of high-nitrogen fertilizer like blood meal or fish meal are very helpful if done about once a month until bulbing begins.

Scallions can be planted from mid-April through August, using different varieties as the season goes on. I like to use sweet Spanish onions for the first crop, Lisbons for the rest of the summer, and an overwintering variety for fall and winter. Scallions are planted much more closely than onions. The rows can be six inches apart, and the plants can be thinned to about a half inch apart in the row. I do not use bulb onion rows as a source of scallions because crowding reduces the final size of the bulbs even though the row is gradually thinned out. Scallions are not as fussy about fertilizers as onions are—it does not matter if they are a little slower growing.

Overwintered onions are best established as late in the summer as possible. They need to be large enough to become fully cold hardy by fall, but no larger than that. I find that an early August planting is perfect. The overwintered crop should not be fertilized until spring, when they should be treated like any other onion. Starting in March, side-dress them with all the fertilizer you can afford. It will pay off with much larger bulbs in June. Overwintered onions can also be grown as a spring scallion crop, as they do not begin bulbing until mid-May but are edible from the end of February on. They make very sweet scallions.

Garden Planning

It is very hard to judge how many onions a family will want, because people's craving for this vegetable is highly variable. You can figure that if they are well fertilized, two pounds of onions per foot of row is a reasonable expectation. For a continuous yield of scallions, make three plantings, one in April for early summer harvesting, one in June for late summer, and one in August for winter and overwintering.

Insects and Diseases

Insects and diseases are not a problem.

Water

If you are short of water, use sweet Spanish types in spring; they will make fairly large scallions before things get too dry, especially if you fertilize them well. Bulb onions take abundant water and may be out of the question. Mulching helps. Sets will produce summer scallions very rapidly, and they take little water. The overwintered onion crop can be started as transplantable seedlings in early August and set out in middle to late September, growing from this point to maturity on rainfall.

Harvest

If bulbing types split into two separate parts or bolt, they will not cure properly. Eat splits as fresh onions. Bolters should be harvested immediately, because once seed production starts the bulb is drained of food and rapidly becomes inedible. Those bulbs that have not split or bolted—most of the crop—are cured to toughen up the skins and lengthen storage. After most of the tops have fallen over, break over the rest. A few days later, pull the bulbs and lay them in the sun to dry for a week before bringing them indoors. Protect the drying onions from rain and dew. If the weather is not sunny and warm, the skins do not cure well, and storage life is greatly reduced. This is why most commercial production is done east of the Cascades. After drying, clip off the tops with scissors and store the onions in onion sacks hung in a cool, dry place. Onion sacks have large openings that allow air to pass freely around the bulbs. Anything that promotes dryness and air circulation will enhance storage by reducing rotting.

Saving Seed

For sweet types and pungent types, select the finest onions that have not split, bolted, or rotted during the winter and plant them out the following spring about six inches apart in rows twelve inches apart. They will sprout, make flowers, and go to seed. When the small black seeds are visible in the seed ball, harvest the stalk and dry it fully indoors. Thresh out the seed by hand and store it. Onions cross-pollinate, but fairly good purity can be had with only a few hundred feet of isolation. Select for size, shape, narrow necks (which promote better storage), and the ability to postpone sprouting until spring. You may not have much luck getting sweets to overwinter in storage without rotting or sprouting. For overwintered bulb onions, replant the bulbs that have not rotted or sprouted by late summer. They will sprout, overwinter, and make seed the following year.

Varieties

Danvers and Southport strains are the standard northern keepers. All seedsmen carry them. New types of hybrid storage onions that have thicker skins and keep longer without spoiling have been developed recently. Most of these have the word "Spartan" in their names, such as Spartan Banner or Spartan Sleeper. The sweet types are all sweet Spanish of different sorts. If they have place names attached, such as Utah or New Mexico, pick the one from the most northerly latitude. Recently, sweet Spanish crosses have appeared. These are hybrids that are half sweet Spanish and half pungent storage type. They are milder than the usual storage onions but keep much better than the old open-pollinated sweet types. Fiesta, El Capitan, Brown Beauty, and Autumn Spice are all of this hybrid type.

Because of their day length sensitivity, be a little cautious about trying onion varieties. Onions are divided into three classes—northern, midlatitude, and southern. The storage types, which bulb on decreasing day length, are all northern types and do well here. The sweets are also decreasing day length onions but bulb on a longer day than storage types. They initiate bulbing in August, before they have had enough time in our latitude to get really large. This is why starting them indoors and transplanting later is so helpful. In the proper latitudes, they would be directly seeded early in March or even in February and make rapid growth from then until late July, when they begin to bulb. Onions developed for southern latitudes bulb on *increasing* day length—about thirteen to fourteen hours, which occurs sometime in April. They are planted in October in Texas and southern California. These strains are not cold hardy enough to survive our winters. The Japanese have developed overwintered onions hardy enough for northern latitudes, and these, too, bulb on increasing day length. Only Johnny's and Territorial sell them. Territorial has tested Kaizuka (JSS) and found that almost all of them split or bolt before maturity—a very bad trait. Imai (TS) is much less prone to these faults in our region.

Scallions generally are onions that are bred not to bulb at all. White Sweet Spanish make fine scallions because of their mild taste and thin skins. There are special nonbulbing strains of sweet Spanish for summertime planting. Lisbon onions also make fine scallions and are fairly winter hardy. I like to make a planting of Lisbons and He-Shi-Ko (Hardy White Bunching) at the same time in August. The Lisbons are faster growing and are harvested in late fall and winter. The He-Shi-Kos overwinter and are harvested in February and March.

Miscellaneous Vegetables

I have included here vegetables that do not obviously belong to a group. There is no point in trying to make generalizations about them.

Asparagus

Asparagus is a perennial plant, storing up a great deal of food in its root system. The roots are prone to rots and diseases that attack under damp conditions. Poorly drained soils do not grow good asparagus, and many plantings west of the Cascades fail after a few years. Commercial production of asparagus is quite extensive on the other side of the mountains, where soils are not waterlogged all winter. Unless you are gardening in sandy soil or on a very well drained slope, with soil at least four feet deep, I would not even attempt a planting. The key to good production is extremely rich soil and a great abundance of nitrogen through the summer. This causes the plant to make vigorous vegetative growth, manufacture a lot of food, and build up its root system in preparation for making next season's shoots.

Culture

In spring, plant asparagus roots in rows about five feet apart. Spread about two inches of compost, ten pounds of lime, and ten pounds of rock phosphate per hundred row-feet in a band about eighteen inches wide. Then as soon as the soil can be worked, dig out a trench about nine inches deep and the width of the compost band. Pile up the soil neatly along the trench. As you dig it out, the compost and rock minerals will be mixed in. Then duplicate the fertilization in the trench. Standing in the trench, spade it up another eight to ten inches deep, and mix the soil amendments into the soil well.

Purchase healthy two-year-old roots from a nursery. Spread out the root carefully, the crown up and the roots fanned out. Place one root every 12 inches down the row. Cover the roots with about 1½ inches of soil from the hill running along the trench. Then sprinkle about ten pounds of bone meal on top of the buried roots. As the shoots begin to emerge from the soil, gradually fill in the trench, leaving about 1 inch of growing shoot exposed. Cut the tops off in late summer, after they have turned brown, and compost them.

Every year or two add ten pounds of lime and ten pounds of rock phosphate to maintain the soil, and mulch the bed annually in the fall with manure at least one inch deep. The asparagus will make seed in small black pods on the drying ferns. Try to prevent this seed from sprouting by harvesting the ferns before the seed begins to fall. If it does sprout, treat the little shoots as though they were weeds and get rid of them. If you do not, the bed will become crowded with too many plants, and the resulting overcompetition will leave the shoots undersized.

Garden Planning

It is a lot of work to establish a bed. You are not likely to succeed if you cut corners or if you have clayey soil. The bed is a perennial and should be productive for at least twenty-five years if you continue to manure and lime it. Consider this when choosing a location in the garden. Twenty feet of row should keep a devout asparagus lover satisfied, once the bed is well established.

Insects and Diseases

Well-drained soils avoid diseases and subsequent loss of the bed.

Water

Asparagus needs abundant water through the season. Its native habitat is along streambeds, where subirrigation keeps it well supplied. The roots go down 4 feet in search of water, so asparagus is an exception to the 2½-foot watering depth "rule."

Harvest

The year you make the bed there will be no harvest. If the bed survives, there also will be very little harvest the second year, because the shoots will be too small and too few and because the roots will not be massive enough to tolerate much picking without being depleted. The second year after planting, begin cutting off the shoots at ground level when they first appear in early spring. Continue the harvest until shoot size declines to below a half inch in diameter. (As the roots become more exhausted, shoot size declines.) Then let the plant make ferns, and keep it well watered. A side-dressing of nitrogen at this time encourages larger and more vigorous fern growth, more food storage in the roots, and a larger crop the following year. This first harvest should not last more than a few weeks. In the third year after the bed is planted, the harvest should last over a month.

Saving Seed

The seeds may be collected toward the end of summer. They can be planted the following spring and new roots started, but it takes two years for these roots to enlarge to transplanting size—like the ones purchased at a nursery. If you want to start your own roots, sow the seed about a half inch deep in rows about twelve inches apart in mid-April. Thin to about three inches apart in the row. Grow them for two years like this, and then carefully dig the roots and transplant them in trenches.

Varieties

Drainage and soil fertilization are more important than variety—any variety should do well on good soil. Oregon State University does recommend Mary Washington or California 500, however.

Sweet Corn

Frankly, I do not understand why many gardeners devote such a large part of their space to sweet corn. It takes up more room for the amount of food it produces than any other garden vegetable. We like a little patch of it to eat raw, but we do not preserve it, preferring to work less ground and get more food for our efforts.

Culture

Plant corn between 15 May and 10 June. Earlier plantings are likely to rot in the ground unless treated seed is used, because corn germinates very poorly in soils below sixty degrees. Do not rush it. If you are determined to have the earliest corn in the neighborhood, try using a very thin sheet of clear plastic about eighteen inches wide over the seeded rows. The plastic heats the soil and is lifted after the seedlings are up and pushing against it. I try to outguess the weather and plant at the end of a rainy spell. If I guess right, the seeds enjoy more soil heat from the sunny days and grow vigorously. Plantings made after 10 June are not likely to ripen unless very early varieties are sown. Plant the seed one to two inches deep and two to three seeds per foot in rows twenty-four to thirty inches apart. Thin to at least eight inches apart in the row when the seedlings are four or five inches tall. If the soil is on the chilly side, plant more seed to make up for what will rot before sprouting. Keep the corn patch free of weeds until the corn is waist high, and then keep out of the patch until harvest. Corn is a shallow-rooted plant, so do not cultivate deeply near the seedlings.

Since it is wind-pollinated, large stands of corn are necessary to obtain sufficient pollen density. If the silks are not fully saturated with pollen, many ears will contain empty rows. A patch four rows wide and ten feet long is minimum; six rows wide and fifteen feet long is much better.

Corn is very demanding of soil. Phosphorus-poor soil will grow a poor crop of almost any vegetable, but it will not grow corn at all. Without abundant phosphorus, corn seedlings become irreparably stunted. Rock phosphate takes over a year to break down enough to supply corn adequately, so if you are just beginning to improve your soil, supplement the rock phosphate with a bone meal treatment, banded below the seed. Sprinkle about four pounds of bone meal in each hundred-foot furrow before you plant. With the bone meal right at hand, the sprouts get an abundant supply of phosphorus when they need it most. After a year or two, bone meal will be unnecessary—if you have used adequate amounts of rock phosphate.

Corn is also highly demanding of nitrogen. Growing a crimson clover cover crop guarantees adequate supplies and helps to make the phosphorus more available in spring. If the corn is suffering from a deficiency of nitrogen, it will be light green and shorter than it should be. For a really impressive corn patch, side-dress the plants with a strong nitrogen source when they are about waist high. Blood meal or fish meal will do very well for this purpose.

Garden Planning

Because corn requires a large patch of ground, it would not seem to adapt well to raised-bed gardening—but it does. Simply take two or three beds side by side and fill in the paths, making one large plot. You have to break the rule about never stepping on the beds, but it can be kept to a minimum. Sowing, one or two cultivations, a side-dressing, and harvest should not compact the soil too much. An early harvest of corn can be followed up with transplanted late brassicas or onions. Otherwise, put it back into crimson clover for the winter to replace what the corn depleted. Corn tends to mature uniformly. If you want an extended harvest, either make several sowings about ten days apart, or plant several varieties at the same time.

Insects and Diseases

Earworm problems are rare in the maritime Northwest. Weekly sprayings of Dipel from the time the silks form until harvest will almost totally eliminate the worms if they do trouble your garden.

Water

Corn is highly demanding of water. The only types that are not have been bred by desert Indians, but these types require much too much heat ever to mature here. Considering the economic value of corn, if you have to skimp on irrigation I suggest you skimp on the sweet corn as well.

Harvest

Pick the ears when the wrappers are slightly browing-off or when the silks are fairly dried out. The kernels should be full and milky.

Saving Seed

Corn pollen is wind carried. Two hundred feet of isolation between varieties will give you fair purity; a thousand feet is required for really pure seed. Most varieties today are hybrids. Little work has been done on open-pollinated strains in the last fifty years. If you have an open-pollinated strain you like, saving seed is very simple: just select as many of the best plants as possible and allow the second and third ears to ripen fully until the frosts come. They will be small and rather unattractive, but the seed from them is as good as what grew on the main ear. Let the cobs dry fully indoors and then remove the seed by hand and store it. I would select for variable maturity, and the good taste and appearance of the main ear. After harvesting the main ears, break over the plants not selected.

Varieties

Fairly early varieties are necessary for successful ripening in the Willamette Valley and farther north. From Roseburg south it might be possible to mature the super-sweet midwestern types. This can happen in the Willamette, too (in a warm summer), but you cannot count on it. From Puget Sound north and along the coast, only very early types can be relied on. There the midseason varieties we depend on in the Willamette are too late many years. The unfortunate thing about this is that the earlier the variety matures, the poorer it tastes, the less sugar it develops, and the smaller the cob is.

Growth of sweet corn is regulated by heat. Plant breeders understand this phenomenon so well that they have developed a precise measurement called "heat units" to specify the requirements of differing varieties. From the last spring frost until the first one of autumn, the Willamette Valley averages about 1,800 HU. Over 2,000 accumulate south of Roseburg. Puget Sound and the coast receive 1,400 in a good year. To get an idea of how little this is, compare those figures with that for Umatilla, Oregon, or Iowa, where 4,000 might build up each summer. The Jubilee strain of corn, for example, needs about 1,600 HU. Very early hybrids need 1,400 HU. The late sweet types that the seed catalogs are always touting as being super sweet take 1,900 to 2,300 HU. They will never get that much heat in the maritime Northwest, no matter how long the frost-free season is. When the seed catalog tells you the number of days to maturity, what they are actually saying is that in a particular location it averages that many days to receive the required heat units. Generally the earliest corns listed take "55 days." Translate that to about 90 days here. Main-season corns are listed at around 80 days. Translate that to about 120 in the Willamette and perhaps 150 in Washington.

Jubilee (TS, STK) is about the latest corn that can be reliably grown in the Willamette, and it is worth chancing in Washington because of its excellent flavor. Stylepack (BUR) is about the same as Jubilee. White Sunglow (BUR) is another main season white corn that matures adequately. Gardeners in Washington and along the coast can depend on Earlivee, Early Sunglow, and Borealis. If the variety takes over 80 days I would be very skeptical about it in the Willamette, and if it requires over sixty-five days I would be cautious in cooler areas. All these varieties are hybrids. For open-pollinated types, Golden Bantam is very nice, and it is in the Jubilee class in terms of maturing. Ashworth (JSS, TS) is a new strain I think is equal to the best hybrids, although it is a little lower yielding. Early Golden Bantam is the one for cool locations. I have found that the later open-pollinated strains like Country Gentleman and most of the Indian corns are not early enough to be truly reliable, though they do well in southern Oregon.

Dill

Dill is a frost-sensitive annual that is very easy to grow. No serious cook and canner should garden without growing some. Fresh dill makes better pickles than any dried product.

Culture

Sow dill about the same time you would plant beans or put out tomato plants. Plant it in rows at least 12 inches apart and bury the seed about ¾-inch deep. Thin the seedlings when they are well established to about 8 inches apart in the row. Dill does not require rich soil to make a crop, but the plants will be much larger if the soil is good.

Garden Planning

I grow about five row-feet of dill each summer. Because I prefer to make my pickles late in the season, I sow the seed about the first of July.

Insects and Diseases

Insects and diseases are not a problem.

Harvest

The best, most aromatic seasoning comes from plants just beginning to flower. If you let them continue past this stage, they begin to go to seed.

Water

Dill needs a great deal of water.

Varieties

There are two basic types of dill, one for seed production and the other for leaf. Seed-producing dill makes very little leaf and an abundance of seed. Leaf-producing dill makes an abundance of leaf and little seed. Unless you find a seed catalog that offers leaf dill, buy your seed right from the spice rack in the supermarket.

Sources

Seeds

The following companies will send you a catalog free of charge:

W. Atlee Burpee Company, Riverside, California 92502
Joseph Harris, Moreton Farm, Rochester, New York 14624
Johnny's Selected Seeds, Albion, Maine 04910
Stokes Seeds, Inc., Box 548, Buffalo, New York 14240
Territorial Seed Company, Box 27, Lorane, Oregon 97451

Fertilizers

The main Northwest source of fertilizers is the Webfoot Fertilizer Company, 201 S.E. Washington, Portland, Oregon 97214. Webfoot sells wholesale only and will not sell to gardeners unless they purchase cooperatively in ton lots. Most garden stores purchase their stocks from Webfoot. Using prepackaged five-pound boxes of simple fertilizers is very expensive, but there is no trouble finding blood meal, cottonseed meal, and bone meal in these sizes. Webfoot sells the same materials in hundred-pound sacks at a much lower cost per pound. If transferred to a metal garbage can with a tight lid, simple fertilizers will last many years. Have your favorite garden store special order for you. Webfoot also sells kelp meal and rock phosphate. Agricultural lime and dolomitic lime are available almost anywhere garden supplies are sold. Bone meal and cottonseed meal often are used as animal feed supplements and can be purchased from feed dealers. If you are really stymied, call Webfoot and ask them for the name of a local distributor.

Insecticides

Rotenone is sold by the Lilly Miller company, which has warehouses in Portland and Seattle. Most garden stores carry their products. They distribute a 1 percent rotenone meant for dusting and a 5 percent mix meant for water spraying. I have had more success using the 5 percent mix as a dust.

Dipel is harder to find, since few garden stores carry it. As more people begin using it, Dipel will become readily available. You will have to hunt for it or urge your local garden store to stock it. Johnny's Selected Seeds sells it by mail-order. Burpee and Harris sell Thuricide, which is the same material under a different and less-known brand name.

Further Reading

Richard Raymond's *Down-to-Earth Vegetable Gardening Knowhow* (Charlotte, Vt.: Garden Way Publishing, 1973) is an interesting home-rolled book that goes into the use of the rototiller as a basic tool. Raymond has some connection with the Troy Bilt Company, the best tiller manufacturer in this country. (Merry Manufacturing in Marysville, Washington, is a close second.) The book is particularly interesting and useful on green manuring and sheet composting using a powerful rototiller.

Although raising grain is not the concern of a city gardener, good green manures are simply grains tilled in before maturity. Gene Logsdon's *Small-Scale Grain Raising* (Emmaus, Pa.: Rodale Press, 1977) might also interest gardeners who hope to be self-sufficient.

Since the climate of the Willamette Valley is very much like that in parts of England and since our basic problems and opportunities have been dealt with by English gardeners for centuries, it follows that Laurence D. Hill's *Grow Your Own Fruit and Vegetables* (London: Faber and Faber, 1971) might have something to teach us. It does. This book must be specially ordered through a good bookstore.

John Jeavon's *How to Grow More Vegetables Than You Ever Thought Possible on Less Land Than You Can Imagine* (Berkeley: Ten Speed Press, 1979) is revised and enlarged from the original hand-rolled version. Ten Speed Press has greatly enhanced the format and afforded Jeavons the opportunity to say much more than the first edition did. This book is for the gardener with a very limited space and an unlimited desire to produce large quantities of food. It is the bible of French Intensive gardening.

Sir Albert Howard is an originator of the organic movement, and *The Soil and Health* (New York: Shocken Books, 1947) is his masterpiece. It contains a fine explanation of soil microlife and its interrelationship with plant health. It is a must for those who consider themselves organic gardeners.

Angelo M. Pellegrini is a Washington gourmet whose main interest in gardening is the culinary enjoyment it can produce. *The Food Lover's Garden* (Seattle: Madrona Publishers, Inc., 1970) is written primarily from his own experience gardening around Puget Sound, though he occasionally gives growing directions for crops such as okra that could not be grown in this region.

Gardening means dealing with plants. Whether or not it is done organically, the principles are the same. It never hurts to have a detailed knowledge of the internal workings of plants in general and their relationship to disease, soil, and the basic elements around them. If you plan to be a serious gardener, read a good botany text. All soils derive originally from rocks. An understanding of the basics of soil formation is very useful to the gardener and is covered in all introductory geology textbooks.

The United States Department of Agriculture began publishing yearbooks in the 1930s. Some are general, others offer specific treatments of soil, insects, water, plant diseases, and animal feeding. Although most of them are out of print, they sometimes are available in libraries or used-book stores.

Index

Notes

Other Books from Pacific Search Press